german in review

german in review

kimberly sparks / van horn vail

middlebury college

HARCOURT BRACE JOVANOVICH, INC.

New York San Diego Chicago San Francisco Atlanta

ISBN: 0-15-529590-X

Library of Congress Catalog Card Number: 67–18539

Printed in the United States of America

preface

This book offers a systematic, workable solution to the problem of providing a truly comprehensive review of German grammar and usage. At the college level the problem is acute, for a review must accommodate students who have been taught basic German by a variety of methods. While the instructor may assume a certain overall class achievement, he knows very little about an individual student's knowledge of a given problem. Therefore, we have presupposed nothing: if necessary, the student can re-acquaint himself with a structural problem from the ground up. The teacher may thus conduct his review at the pace that best challenges the whole class. The method is, in fact, predicated on lively, properly paced classroom drilling; the book offers enough exercises to fill a class hour meaningfully and to insure mastery of the principles involved.

Each chapter proceeds from a step-by-step explanation of a particular grammatical principle to extensive exercises and drills that require the student to apply the principle. Where the chapter subject requires a more detailed explanation, it is discussed in two or three stages with corresponding exercises for each level. For example, the chapter on verbs is divided into three levels: "Present Tense"; "Past, Perfect, and Future Tenses"; and "Separable and Inseparable Prefixes." At each level the student performs the accompanying exercises before going on to the next level.

Important features of the book include:

1.   *A complete and systematic presentation of grammar.*
The grammar presentation is in the form of condensed, programed lectures. The student can prepare himself fully *before* class; the instructor can then use the entire hour for drill.

2.   *A large number and variety of drills.*
Each explanation is followed by a *series of exercises* that drill the student on the different aspects of the problem involved. Pattern drills, completion exercises, substitutions, transformations, and synthetic exercises (dehydrated sentences) are used to prepare the student for the express-in-German drills, the final group of exercises in each drill sequence. These drills use English sentences as *cues* (rather than as translation exercises), since the student has already dealt with the same sentences in the preceding German-German exercises. The express-in-German drills demand *total* performance from the student: one that confirms his knowledge of both the grammar and the vocabulary involved.

3.   *Systematic introduction of vocabulary.*
Vocabulary is systematically introduced in the German-German exercises so that the student is familiar with all new vocabulary items before reaching the express-in-German drills.

4.   *An approach that can be used as a review and as a supplement.*
Besides serving as a review grammar, this book may supplement any basic college text that does not provide sufficient drills to insure a student's mastery of a particular area. It can, in fact, be used to introduce, as well as reinforce, any grammatical area of college German instruction.

5.   *Tapes.*
The student may use the tapes that accompany this book to prepare himself more efficiently for fluent oral performance of the express-in-German drills in each chapter.

A word of warmest thanks is due to Monika Sutter, who has been a strength and comfort throughout this long project. We would also like to acknowledge our special indebtedness to Professor Albrecht Holschuh of Indiana University, whose fine ear and sharp eye were indispensable to us. Were it not for the ecclesiastical overtone, we would call him our chief lector.

KIMBERLY SPARKS
VAN HORN VAIL

contents

german in review

verbs

chapter one

LEVEL ONE

I. PRESENT TENSE

1. Infinitives and Verb Stems

The infinitive is the form of the verb found in dictionaries and word lists.
Most German infinitives end in **–en.** By removing this ending, we arrive
at the *verb stem:*

INFINITIVE	STEM
sagen	**sag–**
finden	**find–**

2. *Basic Forms of the Present Tense*

The present tense is formed by adding the following endings to the stem of the verb:

			sagen to say		
ich	sag	e	wir	sag	en
du	sag	st	ihr	sag	t
er, sie, es	sag	t	sie, Sie	sag	en

If the stem of the verb ends in

−d   or   **−t**

all of the endings begin with **e.** Compare the endings of **sagen** and **finden** (whose stem ends in **−d**) in the following table.

ich sag	e	wir sag	en
find	e	find	en
du sag	st	ihr sag	t
find	est	find	et
er sag	t	sie sag	en
find	et	find	en

The **e** in the 2nd and 3rd persons singular and in the 2nd person plural of **finden** makes the endings pronounceable.

3. *Stem-vowel Change*

Certain verbs change their stem vowels in the *2nd and 3rd persons singular:*

e → i   or   ie

geben to give		**sehen** to see	
ich gebe	wir geben	ich sehe	wir sehen
du **gibst**	ihr gebt	du **siehst**	ihr seht
er **gibt**	sie geben	er **sieht**	sie sehen

e → i	e → ie
brechen to break	befehlen to command
essen* to eat	empfehlen to recommend
helfen to help	geschehen to happen
sprechen to speak	lesen* to read
sterben to die	stehlen to steal
treffen to meet; hit	
vergessen* to forget	
werfen to throw	

EXCEPTIONS: These two verbs change a consonant as well as the stem vowel:

nehmen to take	treten to step
ich nehme	ich trete
du nimmst	du trittst
er nimmt	er tritt

a → ä   and   au → äu

fahren to drive, travel		laufen to run	
ich fahre	wir fahren	ich laufe	wir laufen
du fährst	ihr fahrt	du läufst	ihr lauft
er fährt	sie fahren	er läuft	sie laufen

a → ä	au → äu
fallen to fall	saufen to drink (of animals); booze
fangen to catch	
lassen* to let; allow	
schlafen to sleep	
schlagen to hit	
tragen to carry	
waschen to wash	

---

*See p. 4, "Verb Stems Ending in –s, –ss, –ß, –tz, –z."

EXCEPTIONS: In addition to taking an umlaut, these verbs have unusual endings in the 2nd and 3rd persons singular:

halten to hold		**raten** to advise		**laden** to load	
ich	halt e	rat	e	lad	e
du	hält st	rät	st	läd	st
er	hält	rät		läd	t
wir	halt en	rat	en	lad	en
ihr	halt et	rat	et	lad	et
sie	halt en	rat	en	lad	en

NOTE: Not all verbs with the stem vowels **e, a,** and **au** undergo stem-vowel change. Those that do must be memorized.

4. Verb Stems Ending in –s, –ss, – ß, –tz, –z

Verbs of this type have a –t (instead of –st) ending in the *2nd person singular:*

heißen to be called		**lesen** to read		**sitzen** to sit	
ich	heiß e	les	e	sitz	e
du	heiß t	lies	t	sitz	t
er	heiß t	lies	t	sitz	t

5. Infinitives Ending in –n (rather than –en)

Verbs of this type take an –n (rather than –en) ending in the *1st and 3rd persons plural:*

tun to do		**sammeln** to collect		**plaudern** to chat	
ich	tu e	samm(e)l	e	plaud(e)r	e
du	tu st	sammel	st	plauder	st
er	tu t	sammel	t	plauder	t
wir	tu n	sammel	n	plauder	n
ihr	tu t	sammel	t	plauder	t
sie	tu n	sammel	n	plauder	n

NOTE: Most of these verbs have stems ending –el or in –er. The e preceding the l or r is often omitted in the 1st person singular (ich samm(e)le, plaud(e)re).

6. *Exceptions:* haben, sein, *and* werden

haben to have	sein to be	werden to become
ich habe	bin	werde
du hast	bist	wirst
er hat	ist	wird
wir haben	sind	werden
ihr habt	seid	werdet
sie haben	sind	werden

7. *Basic Word Order in Simple Sentences*

a. *Word order with statements*

When a simple sentence is a *statement* (rather than a question), the *verb* is the *second element* in the sentence. Look at the following example:

1	2	
Er	geht	nach Hause.
Der junge Mann	geht	nach Hause.

In both sentences, the verb is the *second element* (but not necessarily the *second word*). In the second sentence, the phrase **Der junge Mann** has simply been substituted for the word **Er.** As you can see by analogy to English, one could not break up the phrase **Der junge Mann.** Hence this entire phrase is the first element in the second sentence (as **Er** is in the first sentence), and the *verb is still the second element.*

b. *Word order with questions*

There are three ways of forming questions in German:

1. *inversion* (verb first, subject second)

1	2	
Gehen	Sie	jetzt nach Hause?

(Are you going home now?)

Both English and German can form questions by *inverting the normal word order* of the subject and the verb. In such a sentence, the *verb is the first element* (rather than the second element) and is immediately followed by the subject.

NOTE: In English questions the present tense verb form is composed of more than one word (*Are* you *going?*). In German however there is only one word (**Gehen** Sie?).

> **Verstehen** Sie ihn?
> (*Do* you *understand* him?)
>
> **Siehst** du ihn jetzt?
> (*Do* you *see* him now?)
>
> **Fahrt** ihr mit dem Schiff?
> (*Are* you *going* by ship?)

2. question words

A question can also be formed by using a *question word*. In this case

> the *question word* is the *first* element
> the *verb* is the *second* element
> the *subject* is the *third* element

> **Wer** ist das?
> (*Who* is that?)
>
> **Wo** ist Hans?
> (*Where* is Hans?)
>
> **Warum** geben Sie es mir nicht?
> (*Why* don't you give it to me?)
>
> **Wann** kommt er nach Hause?
> (*When* is he coming home?)

3. nicht wahr?

A question can also be formed by adding the words **nicht wahr?** (literally, is it *not true?*) to the end of a statement:

> Sie kommen heute abend, **nicht wahr?**
> (You're coming this evening, aren't you?)

8. Imperatives

The imperative is the form of the verb used to give commands:

> **Sagen** Sie das nicht!
> (Don't say that!)

The imperative is not, however, restricted to commands in the military sense of the word. It can also be used to give instructions, to make suggestions, or even to wish someone well:

INSTRUCTION   Fahren Sie geradeaus, dann rechts!
                (Drive straight ahead, then to the right.)

SUGGESTION   Gehen Sie nach Italien! Es ist großartig!
                (Go to Italy. It's great!)

WISH   Kommen Sie gut nach Hause!
                ([I hope you] get home O.K.)

a. German imperative forms

In German each verb has *three imperative forms* corresponding to the **du-, ihr-,** and **Sie-**forms of address:

du-FORM	Sag(e)	das nicht, Albrecht!
ihr-FORM	Sagt	das nicht, Peter und Kai!
Sie-FORM	Sagen Sie	das nicht, Herr Holzschuh!

1. The **du-**form is composed of:

> *verb stem* + (e)

The ending **e** *must* be used if the verb stem ends in:

> **−t**   (antworte)
> **−d**   (finde)
> **−ig** (besichtige)

In most other cases, the e ending is not used in colloquial spoken German, especially if the verb stem is monosyllabic (**sag, komm, geh**).

2. The **ihr**-form is the same as the regular 2nd person plural form of the verb. It is made up of:

verb stem   +   **–t (sagt, kommt)**

or: *verb stem*   +   **–et** (if the verb stem ends
in **–d** or **–t**:   **antwortet, findet**)

3. The **Sie**-form of the imperative is also the same as the regular present tense form:

verb stem   +   **–en**

But the verb is immediately followed by **Sie**:

Folgen <u>Sie</u> mir, bitte!
(Follow me, please.)

b. Imperatives of verbs with stem-vowel change

1. e → i   or   ie

	e → i		e → ie	
du-FORM	**Gib**	es mir!	**Lies**	es, Thomas!
ihr-FORM	**Gebt**	es mir!	**Lest**	es, Thomas und Ulla!
Sie-FORM	**Geben Sie**	es mir!	**Lesen Sie**	es, Herr Huber!

Verbs that change their stem vowel from e to **i** or **ie** *use the changed stem* (**i** or **ie**) in the **du**-form of the imperative.

The **ihr**-form and the **Sie**-form use the regular infinitive stem.

2. Verbs that take an *umlaut* in the 2nd and 3rd persons singular (e.g. **ich schlafe, du schläfst, er schläft** and **ich laufe, du läufst, er läuft**) do NOT take an *umlaut* in forming the imperative:

du-FORM	**Schlaf** gut, Hans!	**Lauf** schneller!
ihr-FORM	**Schlaft** gut, Freunde!	**Lauft** Schneller!
Sie-FORM	**Schlafen Sie** gut, Herr Lange!	**Laufen Sie** schneller!

Contrast: Du schläfst gut, Hans.   Schlaf gut, Hans!

NOTE: *All* German imperatives require an *exclamation point:*

Laufen Sie schneller!

◻ DRILLS

Verbs with stem vowels that change from **e** to **i** or **ie**

Replace the subjects of the following sentences with the words in parentheses, making all necessary changes in the verb forms. (Verbs with stems ending in s-sounds are also included in these drills. See p. 4.)

1. Wir geben es dir morgen.   (er)
2. Sehen Sie es?   (er)
3. Sie sprechen zu schnell, Herr Müller.   (du . . . Hans)
4. Ich vergesse alles.   (du)
5. Wir lesen einen Roman.   (er)
6. Wann treffen sie ihn?   (du)
7. Ich nehme den Anzug.   (er)
8. Sie werfen Tomaten.   (er)
9. Ich empfehle das Schnitzel.   (der Kellner)
10. Helfen Sie ihm?   (du)
11. Die Jungen essen zu wenig.   (Albrecht)
12. Sie stehlen den Wagen.   (er)
13. Sehen Sie das Haus da drüben?   (ihr)
14. Sie sterben bald.   (er)
15. Warum befehlen Sie das?   (der Leutnant)
16. Ich lese die Zeitung.   (Vater)
17. Was empfiehlt er?   (ihr)
18. Wir geben es einem Freund.   (er)
19. Ich treffe ihn morgen.   (wir, er)
20. Was essen Sie, Herr Reh?   (du . . . Albert)
21. Nehmen Sie den Bus?   (du, er)

Verbs with stem vowels that change from **a** to **ä** or **au** to **äu**

Replace the subjects in the following sentences with the words in parentheses, making the necessary changes in the verb forms. (Verbs with stems ending in s-sounds are also included in these drills. See p. 4.)

1. Wir fahren bald nach Deutschland.   (Erika)
2. Ich schlafe nach dem Mittagessen.   (Peter)
3. Was raten Sie ihm?   (du)
4. Tragen Sie nicht zuviel?   (du)
5. Die Kinder waschen den Wagen für mich.   (Karl)
6. Warum lassen Sie das Kind allein?   (du)
7. Die Bäume wachsen sehr langsam.   (das Gras)

8. Wir laden den Lastwagen. (er)
9. Sie laufen durch den Garten. (Grete)
10. Fahren Sie mit dem Wagen? (ihr)
11. Katzen fangen Mäuse. (unsere Katze)
12. Sie schlagen den Hund nicht. (er)
13. Warum fängst du den Ball nicht? (Sie)
14. Wachsen Blumen hier? (etwas)
15. Ich lade die Pistole. (Holmes)
16. Was halten Sie in der Hand? (du)
17. Schlafen Sie immer so lange? (ihr, du)
18. Ich trage das Gepäck für dich. (er, wir)
19. Wir waschen den Wagen. (ich, er)

Verbs with infinitives ending in −n

1. Was tun Sie da? (du, wir)
2. Ich sammle Briefmarken. (wir, er)
3. Er schmuggelt Zigaretten. (wir, ihr)
4. Wandert er durch die Berge? (ihr, du, Sie)
5. Ich plaudere mit ihr. (wir)
6. Er ändert nichts. (ich, wir)

Haben, sein, werden

1. Was haben Sie da? (er, du, ihr)
2. Die Kinder werden groß. (er, du, ihr)
3. Wann sind Sie zu Hause? (er, du, ihr)
4. Haben Sie einen Wagen? (er, du, ihr)
5. Ich werde müde. (er, wir, die Kinder)
6. Er ist nicht sicher. (ich, wir)
7. Ich habe es nicht. (er, wir)
8. Sind Sie Amerikaner? (du, ihr)
9. Ich werde Arzt. (er)

Imperatives

Supply the suggested imperative forms.

1. (werfen) _____ den Ball, Otto!
   _____ den Ball, Kinder!

2. (helfen) _____ mir bitte, Dieter!
   _____ mir bitte, Herr Kunz!

3. (lesen)   _____ etwas langsamer, Konrad!
                  _____ etwas langsamer, Frau Steltzer!

4. (laufen)   _____ schneller, Hanna!
                  _____ schneller, Herr Litz!

5. (sehen)   _____ her, Frau Huber! (Look here . . . .)
                  _____ her, Klaus!
                  _____ her, Kinder!

6. (essen)   _____ nicht so schnell, Kai!
                  _____ nicht so schnell, Kinder!

7. (schlafen)   _____ gut, Herr Emrich!
                  _____ gut, Freunde!
                  _____ gut, Jürgen!

8. (vergessen)   _____ die Adresse nicht, Hans!
                  _____ die Adresse nicht, Herr Brandt!

9. (empfehlen) _____ mir etwas, Wolf!
                  _____ mir etwas, Herr Scherpe!

10. (fangen)   _____ den Ball, Karl-Heinz!

11. (sprechen)   _____ nicht so laut, Herr Kuhn!
                  _____ nicht so laut, Kinder!
                  _____ nicht so laut, Benno!

12. (schlagen)   _____ den Jungen nicht, Herr Schmidt!

Mixed drills

1. Sie sprechen zu schnell.   (er)
2. Ich schlafe nach dem Mittagessen.   (Peter)
3. Sehen Sie das Haus da drüben?   (du)
4. Ich bleibe hier.   (er)
5. Tragen Sie nicht zuviel?   (du)
6. Ich lese die Zeitung.   (er)
7. Ich vergesse alles.   (du)
8. Wir trinken nur Wasser.   (er)
9. Wann treffen Sie ihn?   (du)
10. Wir laden den Lastwagen.   (er)
11. Sie trinken nicht, sie saufen.   (er)
12. Wir geben es dir morgen.   (er)

13. Ich nehme den Anzug. (er)
14. Was tun Sie da? (du)
15. Haben Sie einen Wagen? (du)
16. Helfen Sie ihm? (du)
17. Die Kinder werden groß. (Karl)
18. Fahren Sie mit dem Wagen? (du)
19. Ich trage das Gepäck für dich. (er)
20. Was essen Sie da, Herr Meyer? (du ... Hans)
21. Er schmuggelt Zigaretten. (wir)
22. Warum lassen Sie das Kind nicht zu Hause? (du)
23. Sie werfen Tomaten. (er)
24. Warum fangen Sie den Ball nicht? (du)
25. Was raten Sie ihm? (du)
26. Ich werde Arzt. (er)
27. Was kosten die Krawatten? (die Krawatte)
28. Sind Sie Amerikaner? (er)
29. Ich empfehle das Schnitzel. (er)
30. Wir spielen Ball. (er)
31. Was halten Sie in der Hand? (du)
32. Nehmen Sie den Bus? (du)
33. Ich werde müde. (er)
34. Wachsen Blumen hier? (etwas)
35. Wandert er durch die Berge? (Sie)
36. Wir fahren bald nach Deutschland. (Georg)
37. Was empfehlen Sie? (du)

Express in German*

1. When are you meeting him, Hans?
2. He speaks too fast.
3. Is he an American?
4. Peter is going to Germany.
5. He'll give it to you tomorrow.
6. She drinks only water.
7. Is Grete at home?
8. What is he carrying?
9. Viktor forgets everything.

---

*NOTE: German commonly uses the present tense to express future time. Although some of the English sentences in these drills are in the future tense, all of their German equivalents may be expressed by using the present tense.

10. Do you see the house over there, Karl?
11. What are you doing there, Mr. Huber?
12. Kai is getting (is becoming) big.
13. Are you taking the bus, Peter?
14. They are wandering through the mountains.
15. Richard sleeps after lunch.
16. He's reading the newspaper.
17. I'm staying here.
18. Are you helping him, Dieter?
19. We're meeting him tomorrow.
20. He's loading the truck.
21. He's throwing tomatoes.
22. What does she recommend?
23. What are you holding in your hand, Theo?
24. He's playing ball.
25. She's getting (becoming) tired.
26. Does he have a car?
27. Why don't you catch the ball, Peter?
28. Why doesn't she leave the child at home?
29. He recommends the schnitzel.
30. What are you eating there, Albert?
31. We're carrying too much.

LEVEL TWO

I. PAST, PERFECT, AND FUTURE TENSES

A. Past tense and present perfect tense of weak [regular] verbs

1. Weak (Regular) Verbs = Verbs with Only One Stem

Weak (regular) verbs are verbs which use the same stem in forming their present, past, and perfect tenses. Both English and German have verbs of this type. In English these verbs add the endings –*ed* or –*d* to form their past and perfect tenses. For example, the infinitive (*to*) *answer* is used to form:

PRESENT TENSE	they *answer*
PAST TENSE	they *answer*ed
PERFECT TENSE	they have *answer*ed

As you can see, the infinitive *answer* (which is also the stem in English) is present in every tense. By adding the appropriate endings (*–ed* or *–d*), we may predict the past and perfect forms of any verb of this type (e.g. they *work*, they *work*ed, they have *work*ed; they *commence*, they *commenc*ed, they have *commenc*ed). Similarly, the past and perfect forms of German weak verbs are *predictable*.

2. Past Tense

The past tense of a *weak verb* is formed by adding *past tense endings* to its stem:

INFINITIVE	STEM
sagen	**sag–**
antworten	**antwort–**

			sagen to say		
ich	sag	te	wir	sag	ten
du	sag	test	ihr	sag	tet
er	sag	te	sie	sag	ten

If the stem of the verb ends in **–d** or **–t**, an e is inserted before these endings to make the verb forms pronounceable:

ich	sag	te	wir	sag	ten
	antwort	ete		antwort	eten
du	sag	test	ihr	sag	tet
	antwort	etest		antwort	etet
er	sag	te	sie	sag	ten
	antwort	ete		antwort	eten

It should be noted that these are the past tense endings *for weak verbs only*.

3. Present Perfect Tense

a. Compound form

The present perfect is a *compound tense* (not a simple one-word form like the present or past tense). It is made up of:

AUXILIARY VERB   and   PAST PARTICIPLE
(the present tense
of **haben** or **sein***)

Er	**hat**	**gesagt**
(He	has	said)

b. Past participles of weak verbs

The past participles of weak (regular) verbs are formed by adding both the prefix **ge–** and the ending **–t** (or **–et** if the stem ends in **–d** or **–t**) to the verb stem:

gesagt   (**ge** sag **t**)
geantwortet   (**ge** antwort **et**)

NOTE: Verbs of foreign origin with infinitives ending in **–ieren** do not add a **ge–** prefix in forming their past participles:

INFINITIVE	PAST PARTICIPLE
rasieren	rasier**t**
studieren	studier**t**

c. Tense formation

In a compound tense it is the *auxiliary* that changes according to person and number (i.e. is conjugated); the past participle remains constant:

ich habe **gesagt**	wir haben **gesagt**
du hast **gesagt**	ihr habt **gesagt**
er hat **gesagt**	sie haben **gesagt**

---

*The choice between the auxiliary verbs **haben** and **sein** is discussed on p. 21.

d. Word order

The past participle is the *last element* in a simple sentence:

> Ich **habe** es ihm gestern **gesagt.**
> (I told him yesterday.)

The auxiliary verb (*here:* **habe**) is the second element in the sentence (i.e. is in the normal verb position).

4. Usage

Conversational German often uses the *present perfect* where English uses the past tense.

I said can be rendered by either

> **Ich sagte**   or   **Ich habe gesagt.**

He didn't answer is either

> **Er antwortete nicht**   or   **Er hat nicht geantwortet.**

The tendency is to use the present perfect in a give-and-take conversational situation and to use the past tense in narration. For this reason, the present perfect is often called the "conversational past" and the past tense is called the "narrative past." Many present perfect sentences in German have no present perfect equivalent in English.

> Ich habe es ihm gestern gesagt*

must be rendered in English by the past tense (I told him yesterday), since the perfect tense (I have told him yesterday) is not an English sentence.

5. Summary

Weak (regular) verbs are verbs that use the *same stem* to form all of their tenses. **Sagen** is a regular verb, and, as you have seen, the stem **sag–** occurs in the present, past, and perfect tenses. The forms of all verbs of this type are predictable; that is, they may be formed from the stem according to the rules just discussed. Given the infinitives **rauchen** (to smoke) and **stören** (to disturb), we know that the past tense forms (3rd person) are rauchte and störte and that the past participles are geraucht and gestört.

---

*NOTE: **Sagen** *must* have a direct object in German: Ich habe **es** ihm gesagt.

B. Past tense and present perfect tense of strong [irregular] verbs

1. *Strong (Irregular) Verbs = Verbs with More Than One Stem*

Many verbs use different stems in forming their present, past, and perfect tenses. Often only the stem vowel is affected, as in the following example in English:

PRESENT	PAST	PAST PARTICIPLE
sing	sang	sung

In other cases more radical changes are involved:

go	went	gone

2. *Past Tense*

a. *Tense formation*

The past tense of strong verbs is formed by adding endings to a *past tense stem that differs from the present tense stem:*

INFINITIVE		PRESENT TENSE STEM (or *stems* where there is stem-vowel change in the present tense)	PAST TENSE STEM
singen	to sing	sing–	sang–
fahren	to ride, travel	fahr– (fähr–)	fuhr–
bitten	to ask, request	bitt–	bat–
lesen	to read	les– (lies–)	las–
nehmen	to take	nehm– (nimm–)	nahm–
kommen	to come	komm–	kam–
gehen	to go	geh–	ging–

The stem changes of irregular verbs are *not predictable* and must, therefore, be *memorized*. In most cases only the stem vowel is affected. There are, however, quite a few verbs that have double consonants in one stem and single consonants in another (e.g. kommen, kam; bitten, bat) and a few with even more radical changes (e.g. gehen, ging).

b. Past tense endings for strong verbs

Strong verbs have their own set of past tense endings (different from those used with weak verbs):

gehen to go					
ich	ging	—	wir	ging	en
du	ging	st	ihr	ging	t
er	ging	—	sie	ging	en

NOTE: The 1st and 3rd person singular forms have no ending.

EXCEPTIONS:

1. If the past tense stem ends in an s-sound (–s, –ss, –ß, –z), the past tense ending of the 2nd person singular is –est (e.g. **du lasest**).

2. If the past tense stem ends in –t or –d, the past tense ending of the 2nd person singular is –est (e.g. **du batest**) and the ending of the 2nd person plural is –et (e.g. **ihr batet**).

gehen (normal) lesen (1) bitten (2)					
ich	ging	—	wir	ging	en
	las	—		las	en
	bat	—		bat	en
du	ging	st	ihr	ging	t
	las	est		las	t
	bat	est		bat	et
er	ging	—	sie	ging	en
	las	—		las	en
	bat	—		bat	en

The **e** is inserted before these endings to make the verb forms pronounceable.

3. Present Perfect Tense

a. Compound form

Like the present perfect tense of weak verbs, the present perfect of strong (irregular) verbs consists of:

AUXILIARY VERB	and	PAST PARTICIPLE
(the present tense		
of **sein** or **haben**)		
Er is**t**		**gegangen.**
(He has		gone.)

As you can see from the example of **gehen, ging, gegangen,** the stem of the *past participle* of a strong (irregular) verb is *not predictable*. Thus the past participle, like the past tense stem, *must be memorized.*

b. Past participles of strong verbs

With the exception of a small group of verbs (which is discussed below), the past participles of strong verbs begin with a **ge–** prefix and take an **–en** ending:*

INFINITIVE	PAST TENSE	PAST PARTICIPLE
gehen	ging	**ge**gangen
fahren	fuhr	**ge**fahren
bitten	bat	**ge**beten
nehmen	nahm	**ge**nommen

c. Word order

A past participle is the *last element* in a simple sentence:

Er hat es gestern **genommen.**
(He took it yesterday.)

4. Mixed Verbs (*a sub-group of strong verbs*)

There are eight verbs that follow a pattern of their own. *They change their stems* (as do all strong verbs), but, instead of adding the endings for strong verbs, *they take the endings used with weak verbs:*

---

*Verbs with separable and inseparable prefixes behave differently. See pp. 32–37.

	bringen to bring	
PAST TENSE	ich brach**te** du brach**test** er brach**te**	wir brach**ten** ihr brach**tet** sie brach**ten**

The past participles of these verbs, like those of weak verbs, begin with a **ge–** prefix and take the ending **–t**:

Ich habe gebracht.

The six most common verbs that behave this way are:

INFINITIVE		PAST TENSE	PAST PARTICIPLE
brennen	to burn	**brannte**	**gebrannt**
bringen	to bring	**brachte**	**gebracht**
denken	to think	**dachte**	**gedacht**
kennen	to be acquainted with, know	**kannte**	**gekannt**
nennen	to call, name	**nannte**	**genannt**
rennen	to run	**rannte**	**gerannt**

NOTE: Each of these verbs uses the *same stem* to form its *past tense* and its *past participle*. In all six cases, the stem vowel for the past tense and the past participle is **a.**

5. *Past and Perfect Tenses of* haben, sein, *and* werden

	haben to have					
PAST TENSE	ich	hat	**te**	wir	hat	**ten**
	du	hat	**test**	ihr	hat	**tet**
	er	hat	**te**	sie	hat	**ten**

As you can see, the past tense of **haben** is formed by adding the *endings used with weak verbs* to a *new past tense stem* (**hat–**).

PRESENT PERFECT	Ich habe **gehabt,** etc.

Gehabt takes the *weak* verb ending: **–t.** Its auxiliary verb is **haben.**

	sein to be			
PAST TENSE	ich war —		wir war en	
	du war st		ihr war t	
	er war —		sie war en	

The past tense of **sein** is formed by adding the *endings used with strong verbs* to a *new past tense stem* (**war–**).

PRESENT PERFECT | ich bin gewesen, etc.

Gewesen takes the *strong* verb ending: **–en.** Its auxiliary verb is **sein.**

	werden to become	
PAST TENSE	ich wurde	wir wurden
	du wurdest	ihr wurdet
	er wurde	sie wurden

The past tense of **werden** is unique.

PRESENT PERFECT | ich bin geworden, etc.

Geworden takes the strong verb ending: **–en.** Its auxiliary verb is **sein.**

C. HABEN or SEIN as auxiliary verbs

Most German verbs take **haben** as their auxiliary in forming the present perfect tense. However, certain verbs require **sein.** Sein must be used as the auxiliary verb when two conditions are met. (N.B. *Both* conditions must be satisfied.)

1. The verb expresses *motion* or *change of condition.*

2. The verb is *intransitive* (i.e. *cannot* take a direct object).

Thus: Er **hat** Bier getrunken.　　　(**Trinken** is transitive.)
(He drank beer.)

Er **hat** gut geschlafen　　　　　(**Schlafen** is intransitive,
(He slept well.)　　　　　　　　but there is no motion or
　　　　　　　　　　　　　　　change of condition in-
　　　　　　　　　　　　　　　volved.)

Er **hat** den Wagen geschoben. (He pushed the car.)	(Motion is involved, but **schieben** is transitive.)
Er **hat** kräftig geschoben. (He pushed hard.)	(**Schieben** is still transitive, i.e. it *can* take an object, even though it does not in this sentence.)
But: Er **ist** schnell gelaufen. (He ran fast.)	(**Laufen** is an *intransitive* verb of *motion*.)
Es **ist** kalt geworden. (It's gotten cold.)	(**Werden** is an *intransitive** verb describing a *change of condition*.)
Er **ist** nach Frankfurt gefahren. (He's driven to Frankfurt.)	(**Fahren** is an *intransitive* verb of *motion*.)
Er **ist** gestorben. (He died.)	(**Sterben** is an *intransitive* verb describing a radical *change of condition*.)

In addition to these types of verbs, the following three verbs also use **sein** as their perfect auxiliary:

sein	to be	Er **ist** nie da gewesen.
bleiben	to stay, remain	Er **ist** hier geblieben.
geschehen	to happen	Was **ist** geschehen?

D. Past perfect tense of weak and strong verbs

a. Tense formation

The past perfect is formed like the present perfect; the only difference is that the *auxiliary verb* (**haben** or **sein**) *is in the past tense:*

PRESENT PERFECT	Ich **habe** es gesehen.	(I have seen it.)
PAST PERFECT	Ich **hatte** es gesehen.	(I had seen it.)

*****Werden** is always intransitive. In the sentence

Er **ist** Journalist geworden
(He's become a journalist)

Journalist is a *predicate* object (nominative case), not a direct object (the accusative is Journalisten).

PRESENT PERFECT	Er **ist** nicht gekommen.	(He hasn't come.)
PAST PERFECT	Er **war** nicht gekommen.	(He hadn't come.)
PRESENT PERFECT	Er **ist** hier gewesen.	(He's been here.)
PAST PERFECT	Er **war** hier gewesen.	(He'd been here.)

b. Word order

The past participle is the *last element* in a simple sentence:

> Er war sehr spät nach Hause **gekommen**.
> (He had come home very late.)

c. Usage: a second past time

Look at the following example:

1ST PAST TIME	Bond **ging** in sein Zimmer. Seine geschulten Augen **sahen** es sofort.	Bond *went* into his room. His schooled eyes *saw* it immediately.
2ND PAST TIME	Ein Smersh-Agent **war** da **gewesen** und **hatte** sein Zimmer **durchsucht**.	A Smersh agent *had been* there and *had searched* his room.

The first two clauses relate something that took place in the past. The verbs, **ging** (*went*) and **sahen** (*saw*), are in the past tense. The action of the second pair of clauses also took place in the past; but it is a period of past time prior to the past time of the first two clauses, that is, a second, earlier period of past time.

2ND PAST TIME   1ST PAST TIME   PRESENT
✕⟵—————✕⟵—————✕

The verbs, **war ... gewesen** (*had been*) and **hatte ... durchsucht** (*had searched*), are in the past perfect. The Smersh agent *had been* in Bond's room and *had searched* it (during a second period of past time).

The same distinction can be seen in the following example:

1ST PAST TIME   2ND PAST TIME

Ich **suchte** ihn im Büro, aber er **war** schon nach Hause **gegangen**.
(I *looked* for him in his office, but he *had* already *gone* home.)

The action of the second clause took place in a second period of past time that preceded the period of past time of the first clause.

E. Future tense = WERDEN and infinitive

a. Tense formation

The future tense is made up of the present tense of the auxiliary verb **werden** *plus an infinitive:*

Ich **werde** wohl kommen.	(I'll probably come.)
Du **wirst** wohl kommen.	(You'll probably come.)
Er **wird** wohl kommen.	(He'll probably come.)
Wir **werden** wohl kommen.	(We'll probably come.)
Ihr **werdet** wohl kommen.	(You'll probably come.)
Sie **werden** wohl kommen	(They'll probably come.)

b. Word order

When the future tense is used, the infinitive is the *last element* in a simple sentence:

Er **wird** wohl morgen **kommen.**
(He will probably come tomorrow.)

As you can see from the examples the *auxiliary* (**werden**) *changes* according to person and number (ich werde kommen, du wirst kommen, etc.), while the *infinitive remains constant.*

c. Usage

Look at the following example:

Ich fahre nächstes Jahr nach Deutschland.
(*I'm going* to Germany next year.)

As you can see, *future time* may be expressed by the *present tense* in both English and German. In fact, the future tense often sounds awkward. For instance, the sentence

I will go to Germany next year

may be grammatically correct (i.e. it uses the future *tense* to express future *time*), but it sounds somewhat stilted. The same is often the case in German.

GENERALIZATION: Conversational German tends to use the *present tense to express future time.*

However, German uses the future tense in the following cases:

1. *in the absence of a time expression*

In the sentence

> Er reist nächstes Jahr durch ganz Europa
> (He's going to travel all over Europe next year)

the time expression **nächstes Jahr** clearly shows that the action is to take place in the *future* (next year). When the time expression is omitted, the action appears to be taking place in the present:

> Er reist durch ganz Europa.

In such a case, **werden** is used to avoid any confusion of time and to place the action clearly in the future:

> Er **wird** durch ganz Europa reisen.

2. werden *and* wohl

> Er **wird wohl** zu Hause bleiben.
> (He'll probably stay at home.)

Werden and **wohl** are used to indicate probability: a judgment or assumption on the part of the speaker.

3. werden *and present time*

> Das wird Ihre Schwester sein.
> (That will be your sister, i.e. I assume that is your sister.)

Werden can be used to indicate an assumption about something connected with the present time. This will occur in such contexts as:

> Who is knocking at the door? *That'll be Peter.*
> Wer klopft an die Tür? **Das wird Peter sein.**

▣ DRILLS

Past tense and present perfect tense of weak verbs

Put the following sentences into the past tense and the present perfect tense.

1. Ich hole den Schlüssel.
2. Wir warten auf dich.
3. Was schenkst du Onkel Max?
4. Wir kaufen ein neues Sofa.
5. Nach dem Essen rauchen wir eine Zigarette.
6. Sagen Sie es Herrn Lange?
7. Das ändert nichts.
8. Wir wandern durch die Berge.
9. Ich lerne das nicht.
10. Großvater reist immer gern.
11. Wann zeigst du ihm die Wohnung?
12. Wir fragen nach der Adresse.
13. Wir spielen Tennis.
14. Ich mache eine kurze Reise.
15. Wir tanzen den ganzen Abend.
16. Erich sammelt alte Speisekarten.
17. Warum antworten Sie nicht auf meine Briefe?
18. Peter macht zu viele Fehler.
19. Wir suchen ihn den ganzen Tag.
20. Hanna plaudert mit ihrem Freund.

Past tense and present perfect tense of strong verbs

Put the following sentences into the past tense and the present perfect tense.

1. Wir geben es ihm Montag.
2. Sie hat Zeit.
3. Er spricht zu schnell.
4. Ich nehme den braunen Anzug.
5. Fahren Sie nach München?
6. Ich bleibe zu Hause.
7. Sie bringt es mir heute.
8. Hilft er dir?

9. Wir essen immer zu Hause.
10. Er läuft sehr schnell.
11. Er ist nicht sicher.
12. Ich schreibe ihm einen langen Brief.
13. Er kommt um acht Uhr.
14. Er liest zuviel.
15. Sie trinkt nur Wasser.
16. Wie heißt der Film?
17. Er wird Arzt.
18. Wir sind zu Hause.
19. Er ruft deinen Namen.
20. Er trägt zu viele Pakete.
21. Wir laden den Lastwagen.
22. Ich komme später.
23. Wo steht er?
24. Ich empfehle das Schnitzel.
25. Er bittet mich um eine Zigarette.
26. Wir gehen nach Hause.
27. Ich denke an etwas anderes.
28. Ich kenne ihn sehr gut.
29. Ich treffe ihn um zehn Uhr.
30. Er steigt aus dem Wagen.
31. Mutti wird böse und wirft die Lampe durch das Fenster.
32. Er schläft zuviel.
33. Sie fahren zu schnell.
34. Er stirbt.
35. Es schlägt drei Uhr.
36. Er ist ein guter Schauspieler.
37. Wir sehen ihn selten.
38. Er tritt durch die Tür.
39. Ich halte nicht viel von ihm.
40. Ich finde seine Adresse nicht.
41. Herr Siebenmann fliegt nach Zürich.
42. Was rätst du ihm?
43. Er schließt die Tür.
44. Jeden Samstag wäscht er den Wagen.
45. Warum laßt ihr das Kind allein?
46. Sie singen und tanzen den ganzen Abend.
47. Er kommt später nach Hause.
48. Sie fährt den Wagen nach München.
49. Sie essen und trinken sehr viel.

Present perfect and past perfect tenses of weak and strong verbs

Put the following sentences into the present perfect tense and the past perfect tense.

1. Er ruft deinen Namen.
2. Er trägt zu viele Pakete.
3. Wir gehen nach Hause.
4. Ich komme später.
5. Ich schreibe ihm einen langen Brief.
6. Er wird Arzt.
7. Wir geben es ihm Montag.
8. Wir suchen ihn den ganzen Tag.
9. Herr Siebenmann fliegt nach Zürich.
10. Ich denke an etwas anderes.
11. Es schlägt drei Uhr.
12. Wir sind zu Hause.
13. Er steigt aus dem Zug.
14. Wir warten auf dich.
15. Hilft es dir?
16. Er fährt nach München.
17. Er läuft sehr schnell.
18. Ich empfehle das Schnitzel.
19. Er zeigt uns die Bilder.
20. Er schläft zuviel.
21. Wir laden den Lastwagen.
22. Ich bringe es Ihnen.
23. Wir tanzen den ganzen Abend.
24. Ich bleibe zu Hause.

Future tense

Put the following sentences into the future tense (**werden**).

1. Sehen Sie ihn?
2. Wir sind zu Hause.
3. Was rätst du ihm?
4. Sie hat Zeit.
5. Helft ihr ihm?
6. Das lesen wir nicht.
7. Ich bringe es dir.
8. Sie tun es nicht.
9. Wir spielen Karten.
10. Siehst du ihn?

Mixed drills *— Do this for Friday*

Put the following sentences into <u>the past tense</u> and <u>the present perfect</u> <u>tense</u>. Both weak and strong verbs are included.

1. Wir warten auf dich.
2. Er spricht zu schnell. *Er sprachte, hat gesprochen*
3. Es ist nicht sicher.
4. Peter macht zu viele Fehler.
5. Ich komme später. *Ich kam später, ich bin gekommen*
6. Wo steht er?
7. Ich hole den Schlüssel. *Ich habe geholt*
8. Er ruft deinen Namen. *hat gerurt*
9. Großvater reist immer gern. *ist gereist*
10. Wie heißt der Film? *hat geheißen*
11. Wir sehen ihn sehr oft.
12. Wir tanzen den ganzen Abend.
13. Sie gibt es ihm Montag. *haben gegessen*
14. Wir essen immer zu Hause.
15. Er schließt die Tür. *getroffen*
16. Ich treffe ihn um zehn Uhr.
17. Erich sammelt alte Speisekarten.
18. Das ändert nichts.
19. Sie hat Zeit.
20. Fahren Sie nach München?
21. Ich lerne das nicht.
22. Er schläft zuviel.
23. Ich finde seine Adresse nicht.
24. Herr Siebenmann fliegt nach Zürich.
25. Was schenkst du Onkel Max?
26. Er stirbt.
27. Er steigt aus dem Wagen.
28. Wir spielen Tennis
29. Er wird Arzt.
30. Er trägt zu viele Pakete.
31. Wir suchen ihn den ganzen Tag.
32. Hilft er dir?
33. Ich bleibe zu Hause.
34. Ich mache eine kurze Reise.
35. Er bittet mich um eine Zigarette.
36. Ich denke an etwas anderes.
37. Wir laden den Lastwagen.
38. Wir kaufen ein neues Sofa.

39. Sie trinkt nur Wasser.
40. Wir gehen nach Hause.
41. Es schlägt drei Uhr.
42. Wir fragen nach der Adresse.
43. Er liest zuviel.
44. Wir wandern durch die Berge.
45. Ich nehme den braunen Anzug.
46. Sie bringt es mir heute.
47. Warum antworten sie nicht auf meine Briefe?
48. Er läuft sehr schnell.
49. Ich schreibe ihm einen langen Brief.
50. Er kommt um acht Uhr.
51. Hanna plaudert mit ihrem Freund.
52. Wir sind zu Hause.
53. Ich kenne ihn sehr gut.
54. Warum lassen Sie das Kind allein?
55. Er fährt meinen Wagen nach Hamburg.
56. Sie essen und trinken sehr viel.
57. Was raten Sie?

Express in German

Express each sentence in the past tense and the present perfect tense.

1. He came later.
2. He slept too much.
3. I gave it to him Monday.
4. What did you give Uncle Max?
5. Where was he standing?
6. I stayed home.
7. We went home.
8. He brought it to me yesterday.
9. I took (**machen**) a short trip.
10. He became a doctor.
11. I was thinking of (**denken an** + *acc.*) something else.
12. He called your name.
13. He spoke too fast.
14. I met him at ten o'clock.
15. We danced all evening.
16. She had time.
17. It wasn't certain.
18. He carried too many packages.

see pp 258, 254 Wie geht's?

19. I didn't learn that.
20. He got out of the car.
21. I knew him very well.
22. What did he advise?
23. He ran very fast.
24. We played tennis.
25. It struck three o'clock.
26. I wrote him a long letter.
27. We were at home.
28. I took the brown suit.
29. She drank only water.
30. Did he help you?
31. Why did you leave the child alone?
32. He read too much.
33. I didn't find his address.
34. Peter made too many mistakes.
35. We always ate at home.
36. We waited for (**warten auf** + *acc.*) you.
37. Why didn't you answer (**antworten auf** + *acc.*) our letters?
38. He came at eight o'clock.
39. We saw him very often.
40. He closed the door. *schließen*
41. We wandered through the mountains.
42. We loaded the truck.
43. He asked me for (**bitten um** + *acc.*) a cigarette.
44. We bought a new sofa.
45. Did he drive to Munich?
46. Grandfather liked to travel (**reisen**).
47. Mr. Siebenmann flew to Zürich.
48. What was the film called?
49. That didn't change anything.
50. We asked him for (**fragen nach** + *dat.*) the address.
51. He drove my car to Hamburg.

9-8-81

LEVEL THREE

I. SEPARABLE AND INSEPARABLE PREFIXES

Many German verbs can combine with prefixes to form new verbs with new meanings. These verb prefixes are of two types:

1. *separable prefixes*, so called because under certain conditions they separate from the basic verb and go to the end of the clause

2. *inseparable prefixes*, so called because they are never separated from the basic verb

Separable prefixes are normally prepositions or adverbs; that is, they are complete words that under other grammatical circumstances exist by themselves:

auf–, mit–, zusammen–, etc.

Inseparable prefixes are pure prefixes; they do not occur as whole words in their own right:

ver–, zer–, ent–, etc.

When a *separable prefix* is added to a verb, the meaning of the new prefixed verb *may* be quite obvious:

zurückkommen   to come back

Zurückkommen, for example, takes its meaning from its two components: **zurück** (back) and **kommen** (to come). In other cases, however, the meaning of a verb combined with a separable prefix may not be obvious at all:

vorkommen   to happen, occur
umkommen   to die

Generally, the meaning of a verb with an *inseparable* prefix is unpredictable:

bekommen   to receive, get
verkommen   to go to ruin, degenerate

A. Separable prefixes

ab–	los–	weg–
an–	mit–	zu–
auf–	nach–	zurück–
aus–	vor–	zusammen–
bei–	vorbei–	

1. Word Order

a. Present tense and past tense

In simple sentences the prefix separates and goes to the very end of the sentence:

> **ankommen**   Er **kommt** um fünf Uhr **an.**
> Er **kam** um fünf Uhr **an.**

b. Compound tenses

In the present perfect and past perfect tenses, the prefix is always attached to the past participle:

kommen	**ankommen**
Er ist **gekommen.**	Er ist **angekommen.**
Er war **gekommen.**	Er war **angekommen.**

NOTE: Most past participles are formed with **ge–**. A separable prefix will always *precede* this **ge–** (**angekommen**).

The compound future tense consists of the auxiliary **werden** plus an infinitive. The prefix is always attached to the infinitive:

> **aufmachen**   Er **wird** das Fenster **aufmachen.**

2. Principal Parts of Verbs with Separable Prefixes

The addition of a prefix (whether separable or inseparable) to a verb does not have any effect on the conjugation of the verb. If the basic verb is strong, the prefixed verb is also strong; if the basic verb is weak, the prefixed verb is also weak:

	INFINITIVE	PAST	PAST PARTICIPLE	3RD PERSON PRESENT
STRONG VERB	**abfahren**	fuhr ab	abgefahren	fährt ab
WEAK VERB	**aufmachen**	machte auf	aufgemacht	macht auf

NOTE 1: In lists of the principal parts of verbs with separable prefixes, the prefix traditionally follows the verb in the 3rd person singular present (**fährt ab, macht zu**) and past (**fuhr ab, machte zu**) in order to show its separation and its respective position in a present or past tense sentence.

NOTE 2: In the vocabulary sections of this text, a dot (·) has been placed between the prefix and the verb when the prefix is separable rather than inseparable (e.g. **an·kommen, auf·machen**).

3. Sein *or* haben

To require the auxiliary **sein,** a verb must fulfill two conditions:

1. It must be intransitive (i.e. not take a direct object).

2. It must indicate *motion or change of condition.*

Otherwise the verb uses the auxiliary **haben.** (See p. 21 "Haben or **sein** as Auxiliary Verbs.")

Adding a prefix to a verb may have an effect upon whether that verb fulfills these conditions (and therefore requires the auxiliary **sein**) or not. For example, **schlafen** (to sleep) is intransitive (it fulfills the first condition because it does not take a direct object) but does not indicate motion or a change of condition. Therefore it takes **haben.** On the other hand, **einschlafen** (to go to sleep) fulfills both conditions: it is *intransitive and indicates a change of condition* (from being *awake* to being *asleep*). For this reason, it takes **sein** as an auxiliary.

Er **ist** eingeschlafen.   (He has gone to sleep.)

but: Er **hat** sehr lange geschlafen.   (He [has] slept a long time.)

One must decide in each individual case whether a given verb (with or without prefix) requires **sein** or **haben.**

4. Stress

Separable prefixes (rather than the stem vowel of the verb) receive the primary stress:

INFINITIVE	PAST PARTICIPLE
ábfahren	ábgefahren
aúfmachen	aúfgemacht

B. Inseparable prefixes

be–	ent–	ge–	ver–
emp–	er–	miß–	zer–

1. Forms and Word Order

Unlike separable prefixes, *inseparable prefixes are always joined to their basic verbs*. For example:

PRESENT	Er **verkauft** es Freitag.	(He's selling it Friday.)
PAST	Er **verkaufte** es Freitag.	(He sold it Friday.)

In fact, an inseparable prefix is so firmly joined to its verb that nothing can separate the two. There is *no* **ge–** *prefix* between the separable prefix and the verb in the past participle:

PRESENT PERFECT	Er **hat** es Freitag **verkauft.**	(He [has] sold it Friday.)
PAST PERFECT	Er **hatte** es Freitag **verkauft.**	(He had sold it Friday.)

Regardless of whether they are strong or weak, *verbs with inseparable prefixes do not take a* **ge–** *prefix in forming their past participles:*

	WITH INSEPARABLE PREFIX	WITHOUT INSEPARABLE PREFIX
STRONG VERB	**bekommen** (got, received) **verstanden** (understood)	**gekommen** (came) **gestanden** (stood)
WEAK VERB	**bestellt** (ordered) **verkauft** (sold)	**gestellt** (placed, put) **gekauft** (bought)

The future tense poses no new problem. As usual, it is composed of **werden** *plus an infinitive*. In the example below, the verb has an inseparable prefix:

FUTURE   Er wird es **verkaufen.**   (He will sell it.)

2. Principal Parts of Verbs with Inseparable Prefixes

Adding a prefix to a verb does not affect the conjugation of the verb. If the basic verb is strong, the prefixed verb is also strong; if the basic verb is weak, the prefixed verb is also weak:

	INFINITIVE	PAST	PAST PARTICIPLE	3RD PERSON PRESENT
STRONG VERB	**bekommen** (to get, receive)	bekam	bekommen	bekommt
WEAK VERB	**verkaufen** (to sell)	verkaufte	verkauft	verkauft

3. Sein or haben

The addition of a prefix (whether separable or inseparable) to a verb gives the verb a new meaning, and this new meaning determines whether the prefixed verb requires **sein** or **haben**. For example, the verb **kommen** is *intransitive* (does not take a direct object) and expresses *motion*. **Kommen** therefore meets both the requirements for the auxiliary verb **sein**. On the other hand, the verb **bekommen** is *transitive* (takes a direct object). Hence its auxiliary is **haben**:

Er **hat** das Paket bekommen.   (He [has] received the package.)

but: Er **ist** gestern gekommen.   (He came yesterday.)

4. Stress

Unlike separable prefixes (which are stressed), *inseparable prefixes are not stressed:*

INFINITIVE	PAST PARTICIPLE
verkaúfen	**verkaúft**
bekómmen	**bekómmen**

EXCEPTION: If the inseparable prefix **miß–** is followed by another inseparable prefix, it must be stressed:

míßverstehen   to misunderstand

5. Unter– *and* über– *as Inseparable Prefixes*

The prepositions **unter** and **über** can function as separable prefixes, but they occur much more commonly as *inseparable prefixes*. When they are separable, they are stressed; when they are inseparable, they are NOT stressed:

> **unterhálten**   to entertain
> **unternéhmen**   to undertake
> **überhólen**   to overtake
> **übersétzen**   to translate

The principal parts of these verbs are:

unterhalten	unterhielt	hat unterhalten	(er unterhält)
unternehmen	unternahm	hat unternommen	(er unternimmt)
überholen	überholte	hat überholt	(er überholt)
übersetzen	übersetzte	hat übersetzt	(er übersetzt)

C. Summary table

Compare the principal parts of **ankommen (kommen** plus a separable prefix) and **bekommen (kommen** plus an inseparable prefix):

	INFINITIVE	PAST	PAST PARTICIPLE	3RD PERSON PRESENT
SEPARABLE	**ankommen**	kam . . . an	angekommen	kommt . . . an
INSEPARABLE	**bekommen**	bekam	bekommen	bekommt

NOTE: *Separable* prefixes are *stressed:* **ánkommen.** *Inseparable* prefixes are *unstressed:* **bekómmen.**

▣ DRILLS

Separable-prefix verbs

Use the following words to make complete sentences in the present, past, and present perfect tenses.

1. Kurt / abholen / mich
2. Du / zuhören / gar nicht
3. Ich / einschlafen / früh
4. Mitkommen / Sie / nicht /?
5. Das / vorkommen / oft
6. Herr Kraus / mitbringen / Blumen
7. Kinder / anziehen / Handschuhe
8. Wir / aufmachen / Tür
9. Warum / weglaufen / Sie /?
10. Ich / zurückbringen / Wagen
11. Wann / aufwachen / du /?
12. Anna / aussehen / sehr gut
13. Wir / ausgehen / nicht oft
14. Film / anfangen / um acht
15. Wir / zumachen / Fenster
16. Zug / abfahren / um zwanzig Uhr
17. Wann / zurückkommen / Kinder /?
18. Hans / loslassen / meine Hand
19. Wegnehmen / ihr / das /? (*present* and *present perfect* only)
20. Frau Müller / nachlaufen / mir

Inseparable-prefix verbs

Make complete sentences in the present, past, and present perfect tenses.

1. Wann / bekommen / Sie / Karten /?
2. Herr Raimund / verbringen / Jahr / Amerika
3. Der Direktor / unterschreiben / Brief / nicht
4. Erkennen / du / mich / nicht /?
5. Übersetzen / er / Brief / für dich /?
6. Wir / unternehmen / lange Reise
7. Ich / besprechen / Problem / mit ihm
8. Wagen / gebrauchen / viel Benzin
9. Sie / verstehen / Film / nicht
10. Der Wind / zerstören / Haus

Mixed drills

Make complete sentences in the present, past, and present perfect tenses.

1. Wir / aufmachen / Tür
2. Wann / bekommen / Sie / Karten /?
3. Wagen / gebrauchen / viel Benzin
4. Kinder / anziehen / Handschuhe
5. Warum / weglaufen / Sie /?
6. Das / vorkommen / oft
7. Wir / unternehmen / lange Reise
8. Du / zuhören / gar nicht
9. Kurt / abholen / mich
10. Verstehen / Sie / Film / nicht /?
11. Der Wind / zerstören / Haus
12. Ich / einschlafen / früh
13. Herr Kraus / mitbringen / Blumen
14. Mitkommen / Sie / nicht /?
15. Erkennen / du / mich nicht /?
16. Frau Müller / nachlaufen / mir
17. Wir / ausgehen / nicht oft
18. Herr Raimund / verbringen / Jahr / Amerika
19. Ich / besprechen / Problem / mit ihm
20. Wann / aufwachen / du /?
21. Film / anfangen / acht
22. Wann / zurückkommen / Kinder /?
23. Er / unterhalten / uns / gut
24. Ich / zurückbringen / Wagen
25. Übersetzen / er / Brief / für dich /?
26. Zug / abfahren / um zwanzig Uhr
27. Wegnehmen / ihr / das/? (*present* and *present perfect* only)
28. Wir / überholen / einen Mercedes
29. Kurt / abholen / mich
30. Anna / aussehen / sehr gut

Express in German

1. Aren't you coming along?
2. The wind destroyed the house. (*present perfect*)
3. Don't you recognize me?
4. The children put on their gloves. (*past*)
5. I fell asleep early. (*present perfect*)

6. That happens often.
7. We passed a Mercedes. (*past*)
8. You aren't listening, Mrs. Heller.
9. Why did you run away?
10. He entertained us very well. (*present perfect*)
11. I'll discuss it with him.
12. When did you wake up? (*present perfect*)
13. Kurt is picking me up.
14. We didn't go out very often. (*past*)
15. Mr. Raimund is spending a year in America.
16. We ran after her. (*present perfect*)
17. The movie starts at eight.
18. I translated the letter for him. (*past*)
19. Does the car use much gas?
20. Why did you run away? (*present perfect*)
21. I'll bring it back.
22. Anna is looking very well.
23. They undertook a long trip.
24. The train left at four o'clock. (*present perfect*)
25. When did you get the tickets? (*present perfect*)

adjective
endings

chapter two

LEVEL ONE

I. INTRODUCTION

A. Agreement: gender

The simplest sort of adjective-noun combination is a two-word phrase consisting of a single noun preceded by a single adjective. In English a very common phrase of this kind consists of a noun preceded by the adjective *this:*

this wine

This is an adjective; it *qualifies* or *modifies* the noun *wine*.

The same basic adjective-noun combination occurs in German:

dieser Wein   this wine

When coupled with a singular noun, the English adjective *this* has only one form; in other words, *this* remains *this* no matter what noun it is attached to:

this wine, this beer, this soup

But the German equivalents of *this wine, this beer, this soup* are:

dieser **Wein**   dieses **Bier**   diese **Suppe**

The German adjective takes different forms depending on the noun with which it is associated. This change in form is called *inflection* or *declension*. In this instance, the change has been caused by the *gender* of the nouns: **Wein** is a masculine noun, **Bier** is neuter, and **Suppe** is feminine—der Wein, das Bier, die Suppe.

Thus, the *gender* of a German noun affects the form of the adjective which precedes it. The adjective is therefore said to "agree" with the noun in gender.

B. Agreement: case

Not only does the form of the German adjective reflect the *gender* of the noun it modifies, but it reflects the *case* of the noun as well.

Thus English (where the adjective does not reflect case):

This wine costs too much.   SUBJECT
I like *this wine*.   DIRECT OBJECT
We can begin with *this wine*.   OBJECT OF PREPOSITION

But German (where the adjective DOES reflect case):

Dieser Wein kostet zuviel.   NOMINATIVE SUBJECT
Diesen Wein trinke ich gern.   ACCUSATIVE OBJECT
Wir können mit diesem Wein anfangen.   OBJECT OF PREPOSITION (Here the dative case is used after the preposition **mit,** which requires a dative object.)

C. Agreement: number

In addition to reflecting the *gender* and *case* of the noun it modifies, the German adjective will always reflect the *number* of the noun, i.e. whether the noun is singular or plural:

NOMINATIVE SINGULAR	NOMINATIVE PLURAL
dieser Wein	diese Weine
dieses Bier	diese Biere
diese Suppe	diese Suppen

The same plural forms serve all three genders.

The above examples show one adjective (**dieser**) in five different forms:

dieser   dieses   diese   diesen   diesem

Part of the adjective has remained constant in form throughout these changes: **dies–** is common to all five of the forms and constitutes the *stem* (unchanging part) of the adjective. The adjective *endings* are:

–er   –es   –e   –en   –em

II. STRONG DECLENSION OF ADJECTIVES

In the simple adjective-noun combinations just discussed (**dieser Wein,** etc.), the adjective takes a set of endings called *strong endings*. This is the fullest, most explicit set of endings in German: *the endings of this set show as much as German can show about gender, case, and number.* The following table summarizes all these endings:

	Singular		
	MASCULINE	NEUTER	FEMININE
NOMINATIVE	dieser Wein	dieses Bier	diese Suppe
ACCUSATIVE	diesen Wein	dieses Bier	diese Suppe
DATIVE	diesem Wein	diesem Bier	dieser Suppe
GENITIVE	dieses Wein(e)s	dieses Bier(e)s	dieser Suppe

	Plural
	ALL GENDERS
NOMINATIVE	diese Weine, Biere, Suppen
ACCUSATIVE	diese Weine, Biere, Suppen
DATIVE	diesen Weinen, Bieren, Suppen
GENITIVE	dieser Weine, Biere, Suppen

Notice how similar this kind of declension is to the declension of the definite article **der, das, die.** The following table will show you just how similar:

| | Strong Endings | | | | Definite Article | | | |
	MASC.	NEUT.	FEM.	PL.	MASC.	NEUT.	FEM.	PL.
NOM.	–er	–es	–e	–e	der	das	die	die
ACC.	–en	–es	–e	–e	den	das	die	die
DAT.	–em	–em	–er	–en	dem	dem	der	den
GEN.	–es	–es	–er	–er	des	des	der	der

III. THE DER-WORDS

The following adjectives *always take strong endings.* They are called **der**-words.

> **der**   the *or* that
> **dieser**   this
> **jeder**   each *or* every
> **welcher**   *the question word* which

At this point master the *strong declension* of adjectives by drilling the following simple combinations of a **der**-word and a noun.

◻ DRILLS

Masculine singular strong endings

Supply the required endings.

NOM.	dieser
ACC.	diesen
DAT.	diesem

NOMINATIVE
1. Dies____ Film ist sehr gut.
2. D____ Brief ist schon da.
3. Welch____ Zug ist das?
4. Jed____ Student weiß das.
5. Wie gefällt dir dies____ Wein?

ACCUSATIVE
1. Wir sehen dies____ Film morgen.
2. Ich kaufe d____ Wein nicht.
3. Welch____ Wein trinkst du?
4. Der Professor kennt jed____ Student____.*
5. Arbeiten Sie für dies____ Mann?

DATIVE
1. Ich fahre mit d____ Zug.
2. Ich weiß nichts von dies____ Student____.
3. Mit welch____ Zug fährst du?
4. Er hilft jed____ Student____ gern.
5. Antworten Sie d____ Mann!

MIXED CASES
1. Kaufst du dies____ Tisch?
2. Sag das d____ Vater nicht!
3. Was kostet dies____ Wein?
4. Welch____ Film ist das?
5. Er fährt mit d____ Zug.
6. Erich sieht jed____ Sportfilm.

Neuter singular strong endings

NOM.	dieses
ACC.	dieses
DAT.	diesem

*Student is a so-called weak noun. Weak nouns take the ending –en in all forms except the nominative singular.

	Singular	Plural
NOM.	der Student	die Studenten
ACC.	den Studenten	die Studenten
DAT.	dem Studenten	den Studenten
GEN.	des Studenten	der Studenten

NOMINATIVE

1. D_____ Bild kostet nur zwei Mark.
2. Dies_____ Bier ist sehr gut.
3. Welch_____ Haus ist das?
4. Jed_____ Kind liebt Schokolade.
5. Gefällt Ihnen dies_____ Buch?

ACCUSATIVE

1. Liest du dies_____ Buch?
2. D_____ Bier finde ich nicht gut.
3. Welch_____ Haus kauft er?
4. Lesen Sie jed_____ Wort!
5. Hast du etwas für d_____ Kind?

DATIVE

1. Fährt er mit dies_____ Schiff?
2. Sie kommt gerade aus d_____ Haus.
3. Schokolade gefällt jed_____ Kind.
4. Welch_____ Kind gibst du das?
5. Er antwortet d_____ Mädchen nicht.

MIXED CASES

1. Dies_____ Bier ist nicht gut.
2. Welch_____ Haus kaufst du?
3. Lesen Sie d_____ Buch?
4. Jed_____ Kind gibt er etwas.
5. Mit welch_____ Schiff fährst du?
6. Warum antwortest du d_____ Mädchen nicht?

Feminine singular strong endings

NOM.	diese
ACC.	diese
DAT.	dieser

NOMINATIVE

1. Dies_____ Dame kommt aus Frankreich.
2. D_____ Frau arbeitet zuviel.
3. Welch_____ Zeitung ist das?
4. Jed_____ Suppe gefällt ihm.
5. Dies_____ Krawatte kostet zuviel.

ACCUSATIVE
1. Siehst du d_____ Dame da?
2. Lesen Sie dies_____ Zeitung!
3. Welch_____ Krawatte kaufen Sie?
4. Er kennt jed_____ Straße.
5. Ich kenne dies_____ Stadt nicht gut.

DATIVE
1. Helfen Sie dies_____ Dame!
2. Fährst du mit d_____ Straßenbahn?
3. Aus welch_____ Stadt kommt er?
4. Er antwortet d_____ Frau nicht.
5. Das kommt mit d_____ Zeit.

MIXED CASES
1. Antworte d_____ Dame!
2. Gefällt dir dies_____ Krawatte?
3. Fährst du nicht mit d_____ Straßenbahn?
4. Welch_____ Zeitung lesen Sie?
5. Das Paket ist für dies_____ Dame.
6. D_____ Straßenbahn ist noch nicht da.

Plural strong endings (all genders)

NOM.	diese
ACC.	diese
DAT.	diesen

NOMINATIVE
1. D_____ Bücher sind schon da.
2. Dies_____ Häuser kosten zuviel.
3. Welch_____ Züge fahren nach Berlin?
4. Gefallen dir dies_____ Krawatten nicht?

ACCUSATIVE
1. Dies_____ Bücher lesen wir nicht.
2. Siehst du d_____ Häuser da?
3. Welch_____ Zeitungen meinst du?
4. Haben sie Post für dies_____ Leute?

DATIVE
1. Er spielt mit d____ Kinder____.*
2. Wer wohnt in dies____ Häuser____?
3. Was sagen wir d____ Eltern?
4. Man kann dies____ Leute____ nicht helfen.

MIXED CASES
1. Was geben wir d____ Kinder____?
2. Dies____ Bücher sind zu teuer.
3. Welch____ Zeitungen lesen Sie?
4. Haben Sie Post für dies____ Leute?
5. Sehen Sie d____ Häuser da?
6. Dies____ Leute____ kann man nicht helfen.

Mixed drill (all genders; nominative, accusative, and dative cases; singular and plural)

1. Dies _es_ Bier ist nicht gut.
2. Mit welch _em_ Schiff fahren Sie?
3. Wir sehen dies _en_ Film nicht.
4. Haben wir etwas für d _ie_ Kinder?
5. D _er_ Zug ist schon da.
6. Welch _es_ Haus kaufst du?
7. Wer wohnt in dies _en_ Häuser _n_?
8. D _ie_ Bücher sind hier.
9. Er antwortet d _er_ Frau nicht.   _dative_
10. Welch _er_ Wein gefällt dir am besten?
11. Er spielt mit d _em_ Kinder _n_.
12. Er hilft jed _em_ Student _en_.
13. Was sagen wir d____ Eltern?
14. Welch____ Wagen kauft ihr?
15. Lesen Sie jed____ Wort!
16. Welch____ Zeitung lesen Sie?
17. Er kommt gerade aus d____ Haus.
18. Arbeiten Sie für dies____ Mann?

_____

*With the exception of nouns whose plural forms end in –s (**Radios, Hotels**), all German nouns have *dative plural* forms ending in –n.

NOM.   die Kinder
ACC.   die Kinder
DAT.   den Kindern

19. Kennst du dies____ Dame?
20. Dies____ Leute____ kann man nicht helfen.
21. Jed____ Zeitung liest er gern.

Express in German

1. Do you know this lady?
2. The train is already there. *Der Zug ist schon da*
3. Who lives in these houses?
4. Which car are you buying (*or* going to buy)? *Welches Auto wirst du kaufen?*
5. Read every word.
6. The books are here.
7. He's coming out of the house now.
8. He's not answering (*or* going to answer) the woman.
9. Which house are you buying (*or* going to buy)?
10. Do you work for this man?
11. What ship are you going with?
12. What newspaper are you reading?
13. This beer isn't good.
14. One can't help these people.
15. We're not seeing (*or* going to see) this film.
16. Which wine do you like best?
17. Do we have something for the children?
18. He's playing with the children.
19. He helps every student.

Genitive strong endings

	MASC.	NEUT.	FEM.	PL.
GEN.	dieses	dieses	dieser	dieser

MASCULINE

1. Er kommt Ende d____ Monat____.*
2. Das Ende d____ Film____ ist schlecht.
3. Während d____ Tag____ sieht man ihn nicht.

---

*NOTE: Masculine and neuter nouns take an –(e)s ending in the genitive singular. Generally, the ending –es is used with nouns of one syllable (**Waldes, Brotes**) and all nouns ending in an s-sound (**Gesetzes**). Otherwise, the ending –s is used. (In *spoken* German the –s ending is also found with nouns of one syllable, e.g. **Weins**.)

NEUTER
1. Während d____ Semester____ wohnt er zu Hause.
2. Die Farbe dies____ Auto____ gefällt mir nicht.
3. Wegen d____ Wetter____ bleiben wir zu Hause.

FEMININE
1. Während d____ Woche gehe ich nicht ins Kino.
2. Ende dies____ Woche kommt er nach Hause.
3. Kennst du den Namen dies____ Dame?

PLURAL
1. Wer sind die Eltern dies____ Kinder?
2. Wer ist der Autor dies____ Geschichten?
3. Während d____ Wintermonate lebt er in Wien.

Mixed drill on genitive (all three genders, singular and plural)

1. Ende dies____ Woche kommt er nach Hause.
2. Wer ist der Autor dies____ Geschichten?
3. Während d____ Tag____ sieht man ihn nicht.
4. Kennst du den Namen dies____ Dame?
5. Das Ende dies____ Film____ ist schlecht.
6. Die Farbe dies____ Auto____ gefällt mir nicht.
7. Wegen d____ Wetter____ bleiben wir zu Hause.
8. Während d____ Woche gehe ich nicht ins Kino.
9. Wer sind die Eltern dies____ Kinder?
10. Er kommt Ende d____ Monat____.

LEVEL TWO

I. THE DER-WORDS AS LIMITING WORDS: THE WEAK DECLENSION OF ADJECTIVES FOLLOWING DER-WORDS

A. Introduction

So far we have restricted ourselves to *two-word* combinations of a **der**-word (**der, dieser, jeder, welcher**) and a noun (**Wein, Bier, Suppe,** etc.): **dieser Wein.**

The **der**-words always take strong endings:

> dieser Wein
> diesen Wein
> diesem Wein
> dieses Wein(e)s

But look at *three-word* phrases consisting of a **der**-word *plus another adjective* plus a noun:

> dieser gute Wein
> diesen guten Wein
> diesem guten Wein
> dieses guten Wein(e)s

In the phrases above, **dieser** has full *strong endings*, but the endings of the adjective **gut** are less explicit (i.e. less precisely reflective of gender, case, and number). Such less explicit endings are called *weak endings*.

B. Forms

Weak endings occur in the following pattern:

	Singular			Plural
	MASC.	NEUT.	FEM.	ALL GENDERS
NOM.	−e	−e	−e	−en
ACC.	−en	−e	−e	−en
DAT.	−en	−en	−en	−en
GEN.	−en	−en	−en	−en

NOTE: The ending **−e** is required in the

> masculine: nominative
> neuter: nominative and accusative
> feminine: nominative and accusative

In all other instances the weak ending is **−en.**

C. Usage

1. Two Different Kinds of Adjectives

*a. Limiting adjectives (the **der**-words)*

All the **der**-words are limiting words (or limiting adjectives); that is, they place a limit on the nouns they modify:

der Wein	*the* or *that* wine (not any old wine)
dieser Wein	*this* wine (ditto)
jeder Wein	*each* or *every* wine (an all-inclusive limit)
welcher Wein	*which* wine (which particular one?)

In the examples above, **welcher** is used to ask a person to specify *which* particular wine he is referring to. All the other **der**-words are used to *answer the question* "Which wine?" The answers—*this* wine, *that* wine, *every* wine, and *the* wine—specify *which particular wine* is meant.

b. Descriptive adjectives

Descriptive adjectives answer the question "What kind of...?" If a person asks "*What kind of* wine do you want?" a possible answer is "Red wine." The question "What kind of wine?" asks you to *describe* the sort of wine you want (not to specify *which* particular wine). To do this you use descriptive adjectives (e.g. red, smooth, old).

2. The Effect of Limiting Words on Adjective Endings

As you have seen, there is an essential difference in meaning between limiting adjectives and descriptive adjectives. Still more important, however, is the difference in the way they affect adjective endings.

GENERAL RULE: When a limiting word takes a strong ending the adjectives that follow it take weak endings:

STRONG ENDING	WEAK ENDING
dies**er**	gut**e** Wein

SPECIFIC RULE: **Der**-words are limiting words that *always* take *strong endings*.

CONCLUSION: Therefore, *all* adjectives that follow **der**-words must take weak endings.

Look at the following table that shows the limiting word **dieser** followed by adjective-noun combinations:

		Singular	
	MASCULINE	NEUTER	FEMININE
NOM.	dieser gute Wein	dieses gute Bier	diese gute Suppe
ACC.	diesen guten Wein	dieses gute Bier	diese gute Suppe
DAT.	diesem guten Wein	diesem guten Bier	dieser guten Suppe
GEN.	dieses guten Wein(e)s	dieses guten Bier(e)s	dieser guten Suppe

	Plural
	ALL GENDERS
NOM.	diese guten Weine (Biere, Suppen)
ACC.	diese guten Weine
DAT.	diesen guten Weinen
GEN.	dieser guten Weine

As you see from the tables:

1. The limiting word **dieser** always takes strong endings (as do all **der**-words).

2. The adjectives following the **der**-word take weak endings (–e or –en).

The same pattern holds true for any number of adjectives following a **der**-word:

> der neue grüne Wagen (masc.: nom.)
> das gute frische Brot (neut.: nom. and acc.)
> die guten alten Zeiten (plural: nom. and acc.)

II. ANOTHER SET OF LIMITING WORDS: THE EIN-WORDS

A. The EIN-words

Another group of words limits adjectives in almost the same way as the **der**-words do. This second group is made up of the **ein-** or **kein**-words, so called because they are all declined like **ein,** or better yet like **kein**—since **ein** lacks a plural. The **ein**-words are:

> **ein**   a, an
> **kein**   not a, no

and *all the possessive adjectives:*

mein	my	**unser**	our
dein	your	**euer**	your
sein	his	**ihr**	their
ihr	her	**Ihr**	your (polite form)
sein	its		

NOTE: The **er** at the end of **unser** and **euer** is *part of the stem.* It is NOT *an ending!*

B. Comparison of DIESER and KEIN

There is a slight but very important difference between **der**-words and **ein**-words. Compare the *endings* of **dieser** (a **der**-word) with those of **kein** (an **ein**-word):

	Singular					
	MASCULINE		NEUTER		FEMININE	
NOM.	dieser	kein ☐	dieses	kein ☐	diese	keine
ACC.	diesen	keinen	dieses	kein ☐	diese	keine
DAT.	diesem	keinem	diesem	keinem	dieser	keiner
GEN.	dieses	keines	dieses	keines	dieser	keiner

	Plural	
	ALL GENDERS	
NOM.	diese	keine
ACC.	diese	keine
DAT.	diesen	keinen
GEN.	dieser	keiner

The table above shows the following:

1. **Der-**words: **der**-words *always* take *strong* endings.

2. Ein-words:

   a. Ein-words (such as **kein**) use only their stems, with *no ending*, in the

        masculine: nominative
        neuter: nominative and accusative

   b. In all *other instances*, **ein**-words take *strong endings*.

To summarize: **Der**-words and **ein**-words take the *same* (strong) *endings*, EXCEPT in those three instances where **ein**-words take no endings at all:

	MASCULINE		NEUTER	
NOM.	dieser	kein □	dieses	kein □
ACC.			dieses	kein □

C. Endings on adjectives that follow EIN-words

The same general rule applies to **ein**-words as well as to **der**-words:

1. *When a limiting word takes a strong ending, the adjectives that follow it take weak endings.* Thus, whenever an **ein**-word takes a strong ending, the adjectives following it must take weak endings.

As you have just seen, however, there are three instances where a limiting word takes no ending at all. **Ein**-words take no endings in the

        masculine: nominative
        neuter: nominative and accusative

A specific rule governs this situation:

2. *In those three instances where a limiting word uses only its stem (i.e. has no ending), the adjectives that follow will take* STRONG *endings:*

NOM.	ein	alter	Freund	NOM.	ein	altes	Haus
	sein	alter	Freund		sein	altes	Haus
	unser	alter	Freund		unser	altes	Haus
				ACC.	ein	altes	Haus
					sein	altes	Haus
					unser	altes	Haus

III. ADJECTIVE-NOUN COMBINATIONS WITHOUT LIMITING WORDS

Although most adjective-noun phrases begin with a limiting word (a **der**-word or an **ein**-word), many do not:

> **Frisches Brot** esse ich gern.
> (I like fresh bread.)

> Thomas Mann schreibt **lange Sätze.**
> (Thomas Mann writes long sentences.)

> Jeden Tag bekommen wir **gute, frische Milch.**
> (Every day we get good, fresh milk.)

> Was machst du, **kleiner Mann?**
> (What are you doing, young man?)

When there is no limiting word present, all adjectives preceding a noun take *strong endings*. This is also true of all adjectives in a series:

> **Guter,** alter, treuer Franz!
> (Good, old, faithful Franz!)

IV. VIELE, WENIGE, ANDERE, EINIGE, MEHRERE

Viele, wenige, andere, einige, and **mehrere** are all plural expressions. *They do not act as limiting words;* that is, adjectives that follow them take *strong* endings:

> Ich habe mehrere gute Freunde in Berlin.
> (I have several good friends in Berlin.)

> Er hat viele alte Freunde.
> (He has many old friends.)

Alle, however, *does* act as a limiting word:

> Nicht alle guten Dinge sind teuer.
> (Not all good things are expensive.)

The following scale, which proceeds from *none* to *all*, will help you keep these straight.

keine	no, not a	*a limiting word*	keine guten Freunde
wenige	few		wenige gute Freunde
einige	some		einige gute Freunde
andere	other	*not limiting words*	andere gute Freunde
mehrere	several		mehrere gute Freunde
viele	many		viele gute Freunde
alle	all	*a limiting word*	alle guten Freunde

The extremes **alle** and **keine** indicate a definite number (*all* of a certain group or *none* of a certain group) and are limiting words. The words indicating an indefinite number or an approximation between these definite extremes (*few, some, other, several, many*) are *not* limiting words.

solcher
mancher

V. NOTES ON SPECIAL CONSTRUCTIONS

A. SOLCHER and MANCHER: two more limiting words

In the plural, these two adjectives function as normal limiting words:

Solche langen Bücher lese ich nicht gern.
(I don't like to read such long books.)

Manche alten Leute verbringen den Winter in Florida.
(Many old people spend the winter in Florida.)

In the singular, **mancher** means *many a* and uses the *strong* endings of a **der**-word:

mancher Mann	many a man
manche Frau	many a woman
manches Kind	many a child

and **solcher** means *such* and takes the same (strong) endings:

solcher Unsinn   such nonsense

When used with another adjective in the singular, however, **mancher** becomes **manch ein** (many a) and **solcher** becomes **so ein** (such a). They decline like this:

NOM.	so ein langes Buch	manch ein guter Mann
ACC.	so ein langes Buch	manch einen guten Mann
DAT.	so einem langen Buch	manch einem guten Mann

So and **manch** remain constant and the expression behaves just like an ein-phrase. **Solcher** and **so ein** are common and useful; **mancher** and **manch ein,** however, have an archaic ring.

B. Masculine and neuter genitive singular

Any adjective-noun phrase that begins with a limiting word is completely regular. Look at the following example:

> der Geruch des frischen Heus
> (the smell of the fresh hay)

But when there is no limiting word, you will find the adjective with a weak genitive ending, where you would—according to the "rules"—expect a strong genitive ending:

> der Geruch frischen Heus
> (the smell of fresh hay)

instead of: der Geruch frisches Heus

This exception applies only to the *genitive singular of masculine and neuter nouns.* Since it is a fairly uncommon construction, it is best to learn such expressions as *idioms* when they crop up, rather than as basic structural problems.

VI. PREDICATE ADJECTIVES

> Der Wein ist **gut.**
> (The wine is good.)

> Deine Suppe wird **kalt.**
> (Your soup is getting cold.)

> Ich finde das Buch **interessant.**
> (I find the book interesting.)

The boldface words are *predicate adjectives*. A predicate adjective is an adjective that *does not immediately precede the noun it modifies*. Predicate adjectives are found only with linking verbs such as:

>**sein**   to be
>**werden**   to become, get
>**finden**   to find

As the examples show, predicate adjectives take *no endings:* they consist only of the adjective stem.

VII. SUMMARY

1. There are two types of limiting words:

der-words	and	**ein**-words
der		**ein**
dieser		**kein**
jeder		and all posses-
welcher		sive adjectives

2. *Limiting words* take   (*a*) strong endings

   or   (*b*) no endings at all (in only 3 instances)

   a. When a limiting word has a strong ending, the adjectives that follow it take *weak endings:*

	Singular			*Plural*
	MASC.	NEUT.	FEM.	ALL GENDERS
NOM.	−e	−e	−e	−en
ACC.	−en	−e	−e	−en
DAT.	−en	−en	−en	−en
GEN.	−en	−en	−en	−en

   b. When a limiting word has no ending at all, the adjectives that follow it must take *strong endings*. There are only 3 instances where a limiting word takes no ending: **ein**-words in the

masculine nominative	(ein **alter** Wein)
neuter nominative	(ein **gutes** Bier)
neuter accusative	(ein **gutes** Bier)

In all other instances, limiting words take strong endings and are therefore followed by adjectives with weak endings.

3. *no limiting word*

When an adjective-noun combination does *not* begin with a limiting word the adjectives take strong endings. Such combinations are of the following two types:

    a. combinations beginning with a descriptive adjective:

> gute alte Weine
> armer Hans!

    b. combinations beginning with **viele, wenige, andere, einige,** or **mehrere:**

> viele alte Weine

4. *Predicate adjectives* do not take adjective endings.

VIII. SUMMARY TABLES FOR VARIOUS ADJECTIVE-NOUN COMBINATIONS

MASCULINE

	with **der**-words	with **ein**-words
NOM.	dieser alte Wein	ein alter Wein
ACC.	diesen alten Wein	einen alten Wein
DAT.	diesem alten Wein	einem alten Wein
GEN.	dieses alten Wein(e)s	eines alten Wein(e)s

	with NO limiting word
NOM.	alter Wein
ACC.	alten Wein
DAT.	altem Wein
GEN.	alten Wein(e)s (See p. 58.)

NEUTER

	with **der**-words	with **ein**-words
NOM.	dieses gute Bier	ein gutes Bier
ACC.	dieses gute Bier	ein gutes Bier
DAT.	diesem guten Bier	einem guten Bier
GEN.	dieses guten Bier(e)s	eines guten Bier(e)s

	with NO limiting word
NOM.	gutes Bier
ACC.	gutes Bier
DAT.	gutem Bier
GEN.	guten Bier(e)s (See p. 58.)

FEMININE

	with **der**-words	with **ein**-words
NOM.	diese gute Suppe	eine gute Suppe
ACC.	diese gute Suppe	eine gute Suppe
DAT.	dieser guten Suppe	einer guten Suppe
GEN.	dieser guten Suppe	einer guten Suppe

	with NO limiting word
NOM.	gute Suppe
ACC.	gute Suppe
DAT.	guter Suppe
GEN.	guter Suppe

PLURAL
(all three genders)

	with **der**- or **ein**-words	after **viele, wenige, andere, einige, mehrere**
NOM.	diese alten Leute keine alten Leute	viele alte Leute
ACC.	diese alten Leute keine alten Leute	viele alte Leute

DAT.	diesen alten Leuten	vielen alten Leuten
	keinen alten Leuten	
GEN.	dieser alten Leute	vieler alter Leute
	keiner alten Leute	

with NO limiting word

NOM.	alte Leute
ACC.	alte Leute
DAT.	alten Leuten
GEN.	alter Leute

▣ DRILLS

NOTE: Genitive patterns will be drilled separately at the end of this section.

Masculine singular with **der**-words

Supply the correct endings.

NOMINATIVE
1. D____ ander____ Handschuh ist da drüben.
2. Wem gehört dies____ neu____ Wagen?
3. Welch____ alt____ Mann?
4. Wo ist d____ letzt____ Brief von Hans?

ACCUSATIVE
1. Er kauft d____ neu____ Wagen nicht.
2. Wollen Sie dies____ braun____ Anzug?
3. Welch____ alt____ Mann meinst du?
4. Der Brief ist für d____ alt____ Herr____.

DATIVE
1. Helfen Sie d____ alt____ Herr____!
2. Er sagt es d____ ander____ Mann.
3. Er fährt mit d____ neu____ Zug.

Masculine singular with **ein**-words

NOMINATIVE
1. Das ist ein neu____ Wagen.
2. Das ist kein billig____ Wein.

3. Wo ist mein neu____ Anzug?
4. Dein alt____ braun____ Mantel ist da drüben.
5. Das ist sein letzt____ Brief.

ACCUSATIVE

1. Ich kaufe ein____ neu____ Anzug.
2. Ich sehe kein____ rot____ Wagen.
3. Sehen Sie mein____ ander____ Handschuh?
4. Verkauft ihr euer____ alt____ Wagen nicht? (eur____!)*
5. Haben Sie etwas für ein____ arm____ Mann?

DATIVE

1. Er zeigt es ein____ ander____ Kunde____.
2. So etwas gefällt kein____ alt____ Mann.
3. Ich gehe zu ein____ alt____ Freund.

Masculine singular (mixed drills)

1. Sehen Sie d_en_ ander_en_ Handschuh?
2. Das ist sein letzt_er_ Brief.
3. Ich sehe kein_en_ rot_en_ Wagen.
4. Er fährt mit d_em_ neu_en_ Zug.
5. Welch_en_ alt_en_ Mann meinst du? _du is subject_
6. Dein alt____ braun____ Mantel ist da drüben.
7. Hilf d_em_ alt_en_ Herr_n_!
8. Verkauft ihr euer_n_ alt_en_ Wagen nicht? (eur____!)
9. Wem gehört dies_er_ neu_er_ Wagen? _Wagen is subject_
10. Er zeigt es ein_em_ ander_en_ Kunde_n_.
11. Ich meine d_en_ ander_en_ Brief.
12. Kaufen Sie ein____ neu____ Anzug?
13. Das ist kein____ billig____ Wein.
14. Haben Sie etwas für ein____ arm____ Mann?
15. Hat er gut____ Wein?

Neuter singular with **der**-words

NOMINATIVE

1. D____ braun____ Paket gehört mir.
2. Welch____ alt____ Buch?
3. Wie schnell fährt dies____ neu____ Auto?

---

*NOTE: Adjectives ending in –euer (e.g. **euer, teuer**) drop the second e when an adjective ending is added (e.g. **eure, teure**).

ACCUSATIVE
1. Ich sehe d____ ander____ Mädchen nicht.
2. Welch____ neu____ Haus meinen Sie?
3. Ohne dies____ neu____ Buch kann ich nicht weiterarbeiten.
4. Sie nimmt d____ grün____ Kleid.

DATIVE
1. Er spielt mit d____ klein____ Kind.
2. Er antwortet d____ jung____ Mädchen.
3. Er wohnt nicht weit von dies____ neu____ Hotel.

Neuter singular with **ein**-words

NOMINATIVE
1. Das ist ein groß____ Fenster.
2. Das ist kein billig____ Buch.
3. Wo ist euer neu____ Auto?
4. Ist das ihr alt____ Haus?

ACCUSATIVE
1. Ich kaufe kein teuer____ Auto. (teur____!)
2. Ich gebe dir ein gut____ Beispiel.
3. Wir verkaufen unser alt____ Haus.
4. Das ist nichts für ein klein____ Kind.

DATIVE
1. Kommen Sie zu mein____ neu____ Büro!
2. Es ist ein Brief von ein____ deutsch____ Mädchen.
3. Nein, wir fahren mit ein____ ander____ Schiff.

Neuter singular (mixed drills)

1. Ich sehe d____ ander____ Mädchen nicht.
2. Wie schnell fährt dies____ neu____ Auto?
3. Er antwortet d____ jung____ Mädchen.
4. Das ist nichts für ein klein____ Kind.
5. Er wohnt nicht weit von dies____ neu____ Hotel.
6. Das ist kein billig____ Buch.
7. Kommen Sie zu mein____ neu____ Büro!
8. Was für ein alt____ Buch ist das?
9. Nein, wir fahren mit ein____ ander____ Schiff.

10. Ich gebe dir ein gut_____ Beispiel.
11. Sie nimmt das grün_____ Kleid.
12. Es ist ein Brief von ein_____ deutsch_____ Mädchen.
13. Ist das Ihr neu_____ Haus?
14. Er kauft kein teur_____ Auto.
15. Welch_____ neu_____ Haus meinen Sie?

Feminine singular with **der**-words

NOMINATIVE

1. D_____ braun_____ Krawatte kostet fünf Mark.
2. Wem gehört dies_____ alt_____ Uhr?
3. Welch_____ deutsch_____ Zeitung?

ACCUSATIVE

1. Verstehen Sie d_____ alt_____ Frau?
2. Ich kaufe dies_____ billig_____ Krawatte nicht.
3. Zeigen Sie mir d_____ neu_____ Speisekarte!
4. Fahr nicht durch dies_____ groß_____ Stadt!

DATIVE

1. Ich gebe es d_____ neu_____ Sekretärin.
2. Hilf der nett_____ alt_____ Dame!
3. Ich fahre zu d_____ nächst_____ Tankstelle.
4. Was machen wir mit dies_____ häßlich_____ Lampe?

Feminine singular with **ein**-words

NOMINATIVE

1. Das ist ein_____ schön_____ Farbe.
2. Wo ist mein_____ braun_____ Krawatte?
3. Das ist kein_____ neu_____ Übung.
4. Mein_____ alt_____ Uhr geht nicht mehr.

ACCUSATIVE

1. Wo finden wir ein_____ besser_____ Liste?
2. Kaufen Sie kein_____ silbergrau_____ Krawatte!
3. Er kann sein_____ neu_____ Jacke nicht finden.
4. So ein_____ schön_____ alt_____ Stadt sieht man nicht oft.
5. Haben Sie kein_____ frisch_____ Milch?
6. Er liest ein_____ deutsch_____ Zeitung.

DATIVE
1. Er kommt aus ein____ klein____ Stadt in Bayern.
2. Der Brief ist von mein____ klein____ Schwester.
3. Fahren Sie zu ein____ ander.____ Tankstelle!

Feminine singular (mixed drills)

1. D____ braun____ Krawatte kostet fünf Mark.
2. Er kommt aus ein____ klein____ Stadt in Bayern.
3. Fahr nicht durch dies____ groß____ Stadt!
4. Das ist ein____ schön____ Farbe.
5. Was machen wir mit dies____ häßlich____ Lampe?
6. Er liest ein____ deutsch____ Zeitung.
7. Mein____ alt____ Uhr geht nicht mehr.
8. Ich gebe es d____ neu____ Sekretärin.
9. Verstehen Sie d____ alt____ Frau?
10. Der Brief ist von mein____ klein____ Schwester.
11. Zeigen Sie mir d____ neu____ Speisekarte!
12. Das ist kein____ neu____ Übung.
13. So ein____ schön____ alt____ Stadt sieht man nicht oft.
14. Ich fahre zu d____ nächst____ Tankstelle.
15. Wem gehört dies____ alt____ Uhr?

Plural forms with **ein-** and **der**-words

NOMINATIVE
1. Unser____ neu____ Bücher sind schon da.
2. Wo sind mein____ braun____ Handschuhe?
3. Dies____ hoh____ Preise gefallen mir nicht.
4. D____ erst____ Seiten sind schwer.

ACCUSATIVE
1. Ich kann mein____ schwarz____ Handschuhe nicht finden.
2. Morgen bringe ich dir d____ ander____ Pakete.
3. Haben Sie kein____ deutsch____ Zeitungen?
4. Geben Sie mir d____ neu____ Listen!
5. Er trinkt doch kein____ billig____ Weine!

DATIVE
1. Zeigen Sie es kein____ ander____ Kunden!
2. Was machen wir mit dies____ alt____ Bücher____?
3. Dies____ arm____ Leute____ kann man nicht helfen.

Adjective-noun combinations without **der-** or **ein**-words
(i.e. without limiting words)

There are two types:

1. combinations beginning with descriptive adjectives:

   > Guten Wein trinke ich gern.
   > Gute, alte Weine trinke ich gern.

2. combinations beginning with **viele, wenige, andere, einige, mehrere**:

   > Ich kenne viele gute, alte Weine.

NOMINATIVE
1. Frisch____ Brot ist sehr gut.
2. Was machst du da, jung____ Mann?
3. Arm____ Frau Schneider!
4. Viel____ nett____ Mädchen sind da.
5. In dieser Stadt sind mehrer____ schön____ alt____ Häuser.
6. Hoh____ Preise gefallen mir nicht.

ACCUSATIVE
1. Deutschland hat wenig____ hoh____ Gebäude.
2. Ich lese neu____ Romane gern.
3. Kalt____ Bier trinke ich gern.
4. Sie hat mehrer____ groß____ Pakete.
5. Hat er gut____ Wein?
6. Er schreibt nett____ Briefe.
7. Trinken Sie kalt____ Milch?
8. Das Buch hat einig____ gut____ Beispiele.

DATIVE
1. Schön____ Damen sagt man nicht nein.
2. Man soll arm____ Leute____ helfen.
3. Sie schreibt mit rot____ Tinte.
4. Er hat Freunde in mehrer____ europäisch____ Städten.

Plural (mixed drills)

This exercise includes (*a*) nouns limited by **der-** or **ein-**words, (*b*) nouns preceded by words like **viele** that do not limit the adjective endings, and (*c*) phrases beginning with descriptive adjectives.

1. Morgen bringe ich dir d____ ander____ Pakete.
2. Schön____ Damen sagt man nicht nein.
3. Unser____ neu____ Bücher sind da.
4. Was machen wir mit dies____ alt____ Bücher____?
5. In dieser Stadt sind mehrer____ schön____ alt____ Häuser.
6. Ich lese neu____ Romane gern.
7. Welch____ alt____ Briefe meinst du?
8. Er beginnt mit d____ neu____ Übungen.
9. D____ erst____ Seiten sind schwer.
10. Hoh____ Preise gefallen mir nicht.
11. D____ hoh____ Preise gefallen mir nicht.
12. Deutschland hat wenig____ hoh____ Gebäude.
13. Haben Sie kein____ deutsch____ Zeitungen?
14. Man soll arm____ Leute____ helfen.
15. Wo sind mein____ schwarz____ Handschuhe?

Mixed drills

Gender, number, case, and type of limitation are mixed.

1. Das ist unser neu_er_ Wagen.
2. Ich sehe d_as_ ander_en_ Mädchen nicht.
3. Der Brief ist von mein_er_ klein_en_ Schwester.
4. Unser_e_ neu_en_ Bücher sind da.
5. Er schreibt mit rot____ Tinte.
6. Ist das Ihr alt____ Haus?
7. Tübingen ist ein_e_ schön_e_ alt_e_ Stadt.
8. Morgen bringe ich Ihnen d_ie_ ander_en_ Pakete.
9. Ihr alt_er_ braun_er_ Mantel ist dort drüben.
10. Hat er gut_en_ Wein?
11. Welch____ alt____ Briefe meinst du?
12. Bringen Sie mir d_ie_ neu_en_ Speisekarte!
13. Es ist ein Brief von ein_er_ deutsch_en_ Mädchen.
14. D_ie_ erst_e_ Seiten sind schwer.
15. Wollen Sie dies_en_ braun_en_ Anzug?

16. Hilf d _em_ alt _en_ Mann!
17. Ich fahre zu d _er_ nächst _en_ Tankstelle.
18. Kalt _es_ Bier trinke ich gern.
19. Haben Sie kein _e_ deutsch _en_ Zeitungen?
20. Was machen wir mit dies____ häßlich____ Lampe?
21. Wir verkaufen unser alt____ Haus.
22. Wo sind mein____ schwarz____ Handschuhe?
23. Kaufen Sie ein____ neu____ Anzug?
24. Welch____ deutsch____ Zeitung meinen Sie?
25. Was machst du da, jung____ Mann?
26. Das ist kein____ schön____ Farbe.
27. Ich sehe kein____ rot____ Wagen.
28. Ich gebe dir ein gut____ Beispiel.
29. Es gibt mehrer____ schön____ alt____ Häuser in dieser Stadt.
30. Wie schnell fährt dies____ neu____ Auto?
31. Frisch____ Brot ist sehr gut.
32. Verkaufen Sie Ihr____ alt____ Wagen nicht?
33. Er kommt aus ein____ klein____ Stadt in Bayern.
34. Schön____ Damen sagt man nicht nein.
35. Das ist kein billig____ Wein.
36. Er kauft kein billig____ Auto.
37. Deutschland hat wenig____ hoh____ Gebäude.
38. Was machen wir mit dies____ alt____ Bücher____.
39. Er wohnt nicht weit von d____ neu____ Hotel.
40. Zeigen Sie es d____ ander____ Kunden! (*plural*)

Express in German *# 1-20 für Freitag*

1. Tübingen is a pretty old city.
2. I'll give you a good example.
3. Fresh bread is very good.
4. Aren't you selling your old car?
5. Our new books are here.
6. He's reading a German newspaper.
7. Do you want this brown suit?
8. The first pages are difficult.
9. It's a letter from a German girl.
10. Where are my black gloves?
11. He writes with red ink.
12. I'll bring you the other packages tomorrow.

13. I don't see the other girl.
14. Help the old man.
15. Show me the new menu.
16. Which old letters do you mean?
17. How fast does this new car go?
18. The letter is from my little sister.
19. What are you doing there, young man?
20. Don't you have any German newspapers?
21. Is that your old house?
22. That's our new car.
23. I like to drink cold beer.
24. That's not a pretty color.
25. Are you buying a new suit?
26. What'll we do with this ugly lamp?
27. There are many pretty old houses in Rothenburg.
28. Does he have good wine?
29. Your old brown coat is over there.
30. He doesn't live far from the new hotel.
31. He comes from a small city in Bavaria.
32. Germany has few tall buildings.
33. What'll we do with these old books?
34. I don't see any red car.
35. We're selling our old house.
36. That's not a cheap wine.
37. Show it to the other customers.
38. He's not buying an expensive car.
39. Which old man do you mean?
40. One doesn't say "no" to beautiful ladies.

▣ DRILLS ON GENITIVE PATTERNS

Adjective-noun combinations introduced by **der-** and **ein-words**[*]

MASCULINE and NEUTER
1. Unser Sommerhaus steht am Rande ein＿＿ groß＿＿ Wald＿＿.
2. Während d＿＿ zweit＿＿ Weltkrieg＿＿ lebten wir in Amerika.

---

[*]NOTE: Masculine and neuter nouns take an –(e)s ending in the genitive singular. Generally, the ending **–es** is used with nouns of one syllable (Wald**es**, Brot**es**) and all nouns ending in an s-sound (Gesetz**es**). Otherwise, **–s** is used.

3. Wie ist der Name d____ neu____ amerikanisch____ Präsidenten?
4. Er saß am Ende ein____ lang____ Tisch____.
5. Wer ist der Verfasser dies____ interessant____ Werk____?
6. Wo sind die Eltern dies____ arm____ Mädchen____?
7. Sie ist die Tochter ein____ berühmt____ Dichter____.
8. Der Garten dies____ alt____ Haus____ ist sehr schön.

FEMININE

1. Wer ist der Autor dies____ schön____ Novelle?
2. Heißt das Stück „Besuch ein____ alt____ Dame" oder „Besuch d____ alt____ Dame"?
3. Er ist Direktor ein____ groß____ Firma.
4. Es ist die Geschichte ein____ wahr____ Liebe.

PLURAL

1. Das sind die Enkelkinder dies____ alt____ Leute.
2. Während d____ letzt____ Wochen haben wir ihn nicht mehr gesehen.
3. Die Resultate sein____ neu____ Experimente sind gut.
4. Trotz d____ viel____ Mücken (*bugs*) gehen wir gern camping.

Adjective-noun combinations beginning with adjectives
other than limiting words (See pp. 56 and 58.)

MASCULINE and NEUTER (weak endings)
1. Wegen schlecht____ Wetter____ sind wir zu Hause geblieben.
2. Ende vorig____ Monat____ bekam ich einen Brief von Vater.

FEMININE and PLURAL (strong endings)
1. Er ist ein Liebhaber klassisch____ Musik.
2. Er ist der Sohn reich____ Eltern.

Genitive (mixed drills)

1. Er saß am Ende ein____ lang____ Tisch____.
2. Die Resultate sein____ neu____ Experimente sind gut.
3. Heißt das Stück „Besuch ein_er_ alt_en_ Dame" oder „Besuch d_er_ alt_en_ Dame"?
4. Wo sind die Eltern dies_es_ arm_en_ Mädchen_s_?
5. Wegen schlecht_es_ Wetter_s_ sind wir zu Hause geblieben.
6. Er ist Direktor ein_er_ groß_en_ Firma.
7. Sie ist die Tochter ein____ berühmt____ Dichter____.
8. Er ist ein Liebhaber klassisch_er_ Musik.

9. Während d_er_ letzt_en_ Wochen haben wir ihn nicht mehr gesehen.
10. Wie ist der Name d_es_ neu_en_ amerikanisch_en_ Präsidenten?
11. Es ist die Geschichte ein_er_ wahr_en_ Liebe.
12. Das sind die Enkelkinder dies_er_ alt_en_ Leute. *(pl)*
13. Unser Sommerhaus steht am Rande ein_es_ groß_en_ Wald_es_.
14. Trotz d_er_ viel_en_ Mücken gehen wir gern camping.
15. Wer ist der Verfasser dies_er_ schön_en_ Novelle?
16. Wer ist der Autor dies_es_ interessant_en_ Werk_es_?
17. Er ist der Sohn reich_er_ Eltern.
18. Der Garten dies_es_ alt_en_ Haus_es_ ist sehr schön.
19. Ende vorig_en_ Monat_____ bekam ich einen Brief von Vater.
20. Während d_es_ zweit_en_ Weltkrieg_____ lebten wir in Amerika.

no article

comparison of adjectives and adverbs

chapter three

I. COMPARISON OF ADJECTIVES

A. Introduction

Both English and German adjectives occur in three basic forms: the positive, the comparative, and the superlative.

	ENGLISH	GERMAN
POSITIVE	cheap	**billig**
COMPARATIVE	cheaper	**billiger**
SUPERLATIVE	cheapest	**billigst–**
POSITIVE	interesting	**interessant**
COMPARATIVE	more interesting	**interessanter**
SUPERLATIVE	most interesting	**interessantest–**

English has two ways of forming the comparative and superlative:

1. cheap, cheap*er*, cheap*est*

The suffixes *-er* and *-est* are added to the positive form of all one-syllable and some two-syllable adjectives.

2. interesting, *more* interesting, *most* interesting

The words *more* and *most* are used with longer adjectives.

B. German forms

German forms its comparative and superlative in only *one* basic way: by the use of suffixes.

The basic pattern:
comparative = adjective + **er**   billiger   interessanter
superlative = adjective + **(e)st**   billigst–   interessantest–

1. The Suffixes –er and –(e)st

1. The comparative stem always ends in **–er**:

POSITIVE	billig	interessant	heiß
COMPARATIVE	billiger	interessanter	heißer

2. The superlative stem always ends in **–st** or **–est**:

POSITIVE	billig	interessant	heiß
COMPARATIVE	billiger	interessanter	heißer
SUPERLATIVE	billigst–	interessantest–	heißest–

–est is used when the positive form ends in **–d, –t,** or an s-sound (**–s, –ss, –ß, –z**).

2. Umlaut

Most *one-syllable* adjectives with the stem vowels **a** and **u** will take an umlaut in the comparative and superlative forms. The stem vowel **o** is only occasionally umlauted.

POSITIVE	alt	lang	jung	kurz	grob
COMPARATIVE	älter	länger	jünger	kürzer	gröber
SUPERLATIVE	ältest–	längst–	jüngst–	kürzest–	gröbst–

The following list shows commonly used adjectives that *must* take umlaut and *do not* take umlaut:

MANDATORY UMLAUT		NO UMLAUT	
alt	old	**flach**	flat
arm	poor	**froh**	happy
dumm	stupid	**klar**	clear
grob	coarse	**rasch**	quick
hart	hard; severe	**roh**	raw; crude
jung	young	**schlank**	slender
kalt	cold	**stolz**	proud
klug	clever	**toll**	crazy
kurz	short	**voll**	full
lang	long	**zart**	tender
scharf	sharp		
schwach	weak		
stark	strong		
warm	warm		

3. Comparative and Superlative Forms of Adjectives Ending in –e, –el, –en, and –er

1. Some adjectives have positive *stems that end in* –e. The comparative simply adds –r (since an –e is already there), and the superlative adds –st.

POSITIVE	leise	weise
COMPARATIVE	leiser	weiser
SUPERLATIVE	leisest–	weisest–

2. Adjectives whose *stems end in* –el form the comparative and superlative like this:

dunkel   dunkler   dunkelst–

NOTE: The e in **dunkel** is dropped in the comparative: dunkler.

3. Adjectives whose *stems end in* –en *or* –er will *often* drop this first e in the comparative:

POSITIVE	trocken	tapfer
COMPARATIVE	trock(e)ner	tapf(e)rer
SUPERLATIVE	trockenst–	tapferst–

4. Irregular Forms

The following adjectives have irregular forms. Memorize them.

POSITIVE	COMPARATIVE	SUPERLATIVE	
groß	größer	größt–	(adds only –t in superlative)
gut	besser	best–	
hoch (hoh)*	höher	höchst–	(drops c from comparative)
nah(e)	näher	nächst–	(adds c in superlative)
viel	mehr	meist–**	

C. Usage

1. Positive, Comparative, and Superlative Forms with Adjective Endings

Billig, billiger, and **billigst** are all stem forms, and as stems they will take normal adjective endings when they precede a noun.

Billig + *endings*

> Dies ist ein billig**er** Anzug.
> Zeigen Sie mir einen billig**en** Anzug!
> Haben Sie billig**e** Anzüge?

Billiger + *endings*

> Dies ist ein billiger**er** Anzug.
> Zeigen Sie mir einen billiger**en** Anzug!
> Haben Sie billiger**e** Anzüge?

Billigst + *endings*

> Dies ist der billigst**e** Anzug.
> Zeigen Sie mir den billigst**en** Anzug!
> Wo sind die billigst**en** Anzüge?

---

*__Hoch__ is irregular in the positive form as well. As a predicate adjective, it is regular: **Die Preise sind hoch.** But when endings are added to **hoch**, the c drops from the stem: **Das sind hohe Preise.**
__Die meisten Leute__ most people *or* **Die meisten Kinder most children: German uses the definite article in such expressions.

2. Positive, Comparative, and Superlative Forms as Predicate Adjectives

a. Positive

Used as a predicate adjective, the positive form takes no endings at all:

Dieser Anzug ist **billig.**
Dieses Hemd ist **billig.**
Diese Jacke ist **billig.**
Die Anzüge finde ich **billig.**

b. Comparative

The comparative form likewise uses only its stem when it is a predicate adjective:

Dieser Anzug ist **billiger.**
Dieses Hemd ist **billiger.**
Diese Jacke ist **billiger.**
Anzüge werden jetzt **billiger.**

c. Superlative

The superlative form, however, behaves somewhat differently:

1. It can occur in a pattern with endings that vary according to gender and number:

Dieser Anzug ist **der billigste.** (This suit is *the cheapest.*)
Dieses Hemd ist **das billigste.**
Diese Jacke ist **die billigste.**
Diese Anzüge sind **die billigsten.**

or:

2. It can occur in a form that does not vary in gender or number. This is the pattern:

am _____ **–en**
am billigsten
am interessantesten
am schönsten

Dieser Anzug ist **am billigsten.** (This suit is *cheapest.*)
Dieses Hemd ist **am billigsten.**
Diese Jacke ist **am billigsten.**
Diese Anzüge sind **am billigsten.**

The **am billigsten** pattern *must* be used when dissimilar things are being compared:

Wir haben Orangen, Äpfel und Bananen. Die Äpfel sind **am billigsten.**

D. Common adjective formulas using positive and comparative forms

größer **als** (larger *than*)	Berlin ist größer **als** München.
billiger **als** (cheaper *than*)	Bier ist billiger **als** Wein.
nicht so groß **wie** (*not as* large *as*)	München ist **nicht so** groß **wie** Berlin.
nicht so billig **wie** (*not as* cheap *as*)	Wein ist **nicht so** billig **wie** Bier.
(genau) so alt **wie** ([*just*] *as* old *as*)	Anna ist **(genau) so** alt **wie** Karl.
(genau) so gut **wie** ([*just*] *as* good *as*)	Sein letztes Buch ist **(genau) so** gut **wie** sein erstes.

NOTE: The *comparative* form is used with **als:**

> **größer** als
> **billiger** als

and the *positive* form is used with **wie:**

> nicht so **groß** wie
> (genau) so **groß** wie

je mehr, **desto** besser
(*the* more *the* better)

„Wieviel Geld willst du?"   „**Je** mehr, **desto** besser."
("How much money do you want?")   ("*The* more *the* better.")

Je mehr Geld er hat, **desto** glücklicher ist er.
(*The* more money he has, *the* happier he is.)

In this construction both adjectives are in the comparative.

immer höher	Die Preise werden **immer** höher.
(higher and higher [ever higher])	(Prices are getting higher and higher.)
immer hübscher	Bettina wird **immer** hübscher.
(prettier and prettier)	(Bettina is getting prettier and prettier.)

Rather than repeating a comparative adjective as English does (e.g. higher and higher), German uses the word **immer** in front of the comparative adjective (**immer** höher).

SUMMARY

größer **als**	larger *than*
(nicht) so groß **wie**	(*not*) *as* large *as*
immer größer	larger and larger
je größer, **desto** besser	*the* larger *the* better

II. COMPARISON OF ADVERBS

A. Forms and functions

The forms of the German *adverb* are essentially the same as those of the *predicate adjective*. The distinction between German adjectives and adverbs is more one of *function* than of form. The predicate adjective modifies a noun or a pronoun; the adverb modifies a *verb* (or another adverb—or even an adjective).

POSITIVE	schnell
COMPARATIVE	schneller
SUPERLATIVE	am schnellsten

ADJECTIVE	Der **VW** ist nicht sehr **schnell.** (**Schnell** modifies **VW.**)
ADVERB	Der VW **fährt** nicht sehr **schnell.** (**Schnell** modifies **fährt.**)

ADJECTIVE	Der **DKW** ist **schneller.**
ADVERB	Der DKW **fährt schneller.**

ADJECTIVE	Der **Mercedes** ist **am schnellsten.**
ADVERB	Der Mercedes **fährt am schnellsten.**

NOTE: The **am** _____**-en** form is the *only* form for the superlative of the adverb:

Heinrich singt **am besten.**	(Heinrich sings [the] best.)
Wer springt **am höchsten?**	(Who jumps [the] highest?)

B. Common adverb formulas using positive and comparative forms

The same formulas are used with adverbs as with adjectives:

als	Du gehst **öfter als** ich ins Kino.
	(You go to the movies *more often than* I do.)
nicht so . . . wie	Er schreibt **nicht so gut, wie** er spricht.
	(He does *not* write *as well as* he speaks.)
(genau) so . . . wie	Karl singt **(genau) so schlecht wie** du.
	(Karl sings [*just*] *as badly as* you do.)
immer −er	Das Orchester spielt **immer besser.**
	(The orchestra is playing *better and better.*)
Je . . . desto . . .	**Je schneller** er läuft, **desto früher** ist er da.
	(*The faster* he runs, *the sooner* he'll be there.)

C. GERN, LIEBER, AM LIEBSTEN

Gern (or **gerne**) is an adverb that imparts the meaning *like to* to the verb:

Ich singe.	(I sing.)
Ich singe **gern.**	(I *like to* sing.)
Er spielt Ball.	(He plays ball.)
Er spielt **gern** Ball.	(He *likes to* play ball.)
Ich trinke Milch.	(I drink milk.)
Ich trinke **gern** Milch.	(I *like to* drink milk.)

Gern has irregular comparative and superlative forms:

Ich trinke **lieber** Kaffee.	(I *prefer to* drink coffee.)
Ich trinke **am liebsten** Wein.	(I *like to* drink wine *best of all.*)

◻ DRILLS

Form drills

1. Luise ist _____ als ihre Schwester.   (ruhig)
   Luise ist **ruhiger** als ihre Schwester.
   (alt, schlank, interessant, klug, hübsch, stark, fröhlich, jung, groß)

2. Die Tage werden immer _____. (ruhig)
   Die Tage werden immer **ruhiger.**
   (lang, schwer, kalt, kurz, schön, hart)

3. Je _____, desto besser. (ruhig)
   Je **ruhiger,** desto besser.
   (rasch, früh, billig, leise, nah, klar, viel, hoch, dunkel)

4. Siegfried ist der _____ von meinen Bekannten. (ruhig)
   Siegfried ist der **ruhigste** von meinen Bekannten.
   (gut, stolz, intelligent, arm, tapfer, schwach, toll, weise, dumm, ehrlich)

Predicate adjectives and adverbs

1. Karl ist _____ sein Bruder.
           (older than)

2. Heute ist es nicht _____ gestern.
           (as warm as)

3. Es wird _____.
           (warmer)

4. Diese Koffer werden _____.
           (heavier and heavier)

5. Im Juni sind die Tage _____ und die Nächte _____.
           (longest)   (shortest)

6. Ich trinke _____ Tee.
           (like to)

7. Was trinken Sie _____?
           (like to [drink] best)

8. Er ißt _____ ich.
           (more than)

9. Die Filme werden _____.
           (longer and longer)

10. Du bist _____ dein Vater.
            (just as stupid as)

11. Harvard ist _____, Oxford ist _____, aber
            (old)   (older)
    Salamanca ist _____.
            (oldest)

12. Hier sitzt man _____.
            (the most comfortably)

13. Gold ist _____ Silber.
            (heavier than)

14. Ihre Frau wird _____, Herr Generaldirektor.
    (prettier and prettier)

15. „Wie singt man das?" „_____, _____."
    (The softer the better)

16. Anna ist _____ Heidi, aber ich finde sie _____.
    (not as pretty as)   (more interesting)

17. Wer ist _____, Werner oder Kurt?
    (stronger)

18. Felix ist nicht _____ seine Schwester.
    (as big as)

19. Meine Augen werden _____.
    (weaker and weaker)

20. Es ist _____, _____ du glaubst.
    (closer than)

21. Die Straßenbahn fährt _____ der Bus.
    (more slowly than)

22. Die U–Bahn fährt _____.
    (fastest)

23. Von den deutschen Filmstars gefällt mir die Dietrich _____.
    (best)

24. Aber Mitzi, Karl ist doch zwanzig Jahre _____ du.
    (older than)

25. Das Matterhorn ist nicht _____ der Mont Blanc.
    (as high as)

26. Wir haben Orangen, Äpfel und Birnen; die Äpfel sind _____
    (the cheapest)

    aber sie sind nicht _____ die Orangen.
    (not as good as)

27. _____ er arbeitet, _____ wird er.
    (The more)   (the more tired)

Adjective endings

1. Es ist _____ Haus in der Stadt.
   (the largest)

2. _____ Mal bleibe ich zu Hause.
   (The next)

3. Er sucht _____ Wohnung.
   (a larger)

4. Franz erzählt _____ Geschichten.
   (the craziest)

5. Ich fahre mit _____ Straßenbahn.
    (the next)

6. _____ Kreisen tut man das nicht.
    (In the best)

7. Haben Sie _____ Messer?
    (a sharper)

8. _____ Leute kaufen den _____ Volkswagen.
    (Most)   (smaller)

9. Ich kenne _____ Mann.
    (no wiser)

10. Es ist _____ Rathaus in Deutschland.
     (the oldest)

11. Es ist _____ Wagen in ganz Italien.
     (the fastest)

12. Ich brauche _____ Mantel.
     (a darker)

Mixed drills

1. Es ist _____, _____ du glaubst.
                      (larger than)

2. Ich kenne _____ Mann.
    (no more intelligent)

3. Er läuft _____ ich.
    (faster than)

4. Das Gepäck wird _____.
                      (heavier and heavier)

5. Er sucht _____ Wohnung.
    (a larger)

6. Was trinken Sie _____?
                      (like to [drink] best)

7. Heute ist es nicht _____ gestern.
                      (as warm as)

8. Die italienischen Filme sind _____.
                                          (the longest)

9. „Wie singt man das?" „_____, _____."
                      (The softer the better)

10. Es ist _____ Haus in der Stadt.
     (the largest)

11. Ich fahre mit _____ Zug.
                      (the next)

12. Er liest _____ ich.
    (more than)

13. Wer läuft _____, Karl oder Helmut?
    (faster)

14. Ich trinke _____ Tee.
    (like to)

15. _____ Leute kaufen _____ Auto.
    (Most)   (a larger)

16. Karl ist _____ sein Bruder.
    (older than)

17. _____ Kreisen tut man das nicht.
    (In the best)

18. Diese Fotos sind _____.
    (sharpest)

19. Franz erzählt _____ Geschichten.
    (the craziest)

20. _____ er arbeitet, _____ wird er.
    (The more)   (the more tired)

21. Kühe sind _____ Tiere.
    (the most stupid)

22. Hier ist das Wasser _____.
    (clearest)

23. Es ist _____ Wagen in ganz Italien.
    (the fastest)

24. Er ist _____ sein Vater.
    (bigger than)

25. Ich brauche _____ Mantel.
    (a warmer)

26. Im Dezember sind die Tage _____ und die Nächte _____.
    (shortest)   (longest)

27. Haben Sie _____ Messer?
    (a sharper)

28. Es ist _____ Rathaus in Deutschland.
    (the oldest)

29. Ihre Tochter wird _____.
    (prettier and prettier)

30. _____ Mal bleibe ich zu Hause.
    (The next)

31. Das sind _____ Anzüge.
    (our best)

Express in German

1. He reads more than I.
2. I like to drink coffee.
3. It's later than you think.
4. He's hunting for (**suchen**) a smaller apartment.
5. Who is stronger, Karl or Helmut?
6. Your daughter is getting prettier and prettier.
7. It's the largest house in Hamburg.
8. The more he works the more tired he gets.
9. I need a warmer coat.
10. He is bigger than his father.
11. He walks slower than I.
12. Most people buy a larger car. *Die Meisten Leute kaufen ein größeres Auto (einen größeren Wagen)*
13. Franz tells the craziest stories.
14. It isn't as warm as yesterday.
15. The luggage is getting heavier and heavier.
16. It's the fastest car in Italy.
17. Karl is older than his brother.
18. The more the better.
19. Those are our best suits.
20. In December the days are shortest and the nights longest.
21. Anna isn't as pretty as Heidi, but I find her more interesting.
22. Do you have a sharper knife?
23. The Italian films are the longest.
24. The next time I'll stay home.
25. Is it closer?

prepositions

chapter four

I. INTRODUCTION

The use of prepositions is a particularly rich and idiomatic aspect of language. One preposition can have many meanings and can be found in various syntactical surroundings. The English preposition *on*, for example, has extremes of meaning ranging from the literal to the figurative; it occurs in formal speech as well as slang; and it has settings and functions ranging from the prepositional phrase to verb prefixes and suffixes:

on the table	on the whole
on wheels	the tax on gasoline
on time	the march on the capital
on my honor	the come-on
on the spot	to put on
	turned on

German prepositions are just as rich and varied as their English counterparts.

The meaning and function of a preposition can be best understood in a preposition's most stable setting, the *prepositional phrase*. Here is a simple example in English:

on the table

On is a preposition; *the table* is the object of the preposition. In this case, the whole phrase functions to answer the question "where," i.e. it functions as an adverb:

Where are my glasses?

They are lying *on the table*. (i.e. there)

Other prepositional phrases specify the "when," "why," or "how" of an action or situation.

Some German examples:

auf dem Tisch   on the table (**Auf** is the preposition and
dem Tisch is its object.)
mit einem Hammer   with a hammer
mit ihm   with him
für mich   for me
wegen des Wetters   because of the weather
auf zwei Wochen   for two weeks
mit großer Mühe   with great effort

These German examples show that the *object of a preposition* can be in various *cases*—any case, in fact, except the nominative:

für **mich**   (accusative)

mit **ihm**   (dative)

wegen **des Wetters**   (genitive)

The choice of case is, however, not free.

GENERAL RULES:

1. The case of the object of a preposition is determined by the preposition, which is said to "govern" or "control" it.

2. While most prepositions govern only one case, certain others govern either of two cases. Here the choice of case is determined by the function of the whole prepositional phrase.

Contractions may occur within a prepositional phrase. **Ins** Haus is a formal and legitimate contraction of **in das** Haus. A list of the most common contractions occurring in formal German follows:

am (an dem)	**im** (in dem)	**vors** (vor das)
ans (an das)	**ins** (in das)	**zum** (zu dem)
aufs (auf das)	**vom** (von dem)	**zur** (zu der)
beim (bei dem)	**vorm** (vor dem)	

Other contractions occur in colloquial speech, more in slurred speech: **fürs** (für das) is on the border between formal and colloquial, while **auf'm** (auf dem) is colloquial to the point of slurring.

This chapter examines the meanings and functions of the most common German prepositions as they occur in prepositional phrases.

LEVEL ONE

I. PREPOSITIONS REQUIRING THE DATIVE

The following prepositions require dative objects: **aus, außer, bei, gegenüber, mit, nach, seit, von, zu.**

A. AUS

Most Common Uses

1. *from* (with place name)

Herr Schmidt kommt **aus** Berlin.   (Mr. Schmidt comes *from* Berlin.)
Das Paket kam **aus** Deutschland.   (The package came *from* Germany.)

In such cases, **aus** indicates *origin*. Note that the first sentence means that Mr. Schmidt was either born in Berlin or that he has been living there for some time. Here context plays an important role. If you grew up in California and were studying in New York, you would answer the New Yorker's question "Where do you come from?" with "From **(aus)** California." If you had lived in New York for some time and met someone in

Washington, you might answer the same question with "From (**aus**) New York, but originally from (**aus**) California."

2. *out of* (location)

Sie kommt gerade **aus** dem Haus.	(She's just coming *out of* the house.)
Ich trinke lieber **aus** der Flasche.	(I prefer to drink *out of* the bottle.)

More Specific Uses

3. *out of* / *of* / *for* (motivation)

Er tat es **aus** Mitleid (Gewohnheit).	(He did it *out of* pity [habit].)
Aus diesem Grund will er bleiben.	(*For* this reason he wants to stay.)

When **aus** is used to indicate motivation (or reasons)—**aus Mitleid** or **aus Furcht**—German does not normally use an article or a demonstrative adjective. This construction parallels the English: *out of pity, out of fear.* However, in the expressions **aus welchem Grund?** and **aus diesem Grund** (*for what reason* and *for this reason*), German and English both use the interrogative and demonstrative adjectives and are again parallel.

4. *made (out) of*

Der Ring ist **aus** Gold.	(The ring is *made of* gold.)
Das ganze Haus war **aus** Holz.	(The whole house was *made of* wood.)

When **aus** (made of) is used in this sense, neither English nor German uses an article.

B. AUSSER

Most Common Uses

1. *except for, besides, but, aside from, other than*

Außer ihm kenne ich niemand in Hamburg.	(*Except for* him I don't know anyone in Hamburg.)
	(*Besides him* I don't know anyone in Hamburg.)
	(I don't know anyone in Hamburg *but him.*)

Note that *besides* means the same thing as *except for* in the above sentences.

2. *besides, in addition to*

Außer ihm kenne ich viele Leute in Hamburg.

(I know a lot of people in Hamburg *besides him.*)

Here *besides* means *in addition to* rather than *except for*.

More Specific Uses

3. *out of*

Er ist **außer Atem (außer Gefahr).**
Der Automat ist **außer Betrieb.**

(He's *out of breath* [*out of danger*].)
(The [coin-operated] machine is *out of order.*)

When **außer** is used in the sense of *out of*, no article is used. In this, German is similar to English.

4. *beside* (*himself*, etc.)

Sie war **außer sich.**

(She was *beside herself.*)

When **außer** is used in this sense, reflexive pronouns are required.

C. BEI

Most Common Uses

1. *at, with* (in the sense of *in someone's house* or *home*)

Er wohnt **bei** seinem Bruder.
Er wohnt **bei** seinen Eltern.

(He's living *at* his brother's [house].)
(He's living *with* his parents.)

These sentences should be contrasted with

Er wohnt mit seinem Bruder zusammen

which means that he is living together with his brother (perhaps in an apartment) rather than living at his brother's house.

2. *near* (with locations)

Unser Haus liegt **beim** Bahnhof.

(Our house is [located] *near* the train station.)

Ippendorf liegt **bei** Bonn.

(Ippendorf is [located] *near* Bonn.)

3. *at* (referring to business or professional establishments)

Um drei Uhr muß ich **beim Arzt** sein. (I have to be *at the doctor's* at three.)
Er ist jetzt **beim Friseur.** (He's *at the barber's* now.)

Note that English uses a possessive (at the *doctor's* or at the *doctor's office*), whereas German does not.

4. *at / for* (with work)

Er ist jetzt **bei der Arbeit.** (He is *at work* now.)
Er arbeitet **bei** (der Firma) (He works *for* [the firm] Mercedes-
Mercedes-Benz. Benz.)

More Specific Uses

5. *with*

Ich habe kein Geld **bei** mir. (I don't have any money *with* me [on me].)

6. *by, in the process of*

Beim Lesen lernt man viel. (*In the process of* [*by*] reading one learns a lot.)

7. *when(ever)* (*in the case of*) (normally with expression of weather.)

Bei schlechtem Wetter bleiben wir (*When* the weather is bad we stay at
zu Hause. home.)

8. *by*

Wie kannst du **bei** dem schlechten (How can you read *by* that bad
Licht lesen? light?)

D. GEGENÜBER

1. *opposite, across from*

Mir **gegenüber** saßen zwei alte (Two old gentlemen sat *across from*
Herren. me.)
Unserem Haus **gegenüber** ist ein (There is a stationery store *across*
Schreibwarengeschäft. *from* our house.)

Gegenüber always follows a pronoun object but may come either before or after a noun object.

E. MIT

Most Common Uses

1. *with*

Er macht das **mit** seinem Bruder zusammen.	(He's doing that [together] *with* his brother.)

2. *by* (means of travel)

Er ist **mit** dem Zug gekommen.	(He came *by* train.)

Where English uses only *by* to indicate means of travel, German uses **mit** and a definite article.

F. NACH

Most Common Uses

1. *to* (destination: with place names)

Fahren Sie **nach** Hamburg (Deutschland, Europa)?	(Are you going *to* Hamburg [Germany, Europe]?)

Nach is used for destinations when referring to towns, cities, states, countries, and continents (i.e. names of towns and of larger units).

Note the following idiom:

Ich gehe **nach Hause.**	(I am going *home.*)

2. *after*

Nach der Arbeit geht er direkt nach Hause.	(He goes right home *after* work.)
Es ist zehn **nach** fünf (Uhr).	(It's ten *after* five [o'clock].)

More Specific Use

3. *according to*

Seinem Brief **nach** geht es ihm gut.	(*According to* his letter he's fine.)

When **nach** means *according to*, it will follow its object.

G. SEIT

Most Common Uses

1. *since* (and a point in past time)

Wir wohnen **seit** dem fünfzehnten April in Koblenz.

(We've been living in Koblenz *since* the fifteenth of April.)

2. *for* (period of time)

Sie wohnt **seit** einer Woche bei uns.

(She's been living at our place *for* a week.)

Note that **seit** requires the present tense if it refers to an action that began in the past and is still going on. In such cases English requires the present perfect.

Sie **wohnt** seit dem 15. (seit einer Woche) bei uns.

(She *has been living* with us since the 15th [for a week].)

H. VON

Most Common Uses

1. *from*

Ich fahre **von** Stuttgart nach Köln.

(I'm driving *from* Stuttgart to Cologne.)

Heute habe ich einen Brief **von** Thomas bekommen.

(I got a letter *from* Thomas today.)

Contrast:

Heute habe ich einen Brief **von Thomas** bekommen. (with persons)
Heute habe ich einen Brief **aus München** bekommen. (with places)

Also Contrast:

Ich komme **aus** Stuttgart. (I come *from* Stuttgart, i.e. I live there.)
Ich fahre **von** Stuttgart nach Köln. (I'm driving *from* Stuttgart to Cologne.)

2. *from, off of*

Das Glas fiel **vom** Tisch.

(The glass fell *off of* [*from*] the table.)

3. *by*

Wir haben drei Novellen **von** Thomas Mann gelesen.

(We read three novellas *by* Thomas Mann.)

4. *of* (possessive)

Er ist ein Freund **von** mir (**von** Karl).   (He's a friend *of* mine [*of* Karl's].)

Note that a possessive (i.e. *mine, Karl's*) follows the English *of*-construction, whereas the German **von** is followed by a simple dative object.

I. ZU

Most Common Use

1. *to* (with places inside a town or city or with persons)

Er fährt **zum** Bahnhof (**zu** seinem Freund).

(He's driving *to* the station [*to* his friend's].)

Ich komme nachher **zu** Ihnen.   (I'll come *to* your place afterwards.)

Note that English uses a possessive (*to his friend's* or *to your place*) when a person's house or home is meant. German uses only a dative object.

Note the following idiomatic uses of **zu** :

Er ist **zu Hause.**	(He's [*at*] *home.*)
Wir gehen **zu Fuß.**	(We're walking [going *on foot*].)
zum Beispiel	(*for example*)
zum Schluß	(*at the end, finally, in conclusion*)

More Specific Uses

2. *at / for* (and occasions)

Sie sind **zu** Weihnachten (**zu** verschiedenen Zeiten) angekommen.

(They came *at* Christmas [*at* different times].)

Was haben Sie **zu** Weihnachten bekommen ?

(What did you get *for* Christmas ?)

(Ich fahre **zum** zweiten Mal nach Deutschland.)

(I'm going to Germany *for the* second time.)

Zu is used with **Zeit** (**zu verschiedenen Zeiten**), **Mal,** and with festivals or occasions (**zu Weihnachten, zu Ostern, zu Pfingsten, zum Geburtstag**).

3. *at* (and prices)

Ich will zehn Briefmarken **zu** zwan-   (I want ten twenty-cent stamps. [I
zig Pfennig.   want ten stamps *at* twenty cents
                                             each].)

▣ DRILLS

Fill-ins

Supply the missing prepositions and, where necessary, the missing articles.

1. Er will jetzt ＿＿＿＿＿＿＿＿ Hause gehen.

2. Ich warte schon ＿＿＿＿＿＿＿＿ fünf Uhr hier.

＿＿＿＿＿＿＿＿(since)

3. Bitte, wie kommt man ＿＿＿＿＿＿＿＿ Rathaus?

＿＿＿＿＿＿＿＿(to the)

4. Das Hotel liegt ＿＿＿＿＿＿＿＿ Bahnhof.

＿＿＿＿＿＿＿＿(near the)

5. ＿＿＿＿＿＿＿＿ wem bist du ins Kino gegangen?

(With)

6. Wie kommt man ＿＿＿＿＿＿＿＿ Labyrinth?   (das)

＿＿＿＿＿＿＿＿(out of the)

7. ＿＿＿＿＿＿＿＿ ihm war niemand da.

(Aside from)

8. Ich bin um drei Uhr ＿＿＿＿＿＿＿＿ Hause angekommen.

＿＿＿＿＿＿＿＿(at)

9. Sie wohnt immer noch ＿＿＿＿＿＿＿＿ Eltern.

＿＿＿＿＿＿＿＿(with her)

10. Wollen Sie ＿＿＿＿＿＿＿＿ Zug fahren?

＿＿＿＿＿＿＿＿(by)

11. Der Zug fährt ＿＿＿＿＿＿＿＿ München ＿＿＿＿＿＿＿＿ Stuttgart.

＿＿＿＿＿＿＿＿(from)＿＿＿＿＿＿＿＿(to)

12. Hast du nichts ＿＿＿＿＿＿＿＿ ihm gehört?

＿＿＿＿＿＿＿＿(from)

13. Ich bin Berliner. Ich komme ＿＿＿＿＿＿＿＿ Berlin.

＿＿＿＿＿＿＿＿(from)

14. Er ist jetzt ＿＿＿＿＿＿＿＿ Friseur.

＿＿＿＿＿＿＿＿(at the)

15. Er ist gerade ＿＿＿＿＿＿＿＿ Friseur gegangen.

＿＿＿＿＿＿＿＿(to the)

16. Meine Brille ist _____ Tisch gefallen.
    (off the)

17. Er ist jetzt _____ Arbeit.
    (at)

18. Dem Bahnhof _____ stand ein gutes Restaurant.
    (across from)

19. Es ist zwanzig _____ acht (Uhr).
    (after)

20. Wir wohnen schon _____ zwei Jahren in Amerika.
    (for)

21. Gestern bekam ich ein Paket _____ Hamburg.
    (from)

22. Wir gehen _____ Fuß.
    (on)

More specific uses

23. Hast du Geld _____ dir? (on you)
24. Dem Fahrplan _____ werden wir bald da sein.
    (according to the timetable)
25. Wir sind jetzt ___außer___ Gefahr. (out of danger)
26. Was haben Sie _____ Ihrem Geburtstag bekommen?
    (for your birthday)
27. _____ diesem Grund studiert er nicht mehr.   (For this
    reason)
28. _____ schlechtem Wetter bleiben wir zu Hause.   (When
    the weather is bad)
29. Gute Mappen sind _____ Leder.   (made of leather)
30. Ich lese das Buch _____ zweiten Mal.   (for the second
    time)
31. Das hast du nur _____ Mitleid getan.   (out of pity)
32. Kommst du nachher _____ mir?   (to my place)
33. Wir waren _____ uns.   (beside ourselves)

Express in German

1. Aside from him nobody came.
2. Do you want to go by train?
3. He's at work now.
4. There's a good restaurant across from the station.
5. We've been living here for two years.
6. He's at the doctor's now.

7. They come from Hamburg.
8. Are you driving to the post office?
9. Is Paul still living with his parents?
10. The boys ran out of the house.
11. Lufthansa flies directly from New York to Frankfurt.
12. I know lots of people in Stuttgart besides her.
13. He sat across from me.
14. With whom did you go to the movies (**ins Kino**)?
15. The library has been closed (**geschlossen**) since *seit* the fifteenth of June.
16. Do you live far from here?   *weit von hier*
17. My glasses fell off the table.   *von dem Tisch*
18. I got a package from Munich.   *aus München*
19. Who was it from?   *Von wem*
20. We're walking. *Wir gehen zu Fuß*   *Wir* *sind* *um zwei Uhr*
21. We arrived (at) home at two o'clock.   *Wir* ~~kommen~~ *zu Hause angekommen.*
22. It's twenty after five.   *nach fünf*
23. Many Americans drink beer out of the bottle.   *aus der Flasche*
24. I'm going home now.   *nach Hause*

More specific uses

bei

25. I don't have any money on me.
zu 26. For Christmas I got a record player (**der Plattenspieler**).
zu 27. We'll come to your place afterwards (**nachher**).
nach 28. According to his letter he's arriving tomorrow.
29. I was beside myself.
30. We're not out of danger yet.
31. When the weather is good we always go swimming.   (*Use a preposition.*)
32. I'm telling you that for the last time.
33. Good briefcases are made of leather.

LEVEL TWO

I. PREPOSITIONS REQUIRING THE ACCUSATIVE

The following prepositions require accusative objects: **bis, durch, für, gegen, ohne, um.**

A. BIS

Most Common Uses

1. *until* (with time expressions)

Ich bleibe **bis** nächste Woche (morgen) hier.	(I'm staying here *until* next week [tomorrow].)

2. *as far as* (with places)

Ich fahre nur **bis** Salzburg.	(I'm only driving *as far as* Salzburg.)

3. *to*

von Kopf **bis** Fuß	(from head *to* foot)
von oben **bis** unten	(from top *to* bottom)

4. *by* (and time)

Es muß **bis** morgen fertig sein.	(It must be done *by* tomorrow.)
Es muß **bis zum** einundzwanzigsten November fertig sein.	(It must be done *by the* twenty-first of November.)

Note that German uses **bis zu** and the *definite article* with dates. **Bis zu** requires a dative object.

More Specific Uses

Bis is often found in conjunction with other prepositions. In such constructions, the final preposition governs the case:

5. **Bis in** = *into*.

Wir tanzten **bis** (spät) **in** die Nacht.   (We danced [late] *into* the night.)

6. **Bis an** = (*right*) *up to* (not with persons).

Das Wasser kam **bis an** die Tür.	(The water came [*right*] *up to* the door.)

B. DURCH

Most Common Use

1. *through*

Wir spazierten **durch** den Park.   (We walked *through* the park.)

More Specific Use

2. *by, by means of* (through the action of)

Ich habe das **durch** Zufall gehört.   (I heard that *by* chance.)
Ich lernte ihn **durch** Freunde kennen.   (I met him *through* friends.)

C. FÜR

Most Common Use

1. *for*

Ist Post **für** mich da?   (Is there any mail *for* me?)
Für vier Mark kriegst du ein gutes   (You can get a good meal *for* four
Essen.   marks.)
Wir sind **für** diesen Vorschlag.   (We are *for* this suggestion.)

More Specific Use

2. *for / by*

Wort **für** Wort   (word *for* word)
Schritt **für** Schritt   (step *by* step)

D. GEGEN

Most Common Uses

1. *against*

Was haben Sie **gegen** dieses Buch?   (What do you have *against* this
book?)

2. *into, (up) against*

Er ist **gegen** einen Baum gefahren.   (He ran *into* a tree.)

More Specific Use

3. *around, about, toward* (up to a certain time or number but not exceeding it)

Es waren **gegen** hundert Leute da.   (There were *about* a hundred people there.)

Wir kamen **gegen** vier Uhr an.   (We arrived *about* [*along toward*] four o'clock.)

In these examples **gegen** means *about* or *approximately*, but in a restricted sense: the number or the time given may not be exceeded (up to four o'clock but not after, up to a hundred people but no more).

E. OHNE

1. *without*

Ohne Geld kann man so etwas nicht machen.   (You [one] can't do something like that *without* money.)

Geh nicht **ohne** mich!   (Don't go *without* me.)

F. UM

Most Common Uses

1. *around*

Er kommt gerade **um** die Ecke.   (He is just coming *around* the corner.)

Sie saßen alle **um** den Tisch.   (They were all sitting *around* the table.)

2. *at* (and time)

Er wird **um** elf Uhr da sein.   (He'll be there *at* eleven o'clock.)

Das geschah **um** die Jahrhundertwende.   (That happened *at* the turn of the century.)

▣ DRILLS

Fill-ins

Supply the missing prepositions and, where necessary, the missing articles.

1. Er ist gerade ＿＿＿＿＿＿＿＿ Ecke gelaufen.
      (around the)
2. Dieser Zug fährt nur ＿＿＿＿＿＿＿＿ München.
      (as far as)

3. Bitte, machen Sie das _____ mich!
   (for)

4. Hier fährt man _____ einen Tunnel.
   (through)

5. Ich habe nichts _____ diese Methode.
   (against)

6. Er ist _____ die Korridore gelaufen.
   (through)

7. _____ einen Bleistift kann ich nicht weiterarbeiten.
   (Without)

8. Können Sie nicht _____ Montag warten?
   (until)

9. Er ist _____ acht Uhr gekommen.
   (at)

10. Ich muß die Bücher _____ einundzwanzigsten Juni
    (by the)
    zurückbringen.

11. Sie ist _____ Straßenlaterne gefahren.
    (into a)

12. Geh nicht _____ deine Jacke!
    (without)

13. Er hat sie _____ Kopf _____ Fuß angesehen.
    (from)   (to)

14. Wer nicht für mich ist, ist _____ mich.
    (against)

15. Es muß _____ nächste Woche fertig sein.
    (by)

16. Georg hat viel Geld _____ seinen neuen Mantel aus-
    (for)
    gegeben.

More specific uses

17. _____ Zufall habe ich das Buch gefunden. (By chance)
18. Er ist nur _____ Tür gekommen. (up to the door, as far
    as the door)
19. _____ sechs Uhr werde ich immer hungrig. (About,
    along toward)
20. Übersetzen Sie nicht Wort _____ Wort! (word for word)
21. Wir arbeiteten _____ spät _____ Nacht.
    (late into the night)

Express in German ✳ *11-11*

1. Don't go without your briefcase (**die Mappe**).
2. What do you have against him?
3. We drove through the mountains. *durch die Berge*
4. Can't you wait until Thursday? *bis*
5. I can't go on working without those books. *ohne diese Bücher*
6. He drove through the city. *durch die Stadt*
7. I don't have any time for you now.
8. It has to be ready by next week.
9. There are (**Es stehen**) many trees around the house. *um das Haus*
10. He bumped into the table.   (**stoßen, stieß, ist gestoßen, er stößt**) *gegen den Tisch*
11. Georg spent a lot of money for his new coat.
12. Is he coming at six? *um sechs?*
13. Can't that wait until tomorrow? *bis morgen*

More specific uses

14. Don't translate word for word. *Wort für Wort*
15. I always get hungry about (along toward) six. *gegen sechs*
16. He came up to the door. *Er kam bis an die Tür*
17. We worked late into the night. *Wir haben spät in die Nacht gearbeitet*
18. I met him through friends.

durch

LEVEL THREE

I. TWO-WAY PREPOSITIONS

Two-way prepositions are prepositions which govern both the dative and accusative cases.

Note the difference between the prepositional phrases used in the following sentences:

LOCATION (where? / **wo?**) He's studying *in the library*.
DIRECTION or DESTINATION (where to? / **wohin?**) He just walked *into the library*.

In the first sentence (He's studying in the library), the prepositional phrase (*in* the library) describes the person's *location*, i.e. where (**wo**) he is.

In the second sentence (He just walked into the library), the prepositional phrase describes the person's destination or the direction in which he was going, i.e. where he was going *to* (**wohin**). The *to* of the preposition *into* is like the *to* of the expression *where to:* it is the sign of motion in a certain direction or toward a certain destination. Where motion of this kind is *not* involved, however, *in* rather than *into* is used; one would not say: He's studying *into* the library.

NOTE: It is not just motion but *motion in connection with a destination or specific direction* that determines whether *into* should be used rather than *in:*

He's been running around *in* the library all day.

In this sentence there is motion *but no destination.* The person is moving around inside the bounds of a certain place, but this place is not his destination. For this reason, one would ask *where* (**wo**) he has been running around, rather than *where* he's been running *to* (**wohin**).

German two-way prepositions (**an, auf, hinter, in, neben, über, unter, vor, zwischen**) make the same kind of distinction. But instead of choosing between two prepositions (as English does in the case of *in* and *into*), German chooses between the dative and accusative cases.

RULES:

1. dative: location

Two-way prepositions require dative objects when the prepositional phrase indicates *location.* In such cases, the phrase answers the question **wo** / *where:*

Wo arbeitet er heute abend? Wahrscheinlich **in der Bibliothek.**
(Where's he studying this evening? Probably in the library.)

Wo ist das Buch? Es liegt **auf dem Tisch.**
(Where's the book? It's lying on the table.)

The question *where* / **wo** does not exclude motion or action: one often asks *where* something is happening:

Er ist den ganzen Tag **in der Bibliothek** herumgelaufen.
(He's been running around in the library all day.)

The prepositional phrase **in der Bibliothek** (in the library) tells *where* / **wo** he's been running (location), not *where to* / **wohin** (direction or destination).

2. accusative: destination / direction

The same prepositions require accusative objects when the prepositional phrase describes *motion toward a destination* or *in a specific direction*. In such cases, the phrase answers the question **wohin** / *where to:*

> **Wohin** ist er gegangen? Er ist gerade **in die Bibliothek** gegangen.
> (Where did he go [to]? He just walked into the library.)

> **Wohin** soll ich das Buch legen? Lege es, bitte, **auf den Schreibtisch!**
> (Where shall I put the book? Put it on the desk, please.)

A. AUF

1. *on* (in the sense of *on top of*)

Auf is used with horizontal surfaces, e.g. a floor, a chair, or a table-top. It may *not* be used with vertical surfaces, e.g. a wall or a blackboard.

(**Wo** + dat.)	Es lag auf **dem** Tisch.	(It was lying on the table.)
(**Wohin** + acc.)	Ich warf es auf **den** Tisch.	(I threw it on [to] the table.)

(**Wo** + dat.)	Er saß auf **dem** Sofa.	(He was sitting on the sofa.)
(**Wohin** + acc.)	Er setzte sich auf**s** Sofa.	(He sat down on the sofa.)

Auf may also be used in more abstract or figurative contexts:

(**Wo** + dat.)	Ich bin auf **dem** Weg nach Hause.
	(I'm on the way home)
(**Wo** + dat.)	Inge ist jetzt auf **einer** Reise.
	(Inge is on a trip now).
(**Wohin** + acc.)	Er geht bald auf **eine** Reise.
	(He's going on a trip soon.)

2. *in* (and languages)

auf deutsch (französisch, norwegisch, etc.)

Contrast:

Er sagte es **auf deutsch.** (He said it *in* German.)
Übersetzen Sie aus dem Englischen **ins Deutsche!** (Translate from English *into* German.)

The second sentence treats the adjectives (**deutsch** and **englisch**) as nouns. For this reason, they are *capitalized* and require adjective endings. After **auf,** however, the names of languages are not capitalized (e.g. **auf deutsch**).

Note the following idiomatic uses of **auf**:

auf dem Land   in the country   **aufs Land**   to the country

B. AN

1. *on, onto*

In contrast to **auf, an** is normally used with *vertical surfaces,* e.g. a wall or a blackboard:

(Wo + dat.)	Es steht an **der** Tafel.
	(It's on the blackboard.)
(Wohin + acc.)	Ich habe es an **die** Tafel geschrieben.
	(I wrote it on [to] the blackboard.)
(Wo + dat.)	Das Bild hing an **der** Wand.
	(The picture was hanging on the wall.)
(Wohin + acc.)	Ich hängte es an **die** Wand.
	(I hung it on the wall.)

2. dative: *at, at the edge of, by*
   accusative: *to, up to, toward*

An is used to indicate borders or perimeters:

	an **der** Grenze	at the border
	am Rand	at the edge
LOCATION	**am** Fluß	at the river
	am Strand	at the beach
	am Fenster	at the window
	am Tisch	at the table

Note that when German uses the dative case (*location*), English uses *at.*

When the accusative is used (*destination*), the English equivalent is usually *to:*

	an **die** Grenze	to the border
	an **den** Rand	to the edge
DESTINATION	an **den** Fluß	to the river
	an **den** Strand	to the beach
	ans Fenster	to the window
	an **den** Tisch	to the table

NOTE: **An** usually means *up to, but no farther than* a given point:

Ich fahre an **die** Grenze.

(I'm going [up] to the border, but not across it.)

Note the following idiomatic uses of **an:**

an **der** Universität	at the university
an **der** Ecke	at the corner
an **die** Arbeit gehen	to go to work

Du **bist** jetzt **an der** Reihe.	(It's your turn now.)
Bald **kommst** du **an die** Reihe.	(It will be your turn soon.)

C. HINTER

1. *behind, in back of*

(**Wo** + dat.)   Er arbeitete hinter **dem** Haus.
(He was working in back of [behind] the house.)

(**Wohin** + acc.)   Er lief gerade hinter **das** Haus.
(He just ran behind the house.)

D. IN

1. dative: *in*
accusative: *in, into, to*

(**Wo** + dat.)   Einmal die Woche ißt er gern in **einem** guten Restaurant.
(Once a week he likes to eat in a good restaurant.)

(**Wohin** + acc.)   Einmal die Woche geht er gern in **ein** gutes Restaurant.
(Once a week he likes to go to a good restaurant.)

(**Wo** + dat.)   Wir wohnen noch in **dem**selben alten Haus.
(We're still living in the same old house.)

(**Wohin** + acc.)   Komm sofort **ins** Haus!
(Come into the house right away.)

(**Wo** + dat.)   Das steht **im** Buch.
(That's in the book.)

(**Wohin** + acc.)   Schreiben Sie nicht in **die** Bücher!
(Don't write in[to] the books.)

Note the following idiomatic uses of **in**:

ins Theater (Konzert) gehen	to go to the theater (concert)
in **der** Schule	in (at) school
in **die** Schule	to school
im 3. Stock	on the 4th (!) floor*
in **der** Schweiz (Türkei, Tschechoslowakei)	in Switzerland (Turkey, Czechoslovakia)

but:

Ich wohne in **der** Hauptstraße. (I live on Main Street.)

Ich wohne Hauptstraße 187.   (I live at 187 Main Street.)

NOTE 1: German does not use a preposition when the street number is given.

NOTE 2: in **der** Schweiz (etc.)   in Switzerland
in **die** Schweiz (etc.)   to Switzerland

Die Schweiz, die Türkei, and **die Tschechoslowakei** require the use of the definite article in *all* cases.

E. NEBEN

1. *next to, alongside of, beside*

(**Wo** + dat.)	Er saß den ganzen Abend neben **ihr.**
	(He sat next to her all evening.)
(**Wohin** + acc.)	Setz dich neben **mich!**
	(Sit down next to me [alongside of me, beside me].)

F. ÜBER

1. *over, above*

(**Wo** + dat.)	Das Bild hing über **meinem** Schreibtisch.
	(The picture hung over my desk.)
(**Wohin** + acc.)	Ich hängte das Bild über **meinen** Schreibtisch.
	(I hung the picture over my desk.)

---

*im dritten Stock: In German, the first (ground) floor is called **das Erdgeschoß,** the second floor **der erste Stock,** the third floor **der zweite Stock,** and so forth. For this reason, the number of the floor is always one less in German than it is in English.

2. *across (over), on the other side of*

(**Wohin** + acc.) Ich ging über **die** Straße (**die** Brücke, etc.).
(I went across the street [the bridge, etc.].)

NOTE: This sentence answers the question **wohin**, e.g. Wohin bist du gegangen? In this case, the idea of direction or destination consists in going *from* one side *to* the other.

3. *More than* = **über** + acc.

Es kostet über fünfzig Mark.	(It costs more than fifty marks.)
Gestern mußte ich über zwanzig Briefe schreiben.	(I had to write more than twenty letters yesterday.)
Er ist über siebzig Jahre alt.	(He's over seventy.)

G. UNTER

1. *under*

(**Wo** + dat.) Der Autoschlosser arbeitete unter **dem** Wagen.
(The mechanic was working under the car.)
(**Wohin** + acc.) Der Ball rollte unter **den** Wagen.
(The ball rolled under the car.)

2. *among*

(**Wo** + dat.) So spricht man nur unter Freund**en.**
(One only says things like that among friends.)

3. *Less than* = **unter** + acc.

Diese Anzüge kosten alle unter hundert Mark. (All these suits cost less than a hundred marks.)

Note the following idiomatic uses of **unter:**

Das ist unter **meiner** Würde. (That's *beneath* my dignity.)
unter **uns** gesagt   (just *between* you and me)
unter **dem** Einfluß von   (under the influence of)

H. VOR

1. *in front of (before)*

(**Wo** + dat.) Die Milchflaschen stehen vor **der** Tür.
(The milk bottles are standing in front of the door.)

(**Wohin** + acc.) Stell die Milchflaschen vor **die** Tür!
            (Put the milk bottles in front of the door.)

Note the following idiom:

        vor **allem**   above *all*

I. ZWISCHEN

1. *between*

(**Wo** + dat.) Ihr Wagen steht zwischen **den** zwei anderen da.
           (Your car is standing between those two over there.)
(**Wohin** + acc.) Stellen Sie den Wagen zwischen **die** zwei anderen da!
           (Park the car between those two over there.)

▣ DRILLS

Fill-ins

Supply the missing preposition and, where necessary, the article or possessive adjective.

1. Meine Serviette ist _____ Tisch gefallen.
               (under the)

2. Komm sofort _____ Haus!
             (into the)

3. Der Mond hing _____ Meer.
            (over the)

4. _____ Bett ist ein Nachttisch.
   (Next to the)

5. Er warf seinen Mantel _____ Bett.
              (onto the)

6. Der Kellner stellte sich _____ Stuhl.
              (behind my)

7. Ich hängte das Bild _____ Schreibtisch.
             (over my)

8. Viele Leute standen _____ Haus.
            (in front of the)

9. Er setzte sich _____ Tisch.
          (at the)

10. Heute stand nichts Neues _____ Zeitung.
    (in the)

11. Er beugte sich _____ Teller.
    (over his)

12. Stell deinen Wagen _____ zwei anderen da!
    (alongside of the)

13. Er stand _____ Fenster.
    (at the)

14. Geh nicht zu nahe _____ Fluß!
    (to the)

15. Er schläft mit dem Bart _____ Decke.
    (under the)

16. Fahren Sie den Wagen _____ Haus!
    (in front of the)

17. Deine Schuhe sind _____ Bett.
    (under the)

18. Deine Mappe liegt _____ Sofa.
    (on the)

19. Eine bekannte Straße in Berlin hieß _____ Linden.
    (Under the)

20. Basel liegt _____ Grenze _____ Deutschland
    (on the)   (between)

    und _____ Schweiz.

21. Stell den Stuhl _____ Sofa und _____
    (between the)   (the)

    Schreibtisch!

22. Die Garage ist gleich _____ Haus.
    (behind the)

23. Er sagte es _____ deutsch.
    (in)

24. Schreiben Sie nicht _____ Bücher!
    (in the)

25. Er ging _____ Brücke.
    (across the)

26. Wir gehen bald _____ Reise.
    (on a)

27. Der Kellner stellte ein Glas Wein _____ alten Herrn.
    (in front of the)

28. Er ging _____ Straßenlaterne auf und ab.
    (under the)

29. Ich war _____ Weg nach Hause.
    (on the)

30. Er hat _____ dreißig Pakete bekommen.
    (more than)

Idiomatic uses

31. Er wohnt _____ Hauptstraße.
    (on)

32. _____ gesagt hat er unrecht.
    (Between you and me)

33. Morgen will ich _____ Land fahren.
    (to the)

34. _____ vergiß deine Bücher nicht!
    (Above all)

35. Er studiert jetzt _____ Universität.
    (at the)

36. Sie wohnt _____ dritten Stock.
    (on the)

37. Das ist _____ Würde.
    (beneath my)

38. Ich fahre nächste Woche _____ Schweiz.
    (to)

39. Gehen wir jetzt _____ Arbeit!
    (to)

40. Wir wollen heute abend _____ Theater gehen.
    (to the)

41. Er wohnt jetzt _____ Land.
    (in the)

42. Er steht _____ Ecke.
    (on the)

Synthetic exercises

Form complete sentences using the following elements. Both dative and accusative prepositional objects are involved.

1. Er / setzen / sich / an / Tisch
2. Neben / Bett / stehen / Nachttisch
3. Gäste / werfen / Mäntel / auf / Bett
4. Stellen Sie / Stuhl / zwischen / Sofa / und / Schreibtisch / !
5. Junge / werfen / Steine / in / Wasser
6. Unser Wagen / stehen / vor / Haus
7. Er / beugen / sich / über / Teller
8. Garage / stehen / hinter / Haus
9. Dein Buch / liegen / auf / Tisch / unter / Zeitung
10. Mein Mann / sein / jetzt / in / Büro

11. Kellner / stellen / Tasse Kaffee / vor / Dame
12. Er / setzen / sich / neben / Freund
13. Lampe / hängen / über / Schreibtisch
14. Ball / rollen / unter / Wagen
15. Wir / verbringen / Sommer / an / See
16. Buch / fallen / hinter / Sofa
17. Er / gehen / gerade / über / Brücke
18. Zwischen / Häuser / liegen / groß / Garten
19. Schreiben / das / an / Tafel /!
20. Ulla / gehen / jetzt / auf / Tennisplatz
21. Kinder / müssen / gehen / jetzt / in / Schule

Idiomatic uses

22. Er / wohnen / in / Hauptstraße
23. Sie / übersetzen / Sätze / aus / Englisch / in / Deutsch
24. Wollen / ihr / nächste Woche / auf / Land / fahren /?
25. Er / stehen / an / Ecke
26. Herr Schelling / sein / jetzt / in / Schweiz
27. Wohnen / du / in / zweiten / Stock /?
28. Wollen / ihr / gehen / heute abend / in / Kino/?

Express in German  *für 11-16*

1. Come into the house immediately!
2. He threw his coat on the bed.
3. He was sitting at the window.
4. He bent over the table.
5. Drive the car up in front of the house.
6. My napkin fell under the table.
7. The garage is behind the house.
8. He received more than thirty letters yesterday.
9. He said that in German.
10. Don't stay in the water too long.
11. Put it on my desk.
12. We went across the bridge.
13. My husband is at the office now.
14. Your book is lying on the table.
15. The night table is next to the bed.
16. He was standing right in front of the door.
17. There are a lot of trees between the two houses.
18. He sat down next to her.
19. Hang it on the wall.

20. He has to go to school now.
21. Ulla is going to the tennis court.
22. Put it behind the house.
23. Put your car between those two over there.
24. Don't write in the books.
25. He walked back and forth under the streetlight.
26. A sign (**das Schild**) hung over the door.
27. It rolled under the car.
28. He's sitting at the table over there.

Idiomatic uses

29. I want to drive to the country tomorrow. *aufs Land*
30. They were standing on the corner. *an der Ecke*
31. I'm driving to Switzerland tomorrow. ~~nach~~ *in die Schweiz*
32. He lives on Main Street. *↙ in der Hauptstraße*
33. Translate it from English into German. *(von) aus dem Englischen ins Deutsche*
34. Do you want to go to the movies this evening? *ins Kino*
35. Prague (**Prag**) is in Czechoslovakia. *in der*
36. Let's go to work now. *Gehen wir jetzt an die Arbeit*
37. That's beneath her dignity. *Das ist unter ihrer Würde*
38. He lives on the fifth floor. (!) *im vierten*
39. Above all don't forget your books.
40. Between you and me, he's wrong. ~~Zwischen~~ *Unter uns gesagt, hat er unrechts*
41. They're studying at the university now. *an der Universität*

LEVEL FOUR

I. PREPOSITIONS REQUIRING THE GENITIVE

The following prepositions require genitive objects: **(an)statt, trotz, während, wegen.**

A. (AN)STATT

1. *instead of*

Anstatt is more formal than **statt**.

> **Statt** eines Radios kaufte ich mir einen Plattenspieler.
> (*Instead of* a radio, I bought a record player.)

NOTE: The genitive case is not used when the noun is not preceded by an article or an adjective.

> Statt **Bier** trinken wir Wein.
> (We'll drink wine instead of beer.)

Idiom: **Stattdessen** = instead of that.

B. TROTZ

1. *in spite of*

> **Trotz** des kalten Sommers haben wir eine gute Ernte gehabt.
> (*In spite of* the cold summer, we had a good harvest.)

Idiom: **Trotzdem** = in spite of that, nonetheless.

C. WÄHREND

1. *during*

> **Während** des Krieges waren wir in der Schweiz.
> (*During* the war we were in Switzerland.)

D. WEGEN

1. *because of, due to, on account of*

Wegen der hohen Preise fahren wir diesen Sommer nicht nach Paris.
(*Because of* the high prices we're not going to Paris this summer.)

Idiom: **Weswegen** = *why, on what account, what for.*

> **Weswegen** machen Sie das?
> (*What* are you doing that *for?*)

Idiom: **meinetwegen, deinetwegen, seinetwegen, ihretwegen, unsretwegen, euretwegen, ihretwegen**

Meinetwegen (etc.) = *for my sake, on my account, because of me.*

Ich hoffe, Sie tun das nicht nur **meinetwegen.**
(I hope you're not doing that just *on my account* [*because of me*].)

Meinetwegen (etc.) = *as far as I'm concerned, for all I care.*

Meinetwegen können Sie machen, was Sie wollen.
(*As far as I'm concerned*, you can do whatever you want.)

▣ DRILLS   *11-16-81*

Fill-ins

Supply the missing elements.

1. _____ trinke ich Wasser.
   (Instead of milk)

2. _____ sehen wir Klothilde sehr selten.
   (During the semester)

3. _____ finde ich den Wagen schön.
   (In spite of the color)

4. _____ kaufe ich mir eine Jacke und Hose.
   (Instead of a new suit)

5. _____ muß er viel reisen.
   (Because of his work)

6. _____ ist er immer pleite (*broke*).
   (In spite of his income [**das Einkommen**])

7. _____ haben wir gutes Wetter gehabt.
   (During the vacation)

8. _____ kann man die Berge nicht sehen.
   (Due to the fog [**der Nebel**])

9. _____ können Sie jetzt nach Hause gehen.
   (For all I care)

10. _____ mag ich ihn immer noch.
    (In spite of that)

11. _Statt dessen_ fuhr er nach Paris.
    (Instead of that)

12. Er tat es _meine tewegen_
    (because of me)

▣ MIXED DRILLS (all levels)

Fill-ins

1. Sie wohnt immer noch _____ Eltern.
   (with her)

2. Können Sie nicht _____ Montag warten?
   (until)

3. Meine Serviette ist _____ Tisch gefallen.
   (under the)

4. Er ist gerade _____ Friseur gegangen.
   (to the)

5. Ich habe nichts _____ diese Methode.
   (against)

6. _____ Bett ist ein Nachttisch.
   (Next to the)

7. Es ist zwanzig _____ acht.
   (after)

8. Komm sofort _____ Haus!
   (into the)

9. Er ist Berliner. Er kommt _____ Berlin.
   (from)

10. Er warf seinen Mantel _____ Bett.
    (onto the)

11. Geh nicht _____ deine Jacke!
    (without)

12. Ich warte schon _____ fünf Uhr hier.
    (since)

13. _____ Arbeit muß er viel reisen.
    (Because of his)

14. Es stehen viele Bäume _____ zwei Häusern.
    (between the)

15. _____ war niemand da.
    (Aside from him)

16. Hängen Sie es _____ Wand!
    (on the)

17. _____ Semesters sehen wir ihn sehr selten.
    (During the)

18. Georg hat viel Geld _____ seinen neuen Mantel aus-
    (for)
    gegeben.

19. Er ist _____ acht Uhr gekommen.
    (at)

20. Er saß _____ Fenster.
    (at the)

21. _____ ist ein gutes Restaurant.
    (Across from the railroad station)

22. Legen Sie es _____ Schreibtisch!
    (on my)

23. _____ fuhr er nach Paris.
    (Instead of that)

24. Er ist _____ Korridor gelaufen.
          (through the)

25. Er stand gleich _____ Tür.
              (in front of the)

26. Wir wohnen _____ zwei Jahren in Amerika.
           (for)

27. Die Garage ist gleich _____ Haus.
               (behind the)

28. Er ist _____ Ecke gelaufen.
        (around the)

29. Hast du nicht _____ gehört?
            (from him)

30. Er beugte sich _____ Tisch.
           (over the)

31. _____ Farbe finde ich den Wagen schön.
   (In spite of the)

32. Er ist jetzt _____ Arbeit.
           (at)

33. _____ Einkommens ist er immer pleite.
   (In spite of his)

34. Wollen Sie _____ Zug fahren?
         (with the)

35. Bitte, machen Sie das _____!
            (for me)

36. Er setzte sich _____ Tisch.
         (at the)

37. Es muß _____ nächste Woche fertig sein.
       (by)

38. Der Zug fährt _____ München _____ Stuttgart.
            (from)   (to)

39. _____ können Sie jetzt nach Hause gehen.
   (For all I care)

40. Wir gehen bald _____ Reise.
          (on a)

41. Ein Schild hing _____ Tür.
         (over the)

42. _____ Nebels kann man die Berge nicht sehen.
   (Due to the)

43. Fahren Sie den Wagen gleich _____ Haus!
               (in front of the)

11 - 16

More specific or idiomatic uses

44. Ich lese das Buch __zum__ zweiten Mal. (for the second time)
45. Übersetzen Sie nicht Wort __für__ Wort! (word for word)
46. Morgen will ich __aufs__ Land fahren. (to the country)
47. Sie wohnt __im__ dritten Stock. (on)
48. __Dem__ Fahrplan __nach__ werden wir bald da sein. (According to the timetable)
49. __Durch__ Zufall habe ich das Buch gefunden. (By chance)
50. Gehen wir jetzt __an die__ Arbeit! (to work)
51. Kommst du nachher __zu mir__? (to my place)
52. Wir arbeiteten __bis__ spät __in die__ Nacht. (late into the night)
53. __Unter uns__ gesagt hat er unrecht. (Between you and me)
54. __Bei__ schlechtem Wetter bleiben wir zu Hause. (When the weather is bad)
55. __Gegen__ sechs Uhr werde ich immer hungrig. (Along toward six o'clock)
56. __Vor allem__ vergessen Sie Ihre Bücher nicht! (Above all)
57. Ich habe kein Geld __bei mir__. (with me)
58. Er ist nur __bis an die__ Tür gekommen. (up to the door)
59. Ich fahre nächste Woche __in die__ Schweiz. (to Switzerland)
60. Gute Mappen sind __aus__ Leder. (made of leather)
61. Übersetzen Sie es __(aus)von dem__ Englischen __ins__ Deutsche! (from English into German)

Express in German

1. Come into the house immediately!
2. They come from Frankfurt.
3. There are (**Es stehen**) a lot of trees between the two houses.
4. During the semester we don't see Klothilde very often.
5. It rolled under the car.
6. What do you have against him?
7. Lufthansa flies directly from New York to Frankfurt.
8. It has to be ready by tomorrow.
9. He was sitting at the window.
10. We've been living here for two years.
11. In spite of his income he's always broke.
12. Don't go without your briefcase.
13. He was standing right in front of the door.

14. My napkin fell under the table.
15. Are you driving to the post office?
16. Put it on my desk.
17. Isn't she coming at eight?
18. In spite of the color I find the car pretty.
19. A sign hung over the door.
20. He bumped against the table.   (stoßen, stieß, ist gestoßen, er stößt)
21. Is Paul still living at his parents' place?
22. Because of the fog one can't see the mountains.
23. He threw his coat on the bed.
24. We arrived home at two o'clock.
25. Aside from him nobody came.
26. We drove through the mountains.
27. Hang it on the wall.
28. My glasses fell off the table.
29. Because of his work he has to travel a lot.
30. He's at work now.
31. I can't go on working without those books.
32. Drive the car right up in front of the house.
33. Instead of that he drove to Paris.
34. He sat across from me.
35. Can't you wait until Thursday?
36. He bent over the table.
37. For all I care he can stay there.
38. There are (**Es stehen**) many trees around the house.

More specific or idiomatic uses

39. I'm driving to Switzerland.
40. He worked late into the night.
41. I don't have any money on me.
42. He lives on the fifth floor.   (!)
43. I'm telling you that for the last time.
44. I always get hungry along toward six.
45. Above all don't forget your books.
46. According to his letter he's arriving tomorrow.
47. Let's go to work now.
48. We aren't out of danger yet.
49. I'm driving to the country tomorrow.
50. I met him through friends.
51. Translate it from English into German.
52. That's beneath her dignity.
53. Good briefcases are made of leather.

noch nicht   not yet
schon   already
nicht mehr   anymore
noch   still

anstatt zu arbeiten

mir gegenüber

time
expressions

10-30-81
Freitag

I. HOURS AND MINUTES

A. Asking the time

The two common ways of asking the time of day are:

> Wie spät ist es? and Wieviel Uhr ist es?
> (What time is it?)

NOTE: In the expression **wieviel Uhr, wieviel** does not take an adjective ending.

B. UM = at

Where English uses the preposition *at* (e.g. *at* eight o'clock), German uses the preposition **um** (**um** acht Uhr):

> Er kommt **um** acht Uhr.
> (He's coming *at* eight o'clock.)

Um is used to indicate *exact* time. To indicate approximate time **gegen** is used:

> Er kommt **gegen** acht Uhr.
> (He's coming *along toward* [*about*] eight o'clock.)

C. Full, half, and quarter hours and minutes

1. Full Hours

> Es ist acht (Uhr). (It's eight [o'clock].)

NOTE 1: **Um** is not used in telling a person the time of day, i.e. in answering the question **Wie spät ist es?** This corresponds to English usage: English does not use the preposition *at* in such cases.

NOTE 2: The word **Uhr** may be omitted, just as the word *o'clock* may be. When it is omitted from the German equivalent of *one o'clock*, however, the word **eins** must be used:

> Es ist **ein** Uhr.   but   Es ist **eins.**

2. Half Hours

In English the *half* hour always refers back to the *last* full hour: it's half *past seven*. In German, however, it refers to the next full hour: it's half (of the way to) eight.

> 7:30   Es ist **halb acht.**
> (It's *half past seven.*)

3. Quarter Hours

The most common way of telling quarter hours is to use the prepositions **nach** (*after* the hour) and **vor** (*before* the hour):

> 8:15   Es ist viertel (ein Viertel) **nach** acht.
> (It's quarter [a quarter] *after* eight.)

> 7:45   Es ist viertel (ein Viertel) **vor** acht.
> (It's quarter [a quarter] *to* eight.)

NOTE: If **ein Viertel** is used, **Viertel** is a noun and is therefore capitalized. If the word **ein** is *not* used, **viertel** is not capitalized.

German has an alternate way of reporting quarter hours that is essentially the same as the way half hours are told. This construction does not use prepositions. All the quarter hours refer to the *next* full hour, rather than to the *last* one:

7:15	Es ist **viertel acht.** (a *quarter* of the way *to eight*)
(7:30	Es ist **halb acht.** [*half* of the way *to eight*])
7:45	Es ist **dreiviertel acht.** (*three quarters* of the way *to eight*)

4. Minutes

Expressions referring to minutes require the preposition **nach** or **vor**:

3:10	Es ist zehn (Minuten) **nach** drei.
3:25	Es ist fünfundzwanzig (Minuten) **nach** drei.
3:35	Es ist fünfundzwanzig (Minuten) **vor** vier.

NOTE 1: **Nach** and **vor** are used like their English equivalents *after* (*past*) and *before* (*to*): **nach** is used up to the half hour and refers to the last full hour (3:29   neunundzwanzig nach drei) and **vor** is used after the half hour and refers to the *next* full hour (3:31   neunundzwanzig vor vier).

NOTE 2: Like the word *minutes*, the word **Minuten** is often omitted.

NOTE 3: Occasionally, the half hour may be used as a reference rather than the full hour. This is the case especially when the approximate time is already known:

> Es ist fünf nach (vor) halb.
> (It's five minutes after [before] the half hour.)

5. Timetable Time

Railroads, bus stations, airports, theaters, etc. use a 24-hour system:

> Der Zug kommt um **20.15** (zwanzig Uhr fünfzehn) in Mainz an.
> (The train arrives in Mainz at *8:15 p.m.*)

NOTE: In such cases, quarters and halves are not used. They are replaced by the numbers 15, 30, and 45:

20:15	zwanzig Uhr fünfzehn
15:30	fünfzehn Uhr dreißig
8:45	acht Uhr fünfundvierzig

II. DAYS AND PARTS OF DAYS

The parts of the day are all *masculine* with the exception of **die Nacht** and **die Mitternacht.**

der Morgen	morning	**die Nacht**	night
der Vormittag	forenoon	**die Mitternacht**	midnight
der Mittag	noon		
der Nachmittag	afternoon		
der Abend	evening		

All expressions referring to whole days are *masculine*. These include:

1. the word *day:* **der Tag**

2. the days of the week:

der Sonntag	der Donnerstag
der Montag	der Freitag
der Dienstag	der Samstag (Sonnabend)
der Mittwoch	

3. dates: der fünfundzwanzigste Mai

A. AM

All time expressions referring to days and parts of days may be used with **am**—with the *exception* of **Nacht** and **Mitternacht.**

The resulting expression may indicate:

1. *a one-time occurrence*

Er kommt **am** Donnerstag (**am** dreiundzwanzigsten Mai, **am** Abend).
(He's coming *on* Thursday [*on* the twenty-third of May, *in* the evening].)

2. *a regularly repeated occurrence*

Die Rechnungen kommen immer am Montag (am ersten Januar, am Morgen).
(The bills always come on Monday [on the first of January, in the morning].)

EXCEPTIONS: **in** der Nacht
um Mitternacht

NOTE: The word is **am** (not **an**) and is a contraction of **an dem.**

As in English, the preposition may be omitted *before days of the week:*

Er kommt Mittwoch. (He's coming Wednesday.)

B. Adverbs of time

These same words can be used as adverbs. The adverb is formed by adding an **–s** ending to the noun. As is always the case in German, adverbs are *not capitalized.*

In contrast to the **am**-expressions, these adverbs may *only* be used to indicate *repeated occurrences:*

Er arbeitet nachmittags (nachts, samstags).
(He works afternoons [nights, Saturdays].)

EXCEPTION: During the day = **tagsüber.**

NOTE: There is no adverbial form of dates. One must say:

Er arbeitet immer am ersten Januar.
(He always works on the first of January.)

III. WEEKS, MONTHS, SEASONS, AND YEARS

The *months* and the *seasons* are all *masculine:*

MONTHS

der Januar	der Mai	der September
der Februar	der Juni	der Oktober
der März	der Juli	der November
der April	der August	der Dezember

SEASONS

der Frühling	spring	der Herbst	autumn, fall
der Sommer	summer	der Winter	winter

The word for *week* is feminine: **die Woche, –n.**

A. IM and IN DER

All the expressions above use the preposition **in** *plus the definite article.* (The contraction **im** is *always* used in place of **in dem.**)

> Er ist **im** März hier gewesen.
> (He was here in March.)

> Er kommt **im** Herbst.
> (He's coming in the fall.)

NOTE 1: **In der zweiten Woche** = in the second week.
Like English, German does not normally use the expression *in the week* without some modification, e.g. in the *second* week of our trip.

During the week = **während** der Woche (the preposition **während** plus genitive case).

In *a* week = in **einer** Woche (**in** plus dative case of the indefinite article).

NOTE 2: Er ist **im Jahr(e) 1959** nach Frankfurt gezogen.
Er ist **1959** nach Frankfurt gezogen.
(He moved to Frankfurt *in 1959.*)

In naming a specific year, German may use either (*a*) the expression **im Jahr(e)** *plus the year* or (*b*) the year alone *without* a preposition. One may *not* refer to years in the way one does in English (e.g. ~~in 1939~~).

IV. DEFINITE AND INDEFINITE TIME

A. Accusative case for definite time

The accusative case is used to indicate definite time when no prepositions are involved:

> **Letzten Sonntag** blieb ich **den ganzen Tag** zu Hause.
> (Last Sunday I stayed home all day.)

> Sie fährt **nächste Woche** nach Deutschland.
> (She's going to Germany next week.)

> Wir gehen **jeden Winter** skilaufen.
> (We go skiing every winter.)

Er hat uns **voriges Jahr** besucht.
(He visited us *last year*.)

NOTE: As you see, an adjective such as **letzt–** (*last*), **nächst–** (*next*),
vorig– (*last*), or **jed–** (*every*) is normally used in such expressions.

B. Combinations of GESTERN, HEUTE, MORGEN, and parts of days

English may combine the words *yesterday* and *tomorrow* with words referring to parts of the day (e.g. *morning, afternoon, evening*) in order to
form more exact time expressions:

> yesterday afternoon
> tomorrow evening

German functions in a similar manner:

> **gestern nachmittag**
> **morgen abend**

Unlike English, however, German uses this same method to form time
expressions referring to *today*. Instead of saying *this* morning, *this* evening,
German says **heute** morgen, **heute** abend.

To form this kind of time expression, one may, with one exception,
choose one word from column A and one from column B.

A	B
gestern	morgen
heute	vormittag
morgen	mittag
	nachmittag
	abend
	nacht

The one exception is the German expression for *tomorrow morning:*
morgen früh.

NOTE: When the parts of the day (e.g. **morgen, vormittag**) are used in
conjunction with **gestern, heute,** or **morgen,** they are adverbs of time rather
than nouns and are therefore *not capitalized*.

heute nacht
can mean last night
or the coming night

morgen früh

C. Genitive case for indefinite time

Such expressions use the word **ein**:

→ **Eines Morgens (eines Tages)** ist er ganz unerwartet angekommen.
(*One morning* [*one day*] he arrived quite unexpectedly.)

V. OTHER COMMON TIME EXPRESSIONS

A. Other time expressions requiring prepositions

As we have seen, a time expression without a preposition uses:

the accusative case for definite time
the genitive case for indefinite time

When a preposition is involved, the rules are as follows.

1. Dative Prepositions and Accusative Prepositions

Obviously, when a preposition requires dative objects only or accusative objects only, the appropriate case *must be used*. For example:

Er wohnt **seit einer Woche** hier.
(He's been living here *for a week*.)

Seit requires a dative object at all times; hence a dative object must also be used in time expressions employing **seit**.

NOTE: **Seit** einer Woche = *for* a week.
Seit requires the present tense if it refers to an action (or a condition) that *began in the past and is still going on*. (German stresses that this action or condition is still going on and uses the present tense to indicate this, whereas English normally uses the present perfect: He *has been living* here for a week.)

2. Two-way Prepositions

When a two-way preposition is used in a time expression, the case is determined as follows.

perfekt – Ich habe schon lange gewünscht.

a. Point in time (when / **wann**) = dative

When referring to a *point in time*, the *dative* case is used. Such sentences will answer the question *when* / **wann.**

→ The point in time may be in the *past:*

> Er ist **vor** einer Woche angekommen.
> Er ist heute **vor** acht Tagen angekommen.
> (He arrived a week *ago*.)

→ or the point in time may be in the *future:*

> Wir fahren **in** einer Woche ab.
> Wir fahren heute **in** acht Tagen ab.
> (We are leaving *in* a week [a week from now].)

NOTE 1: **Vor** plus dative = (a week, etc.) *ago* = past time.
In plus dative = *in* (a week, etc.) = future time.

NOTE 2: Heute vor acht (vierzehn) Tagen = a week (two weeks) ago.
Heute in acht (vierzehn) Tagen = in a week (two weeks), a week (two weeks) from now.

Instead of using the word **Woche,** German often uses **heute vor (in) acht Tagen.** This expression is used for one week **(heute vor acht Tagen)** or for two weeks **(heute vor vierzehn Tagen).** When a larger number of *weeks* is indicated, **Wochen** is used.

b. Period of time (how long / **wie lange**) = accusative

When referring to a *period of time*, the *accusative* case is used with two-way prepositions. Such sentences will answer the question *how long* / **wie lange:**

> Ich fahre **auf** eine Woche nach Frankfurt.
> (I'm going to Frankfurt *for* a week.)

> Ich bin **über** einen Monat da geblieben.
> (I stayed there *over* a month.)

NOTE: **Auf** eine Woche = *for* a week.
Auf must be used with verbs of motion (e.g. **fahren**). With other verbs, such as **sein** and **bleiben,** the accusative of definite time is used:

> Ich blieb **eine Woche** in Frankfurt.
> (I stayed in Frankfurt [*for*] *a week*.)

schon lange Zeit (for a long time)

B. Dates of the month

Note the following ways of asking the date and of giving it:

QUESTION	ANSWER
Der wievielte* ist heute?	Heute ist **der einundzwanzigste (21.)** Juni.
Den wievielten haben wir heute?	Heute haben wir **den einundzwanzigsten (21.)** Juni.
(What's the date [today]?)	(Today's the twenty-first [21st] of June.)

NOTE 1: **Der wievielte (den wievielten)** is the first element if a question is involved. (**Wieviel** is a question word.)

NOTE 2: **der einundzwanzigste Juni**
The word *of* as in *the twenty-first of June* has no corresponding form in German.

C. TAGELANG = for days

The German equivalents to *for days, for weeks, for months, for years*, etc. are adverbs of time (therefore *uncapitalized*). These are formed by adding **–lang** to the *plural form* of the noun.

tagelang	**monatelang**
wochenlang	**jahrelang**

D. Expressions using –mal or MAL

1. **Einmal** = *once, one time* **(–mal)**.

once, one time	**ein**mal
twice, two times	**zwei**mal
ten times	**zehn**mal
a hundred times	**hundert**mal

Expressions indicating the number of times (how many times?) are formed by adding **–mal** to the cardinal number.

NOTE 1: The only exception is **einmal**. (The cardinal number is **eins**.)

---

*Literally, **der wievielte** = *the how-many-eth.*

NOTE 2: In expressions such as *a* hundred times, *a* thousand times, German does not have an equivalent to the English *a* (**hundertmal, tausendmal**).

NOTE 3: German never uses the word ~~Zeit~~ in such a context.

2. **Das erste Mal** = *the first time* (**Mal**).

das dritte (achte, nächste Mal)   the third (eighth, next) time

Here English and German behave similarly. In cases like the one above, **Mal** is a noun and is therefore capitalized.

Again one must remember that German never uses ~~Zeit~~ in this context.

3. **Zum** ersten Mal = *for the* first time (**Mal**).

zum dritten (letzten) Mal   *for the* third (last) time

Contrast:
Das letzte Mal hast du es gemacht. (You did it *the last time*.)
Das sage ich dir **zum** letzten Mal. (I'm telling you that *for the* last time.)

🔲 DRILLS

Hours and minutes

Fill in the blanks. Do *not* use "railroad" time.

1. Er kommt ＿＿＿＿＿. (at eight o'clock)
   ＿＿＿＿＿. (at quarter after seven)
   ＿＿＿＿＿. (at quarter to three)
   ＿＿＿＿＿. (at five-thirty)
   ＿＿＿＿＿. (at ten to nine)
   ＿＿＿＿＿. (at quarter to one)
   ＿＿＿＿＿. (at five after eight)
   ＿＿＿＿＿. (at twenty to five)
   ＿＿＿＿＿. (at six-thirty)
   ＿＿＿＿＿. (at twelve o'clock)

2. Es ist ＿＿＿＿＿. (twenty after two)
   ＿＿＿＿＿. (quarter to six)

———————. (twelve-thirty)
———————. (ten after four)
———————. (twenty-five to ten)
———————. (three-thirty)
———————. (five o'clock)
———————. (eleven-thirty)
———————. (quarter after seven)
———————. (quarter to one)

Days and parts of days

1. Er kommt ——————— (on Friday, on Sunday).
2. Er arbeitet ——————— (Saturdays, Wednesdays, nights).
3. ——————— (Evenings) bleibt er zu Hause.
4. Ich sehe ihn ——————— (on the twenty-fifth).
5. Heute kommt er ——————— (in the afternoon, at midnight).
6. ——————— (During the day) ist es sehr schön.
7. ——————— (Sundays) regnet es immer.
8. Er kommt ——————— (at night, in the evening).
9. Ich fahre ——————— (on Tuesday, on Monday) ab.

Weeks, months, seasons, and years

1. Er kommt ——————— (in May, in December, in August).
2. ——————— (In 1964) war ich in Innsbruck.
3. Wir fahren ——————— (in March, in February, in April) nach Mainz.
4. ——————— (During the week) muß er arbeiten.
5. ——————— (In the fall, in the spring) ist es sehr schön hier.
6. Ich bin ——————— (in 1930) geboren.

Definite and indefinite time

1. Wir gehen ——————— (this evening) ins Kino.
2. Haben Sie ihn ——————— (yesterday afternoon) besucht?
3. ——————— (Tomorrow morning) muß ich arbeiten.
4. ——————— (Next year) bin ich in Berlin.
5. ——————— (One morning) war er einfach nicht mehr da.
6. Besuchen Sie uns ——————— (next week)?

7. Er kommt ＿＿＿＿＿＿＿ (tomorrow evening).
8. Er blieb ＿＿＿＿＿＿＿ (all day) zu Hause.
9. ＿＿＿＿＿＿＿ (One day) ist er weggegangen.
10. So geht es ＿＿＿＿＿＿＿ (every spring).

Other common time expressions

1. Er ist ＿＿＿＿＿＿＿ (a month ago) abgefahren.
2. Ich bin ＿＿＿＿＿＿＿ (over a year) da geblieben.
3. Wir sind nur ＿＿＿＿＿＿＿ (once) in Frankreich gewesen.
4. Ich wohne ＿＿＿＿＿＿＿ (for a month) hier.
5. Er hat ＿＿＿＿＿＿＿ (for years) allein gelebt.
6. Ich fahre ＿＿＿＿＿＿＿ (for a month) nach Wien.
7. ＿＿＿＿＿＿＿ (A year ago) war er noch gesund.
8. ＿＿＿＿＿＿＿ (The next time) bleibe ich zu Hause.
9. ＿＿＿＿＿＿＿ (In a week, in two years) ist er wieder da.
10. Sie ist ＿＿＿＿＿＿＿ (four times) da gewesen.
11. Heute haben wir ＿＿＿＿＿＿＿ (the eighth of January).
12. Ich lese diese Novelle ＿＿＿＿＿＿＿ (for the first time).

Mixed drills

1. Ich wohne _seit einem Monat_ (for a month) hier.
2. Er arbeitet _Montags_ (Mondays).
3. Otto kommt _zehn vor nein_ (at ten to nine).
4. ＿＿＿＿＿＿＿ (The next time) bleibst du zu Hause.
5. Er hat _Jahre lang_ (for years) allein gelebt.
6. Ich fahre _am Donnerstag_ (on Thursday) ab.
7. Ilse kommt _um halb sieben_ (at six-thirty).
8. _Sonntags_ (Sundays) regnet es immer.
9. Frau Jens ist _üb er ein Jahr_ (over a year) in München geblieben.
10. _Tagsüber_ (During the day) ist es sehr schön.
11. Ich bin _um viertel nach e_ (at quarter past one) zurück.
12. _Am 1959_ (In 1959) war es sehr heiß.
13. Heute haben wir _den achten Januar_ (the eighth of January).
14. Liest er das _zum ersten Mal_ (for the first time)?
15. Es ist genau _fünf nach halb_ (twenty-five to ten).
16. Ich sehe ihn _am_ ＿＿＿＿＿＿＿ (on the twenty-fifth).
  fünfund zw

17. _____ (Tomorrow morning) fahren wir ab.
18. Wir haben den Film _____ (three times) gesehen.
19. Es ist _____ (five minutes after three).
20. Ich bin nur _____ (once) da gewesen.
21. Wir fahren _für enJahr_ (for a year) nach Deutschland.
22. _Abends_ (Evenings) bleibt er immer zu Hause.
23. Der Zug ist _vor zehn Minuten_ (ten minutes ago) abgefahren.
24. Arbeiten Sie _nachts_ (nights)?
25. Er kommt _um eins_ (at one).
26. So geht es _____ (every spring). _jeden Frühling_
27. _____ (All morning) blieb er zu Hause. _den ganzen Morgen_
28. _Eines Tages_ (One day) war sie einfach nicht mehr da.
29. _Nächste Woche_ (Next week) kommt er nach Berlin.
30. Warst du _____ (yesterday evening) zu Hause?
31. Hier ist es _im Februar_ (in February) sehr kalt.

Express in German   _10-30-81_.

1. I was born in 1951.
2. He left at ten to nine.
3. In February it's always cold.
4. I've been living here for a month.
5. Were you home yesterday afternoon?
6. They'll be back in two days.
7. He works Mondays.
8. I'm going to Berlin next week.
9. One day he simply went away.
10. You can stay home the next time.
11. For years he lived alone.
12. He worked all week.
13. Did you stay there all morning?
14. We're leaving on Friday.
15. And so it goes every spring.
16. Are you coming at eleven-thirty?
17. It always rains Sundays.
18. We eat at one.
19. The train left ten minutes ago.
20. During the day it's very hot.
21. Does she work nights?

22. Frau Jens stayed here over a year.
23. I've only been there once.
24. I'll be back at quarter after seven.
25. Today is the fourth of July.
26. It was very cold in 1947.
27. It's eight minutes to eight.
28. We've seen that movie five times.
29. She's leaving tomorrow morning.
30. I'm seeing him on the twenty-third.
31. Are you reading that for the first time?
32. It is exactly twenty-five to ten.
33. Where are you going (**hinfahren**) in September?

modal
auxiliaries

chapter six

LEVEL ONE

Look at the following examples:

> I'm going home.
> He's doing it.

These are simple declarative statements of fact. Often, however, one wants
to express more than a simple statement:

> I *must* go home.
> He *can* do it.

As you see, this can be done by using an additional verb (e.g. *must, can*).
Such verbs are called *modal auxiliaries* and are used to express ability (I
can do it), necessity (I *must* do it), possibility (I *may* do it), desire (I *want*
to do it), and so on. These verbs are treated as a group since they all affect
sentence structure in the same way.

II. STRUCTURE OF GERMAN SENTENCES USING MODAL AUXILIARIES

The following sentences are simple declarative statements of fact; they *do not* contain modal auxiliaries:

Ich gehe nach Hause.
Er macht das.

When the modals **muß** (*must*) and **kann** (*can*) are added to them, the following changes take place:

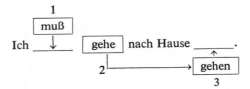

Ich **muß** nach Hause gehen.

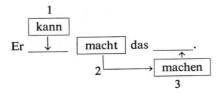

Er **kann** das **machen.**

1. **Muß** and **kann** (conjugated forms of the modals) must occupy the second (or verb) position in the sentence.

2. **Gehe** and **macht,** which were in the second position before, are forced out of this position and are moved to the end of the sentence.

3. Since a modal expression cannot have *two* conjugated verbs, **gehe** and **macht** *appear at the end of their sentences as infinitives:*

Ich muß nach Hause **gehen.**
Er kann das **machen.**

III. OMISSION OF ZU WITH INFINITIVES IN MODAL EXPRESSIONS

I must go home.   Ich muß nach Hause gehen.
(I have *to* go home.)

I can do it.   Ich kann das machen.
(I am able *to* do it.)

Some English equivalents of the German modal auxiliaries require the word *to* (I have *to* go home, I am able *to* do it, I want *to* come along). Others, however, do not (I must go home, I can do it, etc.).

German never uses **zu** before infinitives *in modal expressions.*

IV. FORMS AND MEANINGS OF GERMAN MODALS

A. MÜSSEN

1. *must, have to* (necessity)

PRESENT TENSE		PAST TENSE	
ich muß	wir müssen	ich mußte	wir mußten
du mußt	ihr müßt	du mußtest	ihr mußtet
er muß	sie müssen	er mußte	sie mußten

Ich **muß** jeden Tag früh aufstehen.   (I *have to* get up early every day.)
Wir **mußten** gestern zu Hause bleiben.   (We *had to* stay home yesterday.)

B. KÖNNEN

PRESENT TENSE		PAST TENSE	
ich kann	wir können	ich konnte	wir konnten
du kannst	ihr könnt	du konntest	ihr konntet
er kann	sie können	er konnte	sie konnten

1. *can, to be able to* (ability)

Er **kann** das machen.   (He *can* do it.)
Sie **konnte** sehr gut schwimmen.   (She *could* [was able to] swim very well.)

2. *may, can* (possibility)

Das **kann** sein.	(That *may* be.)
So etwas **kann** nicht vorkommen.	(Something like that *can't* happen.)

3. *to know* (ability)

Er **kann** Deutsch.   (He knows German. [He *can* read it, write it, etc.])

NOTE: German has three words that correspond to the English *know:*

wissen to know a *fact*	Ich **weiß,** wo das ist. (I *know* where that is.)
kennen to know a *person* or to be familiar with a *place* or *subject*	Er **kennt** den Mann (München, die deutsche Romantik) sehr gut. (He *knows* that man [Munich, German Romanticism] very well.)
können to know in the sense of *to have a facility in something*	Er **kann** Bridge. (He *knows* bridge. [He *can* play it.])

C. DÜRFEN

1. *may, to be permitted to, be allowed to* (permission)

PRESENT TENSE		PAST TENSE	
ich darf	wir dürfen	ich durfte	wir durften
du darfst	ihr dürft	du durftest	ihr durftet
er darf	sie dürfen	er durfte	sie durften

Darf ich heute abend ins Kino gehen?	(*May* I go to the movies this evening?)
Gestern **durften** wir nicht ausgehen.	(We *weren't allowed* to go out yesterday.)

NOTE: In colloquial speech one often hears **können** (**Kann** ich heute abend ins Kino gehen?) instead of **dürfen.** This corresponds to colloquial English *Can* I go? instead of the more formal *May* I go?

D. MÖGEN

PRESENT TENSE		PAST TENSE	
ich mag	wir mögen	ich mochte	wir mochten

du magst	ihr mögt	du mochtest	ihr mochtet
er mag	sie mögen	er mochte	sie mochten

(The simple past tense forms of **mögen** are uncommon in spoken German.)

implies an emotional relationship

1. *to like* (liking, fondness)

>Diese Suppe **mag** ich nicht.   (I don't *like* this soup.)
>**Mögen** Sie ihn nicht?   (Don't you *like* him?)

2. *may* (possibility)

>Das **mag** wohl sein.   (That *may* well be.)

NOTE: When **mögen** denotes possibility, it often has a negative connotation and is therefore followed by a qualifying statement:

>Er **mag** wohl viel arbeiten, **aber** er schreibt doch schlechte Prüfungen.
>(He *may* well work a lot, *but* he still writes bad tests.)

In such cases **mögen** *must* be used (rather than **können**).

gern – like doing / you like doing something

E. WOLLEN

gefallen – Das gefällt mir.

PRESENT TENSE		PAST TENSE	
ich will	wir wollen	ich wollte	wir wollten
du willst	ihr wollt	du wolltest	ihr wolltet
er will	sie wollen	er wollte	sie wollten

1. *to want to* (desire, volition)

>Er **will** diesen Sommer nach Deutschland fahren.
>(He *wants to* go to Germany this summer.)

>Das **wollte** ich dir sagen.
>(I *wanted to* tell you that.)

2. *to claim to, consider oneself* (assertion, opinion)

Er **will** ein großer Musikfreund sein.
(He *claims to* be [*considers himself, thinks* he is] a great music lover.)

F. SOLLEN

PRESENT TENSE		PAST TENSE	
ich soll	wir sollen	ich sollte	wir sollten
du sollst	ihr sollt	du solltest	ihr solltet
er soll	sie sollen	er sollte	sie sollten

1. *to be supposed to* (obligation)

> Er **soll** um fünf Uhr kommen.
> (He *is supposed to* come at five o'clock.)
>
> Wir **sollten** das schon gestern machen.
> (We *were supposed to* do that yesterday.)

2. *to be said to, be supposed to* (supposition)

> Dieser Film **soll** sehr gut sein.
> (This film *is said to* be [*is supposed to* be] very good.)

3. *shall*

> Wo **soll** ich es hinstellen?
> (Where *shall* I put it?)

G. Forms of German modals (summary)

1. Stems of the Modals

Five of the German modals have *two stems:* one stem for the infinitive and the plural forms and a different stem for the singular forms:

INFINITIVE	PLURAL STEM	SINGULAR STEM
müssen	müss–	muß–
können	könn–	kann–
dürfen	dürf–	darf–
mögen	mög–	mag–
wollen	woll–	will–

The one remaining modal has only *one* present tense stem:

INFINITIVE	PLURAL STEM	SINGULAR STEM
sollen	soll–	soll–

2. Present Tense Forms

The present tense endings of the modals are unusual: the 1st and 3rd persons singular *take no endings,* i.e. they use only the stem:

ich kann	—	wir könn	en
du kann	st	ihr könn	t
er kann	—	sie könn	en

3. Past Tense Forms

The past tense forms of the German modals have only *one stem*. The past tense is formed by adding the following endings to this stem:

ich konn	te	wir konn	ten
du konn	test	ihr konn	tet
er konn	te	sie konn	ten

V. OMISSION OF INFINITIVES IN MODAL EXPRESSIONS

He must *go* home.	Er muß nach Hause gehen.
	Er muß nach Hause.
He can *do* it.	Er kann das machen.
	Er kann das.

In German the infinitive may be omitted from modal expressions:

1. when a goal or destination is explicitly stated in the sentence:

    Ich muß nach Hause **gehen.**   Ich muß nach Hause.

2. when the idea of *to do* (**machen, tun**) is present:

    Er kann das **machen.**   Er kann das.

3. when the context would make the infinitive repetitious or superfluous:

Does he have to stay home today?   Muß er heute zu Hause bleiben?
Yes. He *has to.*   Ja, er **muß.**

NOTE: Example 3 is similar to English usage, whereas 1 and 2 are not.

▣ DRILLS

Form drills

Insert the modal auxiliaries into the following sentences. The tense required is indicated by the tense of the verb in the basic sentence: when this verb is in the past tense, the modal must also be in the past tense.

Examples: Ich **gehe** nach Hause. (müssen)
Ich **muß** nach Hause gehen.

Er **tat** es. (können)
Er **konnte** es tun.

1. Sie kommt mit. (dürfen)
2. Ihr schämt euch. (sollen)
3. Warum warten wir so lange? (müssen)
4. Siehst du das Bild? (können)
5. Schreibst du einen Brief? (wollen)
6. Ich las das Buch gestern. (müssen)
7. Peter geht heute abend ins Kino. (dürfen)
8. Meine Schwester spielt Klavier. (können)
9. Sie machte einige Einkäufe. (wollen)
10. Kommt er morgen an? (sollen)
11. Er ist wohl ein guter Lehrer. (mögen)
12. Sie aß nur wenig. (können)
13. Thomas ist jetzt in Tübingen. (sollen)
14. Ihr steht immer früh auf. (müssen)
15. Wir bezahlten die Rechnung nicht. (können)
16. Er kam um fünf Uhr. (sollen)
17. Hier raucht man nicht. (dürfen)
18. Du hast wohl recht. (mögen)
19. Er schwimmt nicht besonders schnell. (können)
20. Er ist ein guter Freund von Adenauer. (wollen)
21. Er setzte sich gleich hin. (müssen)
22. So etwas kommt vor. (können)
23. Ich bin um vier Uhr zu Hause. (sollen)
24. Inge ging gestern nicht aus dem Haus. (dürfen)
25. Ich rief ihn zu Hause an. (wollen)

Synthetic exercises

Construct complete sentences in both the present and the simple past tenses (unless otherwise indicated).

Example: Er / müssen / gehen / nach Hause

Er **muß** nach Hause gehen.
Er **mußte** nach Hause gehen.

1. Ich / müssen / lesen / Buch / schnell
2. Meine Schwester / können / spielen / Klavier
3. Peter / dürfen / gehen / ins Kino
4. Wir / müssen / aufstehen / früh
5. Wollen / du / schreiben / Brief /?
6. Er / können / essen / nur wenig
7. Ihr / sollen / kommen / um fünf Uhr
8. Er / sollen / sein / ein guter Student (*present tense only*)
9. Ich / müssen / gehen / in die Bibliothek
10. Herr Stramm / wollen / bleiben / nicht da
11. Film / sollen / sein / sehr gut (*present tense only*)
12. Ich / dürfen / kommen / etwas später
13. Er / können / schwimmen / nicht besonders gut

Fill-ins

Using the English cues, supply the correct German modal auxiliary.

Example: Ich (had to) _____ nach Hause gehen.
            Ich **mußte** nach Hause gehen.

1. Anita _____ nur wenig essen.
           (could)

2. Er _____ das Buch lesen.
     (was supposed to)

3. _____ jetzt einen Brief schreiben?
    (Do you want to)

4. Sie _____ sehr lange warten.
        (had to)

5. _____ ich noch etwas Brot haben, bitte?
      (May)

6. Er _____ ein großer Musikfreund sein.
      (claims to)

7. Ich _____ ihn gar nicht.
       (like)

8. Wir _____ die Rechnung kaum bezahlen.
      (were able to)

9. Inge _____ gestern nicht aus dem Haus gehen.
    (was permitted to)

10. Ich _____ ihn zu Hause anrufen.
      (wanted to)

11. Er _____ ein sehr intelligenter Mann sein.
       (is said to)

12. Sie _____ einige Einkäufe machen.
        (has to)

13. Er _____ wohl ein guter Lehrer sein, aber er spricht immer
          (may
    Dialekt.

14. Sie _____ um acht Uhr kommen.
       (are supposed to)

15. Das _____ doch nicht wahr sein!
          (can)

16. Warum _____ dieses Buch lesen?
           (do we have to)

17. Sie _____ jetzt gehen.
          (may)

18. Die anderen _____ hier bleiben.
                 (want to)

19. Ich _____ den Mann sehr.
          (like)

Express in German *Do for Wed 2/4/81* *aufstehen*

1. I always *have to* get up early.
2. He *is supposed to* come at five o'clock.
3. Yes, he *may* go to the movies this evening.
4. We *could* hardly pay the bill.
5. He *claims to* be a good friend of yours.
6. Why *did* we *have to* wait so long?
7. He *can't* swim particularly fast.
8. *Were* you *supposed to* visit her yesterday?
9. *May* we come along?
10. *Can* you see the picture?
11. That *can't* be true.
12. He *is said to* be very intelligent.
13. They *wanted to* go shopping.
14. He *may* be nice, but he's not particularly bright.
15. She *wasn't able to* eat much.
16. You *aren't allowed to* smoke here.
17. Why *do we have to* read this book?
18. When *are* we *supposed to* be there?
19. He *wasn't permitted to* do it.

LEVEL TWO

I. COMPOUND TENSES OF MODAL AUXILIARIES

As our starting point we will take

Er muß nach Hause gehen

and form its compound future and perfect tenses.

A. Future with auxiliary WERDEN

In German, the future tense is composed of **werden** *plus an infinitive.* This rule also applies to the future tense of modal auxiliaries:

PRESENT TENSE	Er **muß** nach Hause gehen.
FUTURE TENSE	Er **wird** nach Hause gehen **müssen.**

The only difference between the two sentences is that the modal has changed tenses.

The present tense form: **muß**
has been replaced by: **wird . . . müssen.**

B. Present perfect

Here the principle is essentially the same; i.e. the change may be viewed as a simple replacement:

PRESENT	Ich **muß** nach Hause gehen.	**muß** is replaced by
PRESENT PERFECT	Ich **habe** nach Hause gehen **müssen.**	**habe . . . müssen.***

The past participle of **müssen** is **gemußt.** Therefore, the perfect tense of

Ich **muß**   is   Ich **habe gemußt.**

However, when there is a *dependent infinitive* at the end of the clause:

Ich muß nach Hause **gehen**

---

* Double-infinitive construction.

the perfect tense requires the *infinitive form of the modal* (e.g. **müssen**), rather than a past participle (e.g. **gemußt**), in the final position of the clause. The result is called a *double-infinitive* construction:

Ich habe nach Hause gehen <u>müssen</u>.

One may say that the past participle:

gemußt

"changes into" an infinitive when it appears after a dependent infinitive:

gehen <u>müssen</u>

NOTE: This is true for all modal constructions in perfect tenses:

WITHOUT DEPENDENT INFINITIVE	WITH DEPENDENT INFINITIVE
Ich habe . . . **gekonnt**	Ich habe . . . gehen **können**
Ich habe . . . **gedurft**	Ich habe . . . gehen **dürfen**
Ich habe . . . **gewollt**	Ich habe . . . gehen **wollen**
Ich habe . . . **gesollt**	Ich habe . . . gehen **sollen**
Ich habe . . . **gemocht**	Ich habe . . . gehen **mögen**

NOTE: All modal auxiliaries require **haben** (rather than **sein**) to form their perfect tenses.

C. Past perfect

This tense can be treated like the present perfect; the only difference is that **hatte** replaces **hat**:

WITH DEPENDENT INFINITIVE	Ich **hatte** nach Hause **gehen** <u>müssen</u>.
WITHOUT DEPENDENT INFINITIVE	Ich **hatte** es **gemußt**.

D. Word order in dependent clauses

Look at the following example:

Ich wußte nicht, **daß** er nach Hause gegangen **ist**.

The conjugated verb form is normally in *final position* in subordinate clauses. However, when a double-infinitive construction is involved, the conjugated verb form precedes the two infinitives:

Ich wußte nicht, daß er <u>hat</u> mitkommen wollen.

E. Summary

1. Principal Parts of the Modal Auxiliaries

INFINITIVE	PAST TENSE	PAST PARTICIPLE	3RD PERSON SINGULAR PRESENT
müssen	mußte	gemußt	muß
können	konnte	gekonnt	kann
dürfen	durfte	gedurft	darf
mögen	mochte	gemocht	mag
wollen	wollte	gewollt	will
sollen	sollte	gesollt	soll

2. Tenses of Modal Auxiliaries

WITHOUT DEPENDENT INFINITIVE		WITH DEPENDENT INFINITIVE
Ich **muß** es.	have to (go)	Ich **muß** nach Hause gehen.
Ich **mußte** es.	had to (go)	Ich **mußte** nach Hause gehen.
Ich **werde** es **müssen.**	will have to (go)	Ich **werde** nach Hause gehen **müssen.**
Ich **habe** es **gemußt.**	have had to (go)	Ich **habe** nach Hause gehen **müssen.**
Ich **hatte** es **gemußt.**	had had to (go)	Ich **hatte** nach Hause gehen **müssen.**

a. Tense change

The only elements that change in the sentences above are the forms of the modal (muß, mußte, werde . . . müssen, etc.). All modals form their perfect tenses with **haben** (NOT with **sein**).

> *Hence:*   Ich **habe** es **gemußt.**
> Ich **habe** gehen **müssen.**

b. Double infinitives (perfect tenses)

PRESENT PERFECT	Ich **habe** es **gemußt.**	Ich **habe** nach Hause gehen <u>müssen.</u>
PAST PERFECT	Ich **hatte** es **gemußt.**	Ich **hatte** nach Hause gehen <u>müssen.</u>

When no dependent infinitive is involved, the perfect tense of a modal sentence requires a past participle (Ich habe es **gemußt**).

When a dependent infinitive is used to complete the meaning of the sentence, *the infinitive form of the modal is used instead of a past participle* (Ich habe nach Hause gehen **müssen**).

NOTE: In such cases the *infinitive of the modal* is always the *last word* in its clause and is always immediately preceded by the dependent infinitive (e.g. gehen **müssen**).

▣ DRILLS

Future tense with **werden**

Put the following sentences into the future tense by using the auxiliary **werden.**

> Example: Sie **müssen** wohl nach Hause gehen.
> Sie **werden** wohl nach Hause gehen **müssen.**

1. Er kann wohl um fünf Uhr nicht kommen.
2. Inge darf wohl nicht aus dem Hause gehen
3. Er will ihn wohl morgen treffen.
4. Sie müssen früh aufstehen.
5. Nach so einem Früstück könnt ihr nicht mehr viel essen.
6. Peter will wohl hier übernachten.
7. Sie muß wohl einige Einkäufe machen.
8. Du kannst ihn wohl zu Hause besuchen.
9. Wir müssen lange warten.

Present perfect tense

Put the following sentences into the present perfect tense. (Both sentences requiring a double-infinitive construction and those requiring a past participle of the modal auxiliary are included in this exercise.)

> Examples: Sie **müssen** nach Hause **gehen.**
> Sie **haben** nach Hause gehen **müssen.**
>
> Das **kann** er.
> Das **hat** er **gekonnt.**

1. Wie lange müssen Sie denn warten?
2. Solche Geschichten mag ich nie.
3. Die ganze Familie muß früh aufstehen.
4. Können Sie sie besuchen?
5. Dürfen Sie das machen? Ja, ich darf es.
6. Er will es einfach nicht tun.
7. Dieter kann die Rechnung kaum bezahlen.
8. Ich muß sehr viel lesen.
9. Wollen Sie einen neuen Anzug kaufen?
10. Ich soll es bei Herrn Lange abholen.
11. Wir dürfen nicht aus dem Haus gehen.
12. Wir können den Redner gar nicht hören.
13. Das will ich nicht.
14. Müssen Sie in dem Kurs wirklich viel sprechen?
15. Niemand kann ihr helfen.
16. Er will Tennis spielen.
17. Können Sie das Buch leicht finden?
18. Ich will in die Stadt.
19. Müssen Sie wirklich ins Krankenhaus gehen?

Synthetic exercises

Construct sentences in the present, past, compound future, present perfect, and past perfect tenses, using the following elements.

1. Ich / müssen / lesen / viel
2. Können / du / finden / Buch / leicht /?
3. Niemand / können / helfen / ihm
4. Dürfen / wir / tun / das/?
5. Er / müssen / aufstehen / sehr früh
6. Dieter / können / bezahlen / Rechnung / kaum
7. Wir / dürfen / gehen / nicht / aus ... Haus
8. Seine Frau / wollen / machen / einige Einkäufe
9. Wir / müssen / weggehen / rechtzeitig
10. Warum / ihr / können / bleiben / nicht / länger /?
11. Er / wollen / tun / es / einfach nicht

Express in German

Express in German, using the tense or tenses indicated in parentheses.

1. *Were* you *able to* find the book? (*past* and *perfect*)
2. I *had to* read a lot. (*past* and *perfect*)

3. We *will have to* wait a long time. (*future*)
4. He *had to* get up very early. (*past* and *perfect*)
5. Dieter *could* hardly pay the bill. (*past* and *perfect*)
6. We *weren't allowed to* go out of the house. (*past* and *perfect*) *kaum*
7. I *wanted* (to go) downtown. (*past* and *perfect*) *in die Stadt*
8. *Will* we *be able to* do it? (*future*)
9. No one *was able to* help her. (*past* and *perfect*)
10. She *will probably want to* go shopping. (*future*)
11. I never *liked* stories like that. (*perfect*)
12. He simply *didn't want to* do it. (*past* and *perfect*)
13. *Were* you *permitted to* smoke there? (*past* and *perfect*)
14. *Did* you *really have to* go to the hospital? (*past* and *perfect*)
15. He *will probably want to* spend the night here. (*future*)
16. Why *weren't* you *able to* stay longer? (*past* and *perfect*)
17. *Were* you *allowed to* go along? (*past* and *perfect*)
18. We *will have to* leave on time. (*future*)
19. *Will* we *be allowed to* visit you? (*future*)
20. I *was* hardly *able to* understand him. (*past* and *perfect*)
21. He *didn't want to* do it. (*past* and *perfect*)

LEVEL THREE

I. HELFEN, LASSEN, AND THE SENSES

Structurally, **helfen, lassen,** and the verbs indicating the senses behave like modal auxiliaries:

I hear him coming.	Ich **höre** ihn **kommen.**
I heard him coming (come).	Ich **hörte** ihn **kommen.**
I'll hear him coming (come).	Ich **werde** ihn **kommen hören.**
I (have) heard him coming (come).	Ich **habe** ihn **kommen hören.**
I had heard him coming (come).	Ich **hatte** ihn **kommen hören.**

Like the modals, these verbs require a *double-infinitive construction* to form their perfect tenses *when there is a dependent infinitive* (e.g. **kommen**) *involved:*

Ich habe ihn **kommen hören.**

but: Ich habe es **gehört.**

rauchen

After verbs of this type, English very often uses a present participle (e.g. coming). It should be noted that German always uses a dependent *infinitive* (e.g. **kommen**)—never a present participle:

> Ich höre ihn **kommen**.
> (I hear him *coming*.)

A. The senses

In theory, *any* of the verbs used to indicate the senses function as **hören** does in the examples above. In practice, however, **sehen** and **hören** are the sense verbs most commonly used.

B. HELFEN

> I helped *him* repair *the car*.   Ich half **ihm den Wagen** reparieren.

In the sentences above, both verbs have objects: **ihm** is the dative object of **helfen**, and **den Wagen** is the accusative object of **reparieren**.

C. LASSEN

Lassen has a basic meaning from which more specific meanings are derived: **lassen** ordinarily indicates that the subject is *not* himself performing an action but still retains control over whether the action is performed or not. This may express itself as:

1. *To let or allow* (permission)

> Let the boy play.   Laß den Jungen doch spielen!

NOTE: **Lassen** takes the *accusative case* (e.g. **den Jungen**).

2. *To have* (*something done*); *have or make* (*someone do something*)

> I'm having my son *pick* up the mail.
> Ich lasse meinen Sohn die Post **abholen**.
> (**Sohn** is the object of **lassen**.)

> I'm having the mail *picked* up.
> Ich lasse die Post **abholen**.
> (**Post** is the object of **abholen**.)

NOTE 1: In these sentences, English has two patterns whereas German has only one. If I am having a person *do* something, English uses an in-

Ich lasse mir die Haare schneiden.

rechtzeitig

finitive (I'm having *my son pick up* the mail). If I am having something *done*, the past participle is used (I'm having the mail *picked up*). German uses only the *infinitive form* after **lassen** (Ich **lasse** [meinen Sohn] die Post **abholen**).

NOTE 2: This use of **lassen** indicates that the subject of the sentence is not actually performing the action described but is having or making someone else perform it. The sentence

> I'm having my shoes shined
> Ich lasse mir die Schuhe putzen

shows that my shoes are being shined by someone other than myself. However, I am the one who is having it done; i.e. the decision as to whether this action is performed still rests in my hands.

In some cases English does not show this distinction as clearly as German. Instead of:

> We're *having* a house *built*

one often hears:

> We're *building* a house.

In German, however, this last sentence would mean that we are constructing the house with our own hands. If someone else is doing the work, one must say:

> Wir **lassen** uns ein Haus **bauen.**

▣ DRILLS

Fill-ins

Fill in the blanks, using the present or the simple past tense.

1. Ich _____ den Wagen jetzt wegfahren.
   (hear)
2. Wir _____ ihn in den Zug einsteigen.
   (saw)
3. Er _____ mir die Bücher zurückbringen.
   (helped)
4. _____ du ihn winken?
   (Do you see)

5. Er _____ sich ein Haus bauen.
         (is having)

6. Ich _____ ihr die Pakete tragen.
         (helped)

7. Wir _____ den Kellner die Rechnung bringen.
         (had)

8. _____ Sie ihn die Tür zumachen?
   (Did you hear)

Present perfect tense

Put the following sentences into the present perfect.

1. Das hörte ich ihn öfters sagen.
2. Er ließ uns einen langen Aufsatz schreiben.
3. Ich half ihm das Problem lösen.
4. Wir sahen dich um die Ecke kommen.
5. Willi ließ sich heute die Haare schneiden.
6. Saht ihr die Straßenbahn vorbeifahren?
7. Der Chef ließ uns gestern etwas früher nach Hause gehen.
8. Die Kinder halfen mir den Baum pflanzen.
9. Ich hörte den Wagen wegfahren.
10. Marie ließ sich die Haare machen.
11. Ullrich half seiner Mutter aus dem Wagen aussteigen.
12. Meine Frau ließ die Putzfrau das Wohnzimmer aufräumen.

Future tense with **werden**

Put the following sentences into the future tense, using the auxiliary **werden.**

1. Ich höre ihn klopfen.
2. Vater läßt mich nicht ausgehen.
3. Hilfst du mir die Bücher zurückbringen?
4. Er läßt mich seinen Wagen nehmen.
5. Von hier aus sehen wir ihn hereinkommen.

Synthetic exercises

Use the tense or tenses indicated.

1. Er / helfen / mir / Bücher / zurückbringen (*past* and *present perfect*)
2. Das / hören / ich / öfters / sagen (*present perfect*)

3. Wir / lassen / uns / Haus / bauen (*present, past,* and *present perfect*)
4. Ich / sehen / Straßenbahn / noch nicht / vorbeifahren (*present perfect*)
5. Bernhard / lassen / sich / neu / Anzug / machen (*present, past,* and *present perfect*)
6. Hören / ihr / ihn / mal / spielen /? (*present perfect*)
7. Ich / lassen / mein / Bruder / Arzt / holen (*past* and *present perfect*)
8. Kinder / helfen / mir / Baum / pflanzen (*past* and *present perfect*)
9. Er / lassen / sich / Speisekarte / übersetzen (*present, past,* and *present perfect*)
10. Chef / lassen / uns / gestern / etwas früher / nach Hause / gehen (*past* and *present perfect*)

Express in German

1. I didn't hear you knock. (*perfect*)
2. We didn't see you wave. (*perfect*)
3. He let me read the letter. (*past* and *perfect*)
4. I had my hair cut. (*past* and *perfect*)
5. The children helped me plant the tree. (*past* and *perfect*)
6. Wolfi had himself a new suit made. (*past*)
7. Boy Scouts (**Pfadfinder**) help old ladies carry packages.
8. Did you hear him close the door? (*perfect*)
9. He had the waiter bring the bill. (*past* and *perfect*)
10. The boss let us go home a little earlier yesterday. (*past* and *perfect*)
11. I've seen him do that so often. (*perfect*)
12. Lulu had her hair done yesterday. (*past* and *perfect*)
13. Have you ever heard him play? (*perfect*)
14. Father never lets me go out.
15. My wife had the cleaning woman straighten up (**aufräumen**) the living room. (*past*)
16. We've often heard him say that. (*perfect*)
17. He's having a house built.
18. They helped us solve the problem. (*past* and *perfect*)
19. Karl let me drive his car to Munich. (*past*)
20. I saw her get on the train. (*past* and *perfect*)

passive voice

chapter seven

LEVEL ONE

I. COMPARISON WITH ACTIVE VOICE

SUBJECT	VERB	OBJECT
A lot of students	read	this novel.

The subject is performing the action here (a lot of students *read*), and the object (this novel) is being acted upon.

This same sentence can be put into the *passive voice:*

ACTIVE	PASSIVE
A lot of students *read* this novel.	This novel *is* (*being*) *read* by a lot of students.

The subject of the passive sentence is *not* itself acting; on the contrary, it *is being acted upon,* i.e. it is *passive.* The person(s) performing the action is found in a prepositional phrase following the verb (*by* a lot of students) and is called the "agent."

It is the verb form, however, that really shows whether the sentence is active or passive:

ACTIVE   X *reads* (*is reading*).   Here X is *acting.*
PASSIVE   X *is read* (*is being read*).   Here X is being *acted upon.*

II. FORMATION OF PASSIVE SENTENCES

The German passive sentence follows essentially the same pattern. It can be formed from its active counterpart in three steps:

1. The *accusative object* of the active sentence becomes the *nominative subject* of the passive sentence:

ACTIVE	PASSIVE
Viele Studenten lesen **diesen Roman.**	**Dieser Roman** . . .
(A lot of students read *this novel.*)	(*This novel* . . .)

2. The active verb form is replaced by:

> *a conjugated form of* **werden** + *a past participle*

ACTIVE	PASSIVE
Viele Studenten **lesen** diesen Roman.	Dieser Roman **wird** . . . **gelesen.**

NOTE: **Werden** must agree with the subject of the *passive* sentence. In these examples, the subject of the active sentence is plural whereas the subject of the passive sentence is singular.

ACTIVE	PASSIVE
Viele Studenten **lesen** . . .	Dieser Roman **wird** . . . **gelesen.**
(plural) (plural)	(singular) (singular)

3. The subject of the active sentence is replaced by:

> **von** + *a dative object*

ACTIVE	PASSIVE
Viele Studenten lesen diesen Roman.	Dieser Roman wird **von vielen Studenten** gelesen.

This construction corresponds to the *by*-construction in English:

> von vielen Studenten
> (by a lot of students)

In a passive sentence this dative object (e.g. **Studenten**) is called the agent; that is, it is used to indicate the person or thing peforming the action.

NOTE 1: **durch**-*construction*

> Jedes Jahr werden viele Häuser **durch Feuer** zerstört.

Durch + *an accusative object* can be used to express agency when the agent is an impersonal force such as fire, wind, rain, etc. The **durch**-construction can only be used, however, when the agent is not preceded by a limiting word:

> durch Feuer zerstört
> but: von **dem** Feuer zerstört
>
> durch Bomben zerstört
> but: von **einer** Bombe zerstört

NOTE 2: *omission of the agent*

Whenever the presence of an agent makes a passive sentence sound wooden and unnatural, the agent is simply omitted. This is almost always the case when the agent is a pronoun.

Changing active sentences into passive ones is a useful first approach to the passive voice. But passive sentences have a style and logic of their own: they are not mechanical, point-for-point transformations of active sentences. This becomes clear when one tries to put sentences such as the following into the passive voice:

> Mary loves John.
> I had a good supper last night.

The results are awkward in every sense of the word:

> John is loved by Mary.
> A good supper was had last night by me.

The passive must be drilled primarily within the context of the passive itself. For this reason, we shall take the sentence

> Dieser Roman wird von vielen Studenten gelesen

as our model and form its past, future, and perfect tenses.

A. Past tense

PRESENT   Dieser Roman **wird** von vielen Studenten gelesen.
PAST   . . . . **wurde** . . . . gelesen.

Here the present tense form of **werden:**   **wird**
is replaced by the past tense form: **wurde.**

B. Future with auxiliary

PRESENT   Dieser Roman **wird** von vielen Studenten gelesen.
FUTURE   . . . . **wird** . . . . gelesen **werden.**

The present tense form of **werden:**   **wird**
is replaced by the future tense form: **wird . . . werden.**

C. Present perfect

PRESENT   Dieser Roman **wird** von vielen Studenten gelesen.
PRESENT PERFECT . . . . **ist** . . . . gelesen **worden.**

The principle is again basically the same:
the present tense form: **wird**
is replaced by a present perfect form: **ist . . . worden.**

NOTE: **ist . . . worden**
The normal past participle of **werden** is **geworden.** However, the passive uses a contracted form in which the usual **ge–** prefix is missing:

> **ist** gelesen **worden.**

D. Past perfect

PRESENT PERFECT   **ist . . .** gelesen worden.
PAST PERFECT   **war . . .** gelesen worden.

Dieser Roman **war** von vielen Studenten gelesen **worden.**

III. ENGLISH AND GERMAN PASSIVE FORMS: SUMMARY AND COMPARISON

Compare the German verb forms with the English ones in the following sentences:

This novel *is* (*being*) read by most students.
. . . . *was* (*being*) . . . .
. . . . *will be* read. . . . .
. . . . *has been* read . . . .
. . . . *had been* read . . . .

Dieses Buch **wird** von den meisten Studenten gelesen.
. . . . **wurde** . . . . .gelesen.
. . . . **wird** . . . . .gelesen **werden.**
. . . . **ist** . . . . .gelesen **worden.**
. . . . **war** . . . . .gelesen **worden.**

is (*being*) read	**wird** . . . gelesen
was (*being*) read	**wurde** . . . gelesen
will be read	**wird** . . . gelesen **werden**
has been read	**ist** . . . gelesen **worden**
had been read	**war** . . . gelesen **worden**

You will notice:

1. *Read* and **gelesen** occur in every tense. The past participle is the *unchanging* part of passive constructions in both languages.

2. Whereas English uses a form of *to be* and the past participle to form the passive, German uses a form of:

	werden + PAST PARTICIPLE
PRESENT	wird . . . gelesen
PAST	wurde . . . gelesen
FUTURE	wird . . . gelesen werden
PRESENT PERFECT	ist . . . gelesen worden
PAST PERFECT	war . . . gelesen worden

All changes of tense in the passive affect only the form of **werden** (in German) and the form of *to be* (in English).

3. **ist . . . worden**

Werden uses **sein** as its auxiliary. The passive uses a contracted form of **geworden** in which the usual **ge–** prefix is missing: **ist** gelesen **worden**

war gelesen **worden**

⊡ DRILLS

Active—passive

Put the following active sentences into the passive.

1. Ein Tenor singt diese Rolle.
2. Die Regierung unterstützt die Staatsuniversitäten.
3. Doktor Schwarz behandelt meine Frau.
4. Das Wiener Kammerorchester spielt Beethovens Violinkonzert.
5. Fast alle Studenten lesen dieses Buch.
6. Der Chef erledigt solche Sachen.
7. Der Bayrische Rundfunk bringt heute ein Hörspiel von Günther Eich.
8. Einmal die Woche macht die Putzfrau die Wohnung sauber.

Tense formation (past tense and present perfect tense)

Put the following sentences into the simple past tense and the present perfect tense.

1. Die Tür wird langsam geöffnet.
2. Der Tisch wird beiseite geschoben.
3. Meine Frau wird von Doktor Schwarz behandelt.

4. Beethovens Violinkonzert wird von dem Wiener Kammerorchester gespielt.
5. Das Essen wird um acht Uhr serviert.
6. Unser Wagen wird heute repariert.
7. Die Staatsuniversitäten werden von der Regierung unterstützt.
8. Alles wird gut vorbereitet.
9. Die Briefe werden heute abgeschickt.
10. Am Sonntag wird keine Post gebracht.
11. Die Läden werden immer um fünf Uhr geschlossen.
12. Ihr Mann wird heute begraben.
13. Der Volkswagen wird in Deutschland hergestellt.
14. Zwei Tische werden für uns reserviert.
15. Das wird am Montag erledigt.
16. Eine neue Methode wird dieses Jahr eingeführt.
17. Wir werden sehr oft eingeladen.
18. Das wird schnell gemacht.
19. Die Rechnungen werden am Anfang des Monats geschickt.
20. Eine Sekretärin wird gesucht.
21. Seine Werke werden neu herausgegeben.
22. Werden Briefmarken da verkauft?

Tense formation (future tense)

Put the following present tense sentences into the future tense.

1. Beethovens Violinkonzert wird von Isaac Stern gespielt.
2. Dieser Roman wird wohl in viele Sprachen übersetzt.
3. Der Ring wird wohl nie gefunden.
4. Die Bücher werden bis Freitag zurückgebracht.
5. Das wird am Montag erledigt.
6. So ein Wagen wird nie gestohlen.
7. Es wird heute noch gefunden.

Tense formation (mixed tenses)

Put the following present tense sentences into the tenses indicated in parentheses.

1. Dieses Buch wird von fast allen Studenten gelesen. (*past*)
2. Alles wird gut vorbereitet. (*present perfect*)
3. Die Bücher werden morgen zurückgebracht. (*future*)
4. Die Wohnung wird einmal die Woche saubergemacht. (*past*)
5. Der Tisch wird beiseite geschoben. (*past perfect*)

6. Die Rolle wird von einem Sopran gesungen. (*present perfect*)
7. Das wird nächste Woche erledigt. (*future*)
8. Alle vier Jahre wird ein neuer Präsident gewählt. (*past*)
9. Zwei Tische werden für uns reserviert. (*present perfect*)
10. Er wird heute operiert. (*past*)
11. Unser Wagen wird morgen repariert. (*future*)
12. Die Experimente werden genau beobachtet. (*present perfect*)
13. Er wird nicht eingeladen. (*present perfect*)
14. Wird da kein Wein serviert? (*past*)
15. Die Briefe werden heute abgeschickt. (*present perfect*)
16. Sein neues Buch wird in viele Sprachen übersetzt. (*future*)
17. Eine neue Methode wird dieses Jahr eingeführt. (*past*)

The constant factor: the past participle

Complete the following passive sentences by inserting the required past participle.

1. Hier wird kein Wein ＿＿＿＿＿＿＿.
   (served)
2. Sind Sie noch nicht ＿＿＿＿＿＿ worden?
   (invited)
3. Die Rolle wurde von einem Tenor ＿＿＿＿＿＿.
   (sung)
4. Meine Frau wird von Doktor Schwarz ＿＿＿＿＿＿.
   (treated)
5. Der Tisch war beiseite ＿＿＿＿＿ worden.
   (pushed)
6. Eine neue Methode ist dieses Jahr ＿＿＿＿＿ worden.
   (introduced)
7. Sein Wagen wurde gestern ＿＿＿＿＿＿.
   (stolen)
8. Sind die Bücher schon ＿＿＿＿＿ worden?
   (returned)
9. Alles wird gut ＿＿＿＿＿.
   (prepared)
10. Der Ring wird wohl nie ＿＿＿＿＿ werden.
    (found)
11. Die Staatsuniversitäten werden von der Regierung ＿＿＿＿＿.
    (supported)
12. Unser Wagen wird heute ＿＿＿＿＿.
    (repaired)

13. Herr Müller wird heute _____.
    (buried)
14. In dieser Stadt werden die Läden um fünf Uhr _____.
    (closed)
15. Das wird gleich _____ werden.
    (taken care of)
16. Die Briefe sind schon _____ worden.
    (sent off)
17. Der Volkswagen wird in Deutschland _____.
    (manufactured)

The variable factor: the form of **werden**

Insert the form of the auxiliary **werden** suggested by the English word(s) in parentheses.

1. (is being) Er _____ heute operiert.
2. (was) Unser Wagen _____ gestern gestohlen.
3. (Will be) _____ du von Doktor Schwarz behandelt _____?
4. (has been) Es _____ gefunden _____.
5. (is) Tennis _____ überall gespielt.
6. (was) Das Hotel _____ durch Feuer zerstört.
7. (is) Coca-Cola _____ gewöhnlich aus der Flasche getrunken.
8. (will be) Dieser Roman _____ wohl in viele Sprachen übersetzt _____.
9. (had been) Der Tisch _____ beiseite geschoben _____.
10. (is) Schwarzbrot _____ in Deutschland viel gegessen.
11. (was) Amerika _____ im Jahre 1492 entdeckt.
12. (has been) Eine neue Methode _____ dieses Jahr eingeführt _____.
13. (will be) Das _____ am Montag erledigt _____.
14. (was) Die Tür _____ langsam geöffnet.
15. (are) Die Rechnungen _____ immer am Anfang des Monats geschickt.
16. (Has been) _____ er beim Unfall verletzt _____?
17. (is) Am Sonntag _____ keine Post gebracht.
18. (will be) Wir _____ wohl abgeholt _____.
19. (Are) _____ Briefmarken hier verkauft?
20. (was) Die Ehe _____ in der Kirche geschlossen.
21. (Have been) _____ die Briefe schon abgeschickt _____?

22. (are) In der UNO ＿＿＿＿＿ gemeinsame Probleme besprochen.
23. (had been) Es ＿＿＿＿＿ schon vorher erledigt ＿＿＿＿＿.
24. (will be) Beethovens Violinkonzert ＿＿＿＿＿ von dem Wiener Kammerorchester gespielt ＿＿＿＿＿.
25. (has been) Das Buch ＿＿＿＿＿ von fast allen Studenten gelesen ＿＿＿＿＿.
26. (was) Er ＿＿＿＿＿ nach seiner Adresse gefragt.

Synthetic exercises

Use the following elements to make passive sentences in the tense indicated.

1. Der Wagen / repariert / sofort (*present*)
2. Er / eingeladen / noch nicht (*present perfect*)
3. Er / operiert / wohl heute (*future*)
4. Das / erledigt / schon (*present perfect*)
5. Amerika / entdeckt / 1492 (*past*)
6. Coca-Cola / getrunken / gewöhnlich / aus / Flasche (*past*)
7. In / UNO / gemeinsame Probleme / besprochen (*present*)
8. Briefe / abgeschickt /? (*present perfect*)
9. Dieser Roman / übersetzt / viele Sprachen (*future*)
10. Alles / vorbereitet / gut (*present perfect*)
11. Ehe / geschlossen / in / Kirche (*past*)
12. Tisch / geschoben / beiseite (*past perfect*)
13. Zwei Tische / reserviert / für uns (*present perfect*)
14. Wir / abgeholt / wohl (*future*)
15. Tennis / gespielt / überall (*present*)
16. Er / verletzt / bei / Unfall (*past*)
17. Er / begraben / gestern (*present perfect*)
18. Meine Wohnung / saubergemacht / einmal die Woche (*past*)
19. Volkswagen / hergestellt / in Deutschland (*present*)

Express in German

1. Our car has been stolen. Unser Wagen ist gestohlen würde
2. Tennis is played everywhere. Tennis wird überall gespielt.
3. Haven't you been invited yet? ~~Wirst du nicht~~ Bist du nicht eingeladen worde
4. No mail is delivered (**bringen**) on Sunday.
5. The door was opened very slowly. Die Tur wurde sehr langsam geöffn
6. No wine is served here. Kein Wein wird h
7. That will be taken care of right away.

Das wird leicht erledigt werden.

8. The stores are closed at five o'clock.
9. It's been found.
Future 10. Beethoven's Violin Concerto will be played by Isaac Stern. *wird von IS.* *gespielt werden*
PP 11. Was he injured? *Ist er worden?*
Present 12. Coca-Cola is usually drunk out of the bottle. *wird aus der Flasche getrunken*
Future 13. His new book will probably be translated into many languages.
past 14. The table had been pushed aside.
present 15. Where is the Volkswagen produced?
PP 16. The ring was never found.
PP 17. Everything has been well prepared.
present 18. Is she being treated by Doctor Schwarz?
PP 19. She was buried yesterday.
pres 20. Are stamps sold here?
past 21. The hotel was destroyed by fire.
Future 22. The role will be sung by a tenor.
23. Have the letters been sent off?
24. His car is being repaired today.
past perfect 25. America was discovered in 1492. *entdecken*
PP 26. Two tables have been reserved for us.
27. A new method was introduced this year.
28. State universities are supported by the government.
29. The apartment is cleaned once a week.
30. Have the books been returned?
31. The bills are sent at the beginning of the month.
32. The book was read by almost every student.
33. We'll probably be picked up.
34. He was asked for his address.
35. Has he been operated (on) already?

LEVEL TWO

I. PASSIVE: SPECIAL PROBLEMS

A. The false or apparent passive

1. Passive (Action)

Er repariert den Wagen.   Der Wagen wird repariert.
Sie verkaufen das Haus.   Das Haus wird verkauft.

These examples illustrate true passive sentences formed from their active counterparts. The passive voice focuses attention on an *action* (The car is being repaired. The house is being sold.).

In the following examples, however, the focus is on the result of an action, i.e. on a *condition*.

2. False Passive (*Condition*)

The car is repaired.	Der Wagen ist repariert.
The house is sold.	Das Haus ist verkauft.

These sentences illustrate the false passive: a construction that describes a *condition rather than an action* and is actually not passive at all.

To recapitulate:

1. **Das Haus <u>wird</u> verkauft** means that the house is in the process of being sold.

2. **Das Haus <u>ist</u> verkauft** means that it is already sold (a *condition* rather than an action).

The difference in meaning is clear. If a man says, "Das Haus **wird** verkauft," you still have a chance to buy it. If he says, "Das Haus **ist** verkauft," it is off the market.

Grammatically, the false passive is the same as:

sein + *an adjective*

The past participle functions exactly like an adjective:

Das Haus ist braun.
Das Haus ist verkauft.

This makes forming the past tense quite simple:

Das Haus **war** braun.
Das Haus **war** verkauft.

NOTE: The meaningful distinction between passive (action) and false passive (condition) also holds for past situations:

ACTION   Das Geschäft **wurde** um Punkt fünf Uhr geschlossen.
                (The store was closed on the dot of five.)

CONDITION   Das Geschäft **war** den ganzen Tag geschlossen.
                (The store was closed all day.)

B. Passive with absentee subjects

Passive forms may have a definite subject or an indefinite subject—or even no apparent subject at all.

Most passive sentences do have a definite subject:

| ACTIVE | PASSIVE |
| Man verkauft **den Wagen.** | **Der Wagen** wird verkauft. |

As previously seen, the *accusative* object of an active sentence (e.g. **den Wagen**) appears as the *nominative* subject of the corresponding passive sentence (e.g. **der Wagen**).

But look at the following example:

> Man antwortet ihnen nicht.

In this active sentence there is no *accusative* object! Its passive counterpart would be:

> X wird ihnen nicht geantwortet.

Since a verb (e.g. **wird**) cannot be in the first position of a sentence without making the sentence into a question, **es** is used as the subject:

> Es wird ihnen nicht geantwortet.

NOTE: **Werden** agrees with the indefinite subject **es** (es **wird**).

If another element of the passive sentence (e.g. a dative object, time expression, etc.) can sensibly be put in the first position, this may be done; the **es** is then omitted:

> Ihnen wird nicht geantwortet.

NOTE: As you can see, the result is a sentence without an apparent subject. In this case the subject is *an implied* **es**; *for that reason the verb remains in the* 3rd *person singular:* **wird.**

Further examples:

ACTIVE	PASSIVE
Man tanzt heute abend.	Es wird heute abend getanzt. Heute abend wird getanzt.
Man trank bis spät in die Nacht.	Es wurde bis spät in die Nacht getrunken. Bis spät in die Nacht wurde getrunken.

As before, the passive sentences begin either with:

1. **es** (an indefinite subject)

2. another element of the sentence that can sensibly occupy the first position (*here:* time expressions)

NOTE: These German passive sentences have no literal English translations:

GERMAN PASSIVE	ENGLISH EQUIVALENTS
Es wird heute abend getanzt.	There's a dance this evening. There'll be dancing this evening.
Es wurde bis spät in die Nacht getrunken.	They (we) drank late into the night. They (we) went on drinking late into the night.

▣ DRILLS

Active—passive

Put the following sentences into the passive voice. (Do *not* express the agent, e.g. **von ihm** / *by him*.)

> Example: Ich antworte dem Jungen.
> Dem Jungen wird geantwortet.

1. Wir helfen dem alten Herrn.
2. Sie drohen uns. *threaten*
3. Hier raucht man nicht.
4. Man folgt seinem Beispiel.
5. Man gratuliert ihm zu seinem Geburtstag.
6. Wir widersprechen dem Lehrer nie.
7. Man traut dem Mann nicht.
8. Hier ißt und trinkt man viel.
9. Glaubt man ihm?
10. Man macht nicht auf.

Tense formation (past tense and present perfect tense)

Put the following sentences into the simple past tense and the present perfect tense.

1. Dem Jungen wird geantwortet.
2. Ihm wird für seine Hilfe gedankt.
3. Abends wird nicht aufgemacht.
4. Den alten Leuten wird geholfen.
5. Es wird getanzt und gesungen.
6. Wird ihm nicht getraut? *trusted*
7. Ihnen wird gedroht.
8. Dem Chef wird nie widersprochen.

Synthetic exercises

Form passive sentences in the present, past, and perfect tenses.

1. Sein / Beispiel / gefolgt / immer
2. Mein / Freund / gedankt / für / Hilfe
3. Hier / gegessen / und / getrunken / viel

4. Getraut / Herr Braun / wirklich /?
5. Nachts / aufgemacht / nie
6. Kind / geantwortet / nicht

Express in German

Use passive sentences only.

1. He wasn't helped at all.
2. Is he really trusted?
3. Is there dancing here tonight?   (!)
4. The boss was never contradicted.
5. He was threatened.
6. They were thanked for their help.
7. Is there much drinking at the university?   (!)
8. His good example is being followed.
9. He was congratulated on his eightieth birthday.
10. There's no smoking here.   (!)

False or apparent passive

Express the following in German, using the false or apparent passive (i.e. describe a condition rather than an action).

1. The letter is written.
2. The windows are closed.
3. The door is open.
4. These seats are taken (**belegen**).
5. The bill is paid.
6. The newspapers are sold out (**ausverkaufen**).
7. That is already done.
8. His shoes are polished (**putzen**).
9. The game is lost.
10. Is he well prepared?
11. The table is set (**decken**).

Past tense

Translate the sentences above into German, using the past tense of the false passive.

Express in German

This exercise contains both passive and false passive sentences.

1. The windows were closed all day.
2. The bill is being paid now.
3. The house is sold.
4. My shoes are being repaired.
5. All is lost!
6. The traffic is being held up (**aufhalten**).
7. The books were closed during the class.
8. I am insulted (**beleidigen**).

Mixed drills   *due 9-23-81 Wed*

1. That will be taken care of immediately.
2. Is he well prepared? *adj*
3. Are stamps sold here?
4. He wasn't helped at all.
5. There's no smoking here.   (!)
6. His good example is being followed.
7. All is lost! *adj*
8. The car was repaired immediately.
9. Where is the Volkswagen maufactured?
10. They were thanked for their help.
11. Is there dancing tonight?
12. My wife was treated by Dr. Schwarz.
13. The apartment was cleaned once a week.
14. The table is set. *adj*
15. Is he really trusted?
16. These seats are taken.
17. The hotel was destroyed by fire.
18. Everything was being carefully prepared.

LEVEL THREE

I. THE PASSIVE WITH MODAL AUXILIARIES

A. English and German passive forms

First look at an example, in English and German, of the simplest kind of passive expression:

The house is being sold.   Das Haus wird verkauft.

The passive is often found together with a modal auxiliary, and their association leads to a slightly more elaborate construction. Here is an example:

The house must be sold.   Das Haus muß verkauft werden.

The following table shows what such expressions look like in simple and compound tenses:

The house			Das Haus	
has to	be sold.		**muß**	verkauft werden.
had to	be sold.		**mußte**	verkauft werden.
will have to	be sold.		**wird**	verkauft werden **müssen.**
has had to	be sold.		**hat**	verkauft werden **müssen.**
had had to	be sold.		**hatte**	verkauft werden **müssen.**

Have a careful look at the above table and you will notice:

1. Tense Change

The only elements that change in these sentences are the forms of **müssen** (muß, mußte, wird . . . müssen, etc.) and the forms of *to have to* (has to, had to, will have to, etc.). The rest of the expression (be sold, **verkauft werden**) remains unchanged. In other words, *shifts in tense will affect only the modal part of the expression.*

2. Double Infinitive

has had to be sold   hat verkauft werden müssen
had had to be sold   hatte verkauft werden müssen

Where you might expect **hat verkauft werden gemußt** (**gemußt** is the past participle of **müssen**), you actually find **hat verkauft werden müssen** (i.e. an infinitive form).   This is a so-called double infinitive, a grammatical convention which is explained in detail on page 145, "Compound Tenses of Modal Auxiliaries."

3. Omission of zu with Infinitives in Modal Expressions

It must be sold.   Es muß verkauft werden.
It has *to* be sold.

It should be sold.   Es sollte verkauft werden.
It ought *to* be sold.

German never uses **zu** in modal expressions. (See also p. 137, "Omission of **zu** with Infinitives in Modal Expressions.")

B. The rationale behind the German forms

Note that in each case only a simple change takes place.

1. Present Tense

The previous sections have dealt with passive constructions without modals:

Das Haus wird verkauft.

When a modal is added, the following changes take place:

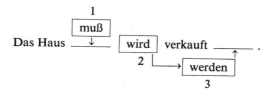

Das Haus muß verkauft werden.

1. **Muß** (a conjugated form of a modal) is needed in the second (or verb) position of the sentence.

2. **Wird,** which was in this position before, is forced out and to the end of the sentence.

3. Because a modal expression cannot have *two* conjugated verb forms, **wird** becomes **werden** (the infinitive form).

NOTE: **verkauft werden** (i.e. past participle + **werden**) is referred to as a *passive infinitive.* Just as

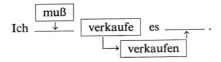

Ich muß es **verkaufen**

results in an active infinitive at the end of the sentence,

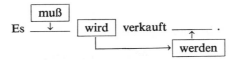

Es muß **verkauft werden**

results in a *passive infinitive.*

As you can see, the infinitive **werden** after the past participle is just the result of the displacement of its conjugated form from the second position in the sentence.

At this point we shall take

Das Haus muß verkauft werden

as our pattern sentence and form its past, compound future, and perfect tenses.

2. Past Tense

PRESENT PASSIVE   Das Haus **muß** verkauft werden.
PAST PASSIVE   . . . . **mußte** . . . .

Here we merely substitute the past tense of the modal (mußte) for its present tense (muß).

3. Future with Auxiliary

PRESENT PASSIVE   Das Haus **muß** verkauft werden.
FUTURE PASSIVE   . . . . **wird** . . . . **müssen.**

Only the modals change tenses in the passive voice; therefore, we may say
that the present form: **muß**
is replaced by: **wird . . . müssen.**

4. Present Perfect

Here the principle is essentially the same. The change may be viewed as a
simple replacement:

Das Haus **muß** verkauft werden.
. . . . **hat** . . . . **müssen.**

NOTE: *double-infinitive construction*
The perfect of **muß** is **hat . . . gemußt.** Here **gemußt** "changes to" **müssen**
because of the infinitive **werden.** (See also p. 145, "Compound Tenses of
Modal Auxiliaries.")

Das Haus <u>hat</u> verkauft **werden** <u>müssen.</u>

5. Past Perfect

This tense can be treated like the present perfect. The only difference is
that **hatte** replaces **hat:**

Das Haus **hatte** verkauft werden müssen.

▣ DRILLS

Form drill (present tense)

Form new sentences by adding to the following passive sentences the
suggested modals.

Example: Das Haus wird verkauft. (müssen)
Das Haus **muß** verkauft werden.

1. Die Übung wird gemacht.   (können)
2. Dem Mann wird geholfen.   (können)
3. Das wird heute erledigt.   (müssen)
4. Das Paket wird heute gebracht.   (sollen)
5. Hier wird nicht getrunken.   (dürfen)
6. Das Mädchen wird eingeladen.   (wollen)

Form drill (mixed tenses)

Give the past and present perfect forms of the following present tense sentences.

Examples: Das Mädchen soll eingeladen werden.
. . . . sollte . . . .
. . . . hat . . . . sollen.

1. Der Brief muß geschrieben werden.
2. Der Wagen kann repariert werden.
3. Dem Mann muß geholfen werden.
4. Das alles muß am Freitag erledigt werden.
5. Der Anzug kann wirklich nicht mehr getragen werden.
6. Er will um Hilfe gebeten werden.
7. Muß es eigentlich gemacht werden?

The constant factor: the passive infinitive

Example: Es kann (be done).
Es kann **gemacht werden.**

1. Das sollte nie (be forgotten).
2. Es muß (be found).
3. Er wollte (be asked).
4. Es darf nicht (be lost).
5. Ihm konnte nicht (be helped).
6. Sie sollte (be invited).
7. Sie wollte (be seen).
8. Hier darf nicht (be sung).
9. Der Wagen mußte (be pushed).
10. Die Sache sollte (be taken care of).
11. Die Fenster müssen (be opened).

The variable factor: the form of the modal

Supply the suggested modal forms.

Example: (had to) Das Haus _____ verkauft werden.
Das Haus **mußte** verkauft werden.

1. (Must) _____ es gleich gefunden werden?
2. (could) Der Wagen _____ nicht verkauft werden.
3. (may) Hier _____ nicht gesungen werden.
4. (had to) Das Fenster _____ geschlossen werden.
5. (has to) Das Bild _____ an diese Wand gehängt werden.
6. (will want to) Das Mädchen _____ wohl eingeladen werden _____.
7. (have had to) Die Aktien _____ verkauft werden _____.
8. (could) Es _____ nicht gemacht werden.
9. (has had to) Das Paket _____ zurückgebracht werden _____.
10. (will have to) Der Brief _____ heute geschrieben werden _____.
11. (could) Ihm _____ nicht geholfen werden.
12. (had to) Es _____ sehr schnell erledigt werden.
13. (has had to) Der Wagen _____ repariert werden _____.
14. (could) Es _____ nicht unter die Tür geschoben werden.

Express in German   *due 9-23*

1. The car had to be repaired. (*past* and *perfect*)
2. That will have to be done at the bank (**bei der Bank**). *gemacht werden müssen*
3. The sofa is supposed to be brought today.
4. She wants to be invited too. *Sie will auch eingeladen werden*
5. That will have to be taken care of.
6. The car couldn't be sold. (*past* and *perfect*) *Das Auto konnte nicht verkauft werden*
7. The letter must be written right away.
8. The suit really could not be worn any more.
9. He wants to be asked for (**bitten um**) help.
10. It had to be said to him six times.
11. The house had to be sold. (*past* and *perfect*)

subjunctive II

chapter eight

LEVEL ONE

I. USE OF THE SUBJUNCTIVE IN CONDITIONAL SENTENCES: INTRODUCTION

A. The subjunctive mood

Mood comes from the word *modus* (mode) and it means *a way*—in this case, a way of talking about things. English and German have two basic moods: *indicative* and *subjunctive*.

The *indicative* is used to make *statements of fact*:

He *needs* the book. He *will buy* it.

The indicative may also be used in conditional sentences (If . . . , then . . .):

> If he *needs* the book, he *will buy* it.

In the example above, it *may be a fact* that he needs the book. (We have implied neither that he does need it nor that he does not need it; we are merely making a statement that *agrees with the possible fact* of his needing the book.)

RULE: The indicative is used to make statements that agree with:

1. facts as they *are* (He needs the book.)
2. facts as they *may be* (If he needs the book . . .)

The *subjunctive,* on the other hand, is used to make *statements that are contrary to fact:*

> If he *needed* the book, he *would buy* it.

The implication is, however, that the person in question *does not need* the book and that he *is not going to buy it.*

Similarly:

> If I knew his address, I would write him.

The implied fact is that I do not know his address and that I will not write him.

And again:

> If I had enough money, I would stay longer.

The fact is that I do not have enough money and therefore cannot stay longer.

The examples above are all present tense situations:

> If I had the money (right *now*), I'd stay longer.
> If he needed the book (right *now*), he'd buy it.

The subjunctive also has past tense forms:

> If I *had had* the money (back *then*), I would *have stayed* longer.
> If he *had needed* the book (back *then*), he would *have bought* it.

B. The English subjunctive in conditional sentences

1. Present Tense

The *present tense* forms of the English *subjunctive* are ordinarily identical with the *past tense* forms of the *indicative*:

PAST INDICATIVE	He *needed* it.
PRESENT SUBJUNCTIVE	If he *needed* it . . .

There is, however, a basic difference in time, and therefore in meaning, between the past tense of the indicative and the present tense of the subjunctive:

PAST INDICATIVE	He *had* enough money (yesterday).
	(*past time* using a *past tense form*)
PRESENT SUBJUNCTIVE	If he *had* enough money (now) . . .
	(*present time* using a *past tense form*)

The present tense of the subjunctive can be easily recognized in English: *past tense forms* are used in a *present tense situation*.

NOTE: There are only a few present subjunctive forms that are different from the past indicative forms:

	PAST INDICATIVE	He *was* here.
but:	PRESENT SUBJUNCTIVE	If he *were* here . . .

2. Past Tense

An analogous situation is found in the *past tense* of the subjunctive.

I saw him

is a simple past tense indicative sentence. If we put this sentence into the *past tense of the subjunctive*, the result is:

If I had seen him (I would have told you).

The *past tense forms of the subjunctive* are identical with the *past perfect forms of the indicative*.

SUMMARY

The English subjunctive as it is used in conditional sentences has two (and only two) tenses:

1. the present tense (whose forms are for the most part identical with those of the past indicative)

2. the past tense (whose forms are identical with the past perfect indicative)

C. The German subjunctive: subjunctive II

As you can see from the following *if*-clauses, German and English follow essentially the same pattern in using the indicative and subjunctive moods in conditional sentences:

PRESENT INDICATIVE   If he *needs* it . . .
                          Wenn er es **braucht** . . .

PRESENT SUBJUNCTIVE   If he *needed* it . . .
                          Wenn er es **brauchte** . . .

PAST SUBJUNCTIVE   If he *had needed* it . . .
                          Wenn er es **gebraucht hätte** . . .

The form of the German subjunctive used in these clauses is called subjunctive II. (Subjunctive I is a less common mood that will be treated in a later chapter.)

1. Word Order

Wenn (*if*) is a subordinating conjunction: it forces the *conjugated verb form to the end of the clause:*

> **Wenn** er es **brauchte,** . . .
> **Wenn** er es **gebraucht hätte,** . . .

(For a detailed explanation of subordinating conjunctions, see p. 224, "Subordinating Conjunctions.")

2. Forms of Subjunctive II

a. Present tense

The present tense of subjunctive II is *derived from the past tense of the indicative.*

1. *weak (regular) verbs*
In the case of weak verbs, the present tense of subjunctive II is identical with the past tense of the indicative.

ich brauchte	wir brauchten
du brauchtest	ihr brauchtet
er brauchte	sie brauchten

2. *strong (irregular) verbs*

To form the present tense of subjunctive II of strong verbs:

a. take the past tense stem of the indicative:

> war
> ging
> sang
> schlug

b. add an umlaut where possible (**a, o,** and **u**):

> wär–
> ging–
> säng–
> schlüg–

c. and add the following subjunctive endings:

ich	wär	e	wir	wär	en
du	wär	est	ihr	wär	et
er	wär	e	sie	wär	en

3. *exceptions*

PAST INDICATIVE	PRESENT SUBJUNCTIVE II
brachte	brächte
dachte	dächte
brannte	(brennte)
kannte	(kennte)
nannte	(nennte)
rannte	(rennte)
half	(hülfe)
stand	(stünde)
starb	(stürbe)
warf	(würfe)
durfte	dürfte
konnte	könnte
mochte	möchte

The forms in parentheses are archaic and are therefore not drilled.

mußte	müßte
hatte	hätte
wußte	wüßte

NOTE: **Sollte** and **wollte** are both past indicative and present subjunctive II.

b. Past tense

The past tense of subjunctive II is *derived from the past perfect tense of the indicative:*

PAST PERFECT INDICATIVE	PAST SUBJUNCTIVE II
Er war gekommen.	Wenn er **gekommen wäre** . . .
Er hatte es gemacht.	Wenn er es **gemacht hätte** . . .

RULE: The past tense of subjunctive II is composed of a form of **wäre** or **hätte** + *a past participle.*

▣ DRILLS

Present subjunctive II of weak verbs

Put the following **wenn**-clauses into the present tense of subjunctive II.

Example: Wenn er es **kauft** . . .
               Wenn er es **kaufte** . . .

1. Wenn wir es **machen** . . .
2. Wenn du **arbeitest** . . .
3. Wenn sie es **braucht** . . .
4. Wenn ihr es ihm **sagt** . . .
5. Wenn du ihm **antwortest** . . .
6. Wenn sie in Stuttgart **wohnt** . . .

Express in German

Express the following *if*-clauses in German, using the present tense of subjunctive II.

1. If he were to buy it . . .
2. If we smoked . . .
3. If she needed it . . .

4. If he loved her . . .
5. If you were to answer him . . .
6. If he were to ask . . .
7. If they worked . . .
8. If I were to translate it . . .

Present subjunctive II of strong verbs

Put the following **wenn**-clauses into the present tense of subjunctive II.

        Example: Wenn er **kommt** . . .
                       Wenn er **käme** . . .

1. Wenn er **geht** . . .
2. Wenn er es mir **gibt** . . .
3. Wenn sie es **tun** . . .
4. Wenn ich es **nehme** . . .
5. Wenn wir es **trinken** . . .
6. Wenn du es **findest** . . .
7. Wenn er einen Anzug **trägt** . . .
8. Wenn sie nach Berlin **fliegt** . . .
9. Wenn wir es **essen** . . .
10. Wenn sie zu laut **singen** . . .
11. Wenn er den Mantel nicht **anzieht** . . .
12. Wenn du den Brief heute nicht **schreibst** . . .
13. Wenn er hier **ist** . . .

Express in German

Express the following *if*-clauses in German, using the present tense of subjunctive II.

1. If he gave it to me . . .
2. If I were to meet (**treffen**) him . . .
3. If they were to sing too loud . . .
4. If he put on the suit . . .
5. If we were to call him . . .
6. If she were to fall . . .
7. If they went . . .
8. If he were to stay . . .
9. If we found it . . .

10. If it were lying on the table ...
11. If she flew to Berlin ...
12. If he read it ...
13. If he were here ...

Present subjunctive II of the exceptions

Put the following **wenn**-clauses into the present tense of subjunctive II.

1. Wenn er es **bringt** ...
2. Wenn wir genug Zeit **haben** ...
3. Wenn er wirklich **muß** ...
4. Wenn er es **weiß** ...
5. Wenn ich daran **denke** ...
6. Wenn wir es **können** ...
7. Wenn ich fragen **darf** ...
8. Wenn sie wirklich **will** ...
9. Wenn wir einen Wagen **haben** ...

Express in German

Express the following *if*-clauses in German, using the present tense of subjunctive II.

1. If he knew it ...
2. If they thought of it ...
3. If we were to bring it ...
4. If he really had to ...
5. If she really wanted to ...
6. If we could do it ...
7. If we had a house ...

Present subjunctive II (mixed drills)

Put the following **wenn**-clauses into the present tense of subjunctive II.

1. Wenn du ihm **antwortest** ...
2. Wenn er nach Hause **geht** ...
3. Wenn er hier **ist** ...
4. Wenn sie nach Berlin **fliegt** ...
5. Wenn ihr es ihm **sagt** ...

6. Wenn sie es **braucht** . . .
7. Wenn wir es **trinken** . . .
8. Wenn er hier **bleibt** . . .
9. Wenn du es **machst** . . .
10. Wenn du es **tust** . . .
11. Wenn ich daran **denke** . . .
12. Wenn wir es **können** . . .
13. Wenn wir es **finden** . . .
14. Wenn er in Stuttgart **wohnt** . . .
15. Wenn ich es **übersetze** . . .
16. Wenn du den Brief heute nicht **schreibst** . . .
17. Wenn er mich **fragt** . . .
18. Wenn ich fragen **darf** . . .
19. Wenn wir es **haben** . . .

Express in German (mixed drills)

Express the following *if*-clauses in German, using the present tense of subjunctive II.

1. If you were to answer him . . .
2. If I might ask . . .
3. If he were to read . . .
4. If they sang too loud . . .
5. If you were to work . . .
6. If she were to fly to Berlin . . .
7. If he knew it . . .
8. If she needed it . . .
9. If he were to bring it . . .
10. If he didn't put on his coat . . .
11. If she lived in Stuttgart . . .
12. If he really had to . . .
13. If he wore a suit . . .
14. If we ate it . . .
15. If she really wanted to . . .
16. If he did it . . .
17. If I found it . . .
18. If he were to stay . . .
19. If you called him . . .
20. If he were here . . .
21. If we had a house . . .

Past subjunctive II of verbs taking **haben**

Put the following **wenn**-clauses into the past tense of subjunctive II.

Example: Wenn er es gefunden **hat** . . .
Wenn er es gefunden **hätte** . . .

1. Wenn du gearbeitet **hast** . . .
2. Wenn er es gesehen **hat** . . .
3. Wenn sie es übersetzt **haben** . . .
4. Wenn er es gemacht **hat** . . .
5. Wenn ihr ihn angerufen **habt** . . .
6. Wenn sie den Brief geschrieben **hat** . . .

Express in German

Express the following *if*-clauses in German, using the past tense of subjunctive II.

1. If he had done it . . .
2. If he had helped us . . .
3. If he had had a house . . .
4. If she had needed it . . .
5. If we had read it . . .
6. If I had brought it . . .

Past subjunctive II of verbs taking **sein**

Put the following **wenn**-clauses into the past tense of subjunctive II.

1. Wenn er gekommen **ist** . . .
2. Wenn sie hier gewesen **sind** . . .
3. Wenn er ihm begegnet **ist** . . .
4. Wenn du Arzt geworden **bist** . . .
5. Wenn sie gestorben **ist** . . .
6. Wenn er gefallen **ist** . . .

Express in German

Express the following *if*-clauses in German, using the past tense of subjunctive II.

1. If she had flown to Berlin . . .
2. If he had come . . .

3. If they had stayed . . .
4. If you had become a doctor . . .
5. If I had fallen asleep (**einschlafen**) . . .
6. If it hadn't happened . . .

Past subjunctive II (mixed drills)

Put the following **wenn**-clauses into the past tense of subjunctive II.

1. Wenn du ihm begegnet **bist** . . .
2. Wenn ihr Geld gehabt **habt** . . .
3. Wenn er Arzt geworden **ist** . . .
4. Wenn sie gelaufen **ist** . . .
5. Wenn sie weniger bezahlt **haben** . . .

Express in German (mixed drills)

Express the following *if*-clauses in German, using the past tense of subjunctive II.

1. If he had come . . .
2. If she'd written the letter . . .
3. If I'd known it . . .
4. If they had understood it . . .
5. If he'd become a doctor . . .
6. If he had run faster . . .
7. If we had called them . . .
8. If she had helped me . . .
9. If you had fallen asleep . . .
10. If he had sold it to me . . .

Present and past subjunctive II (mixed drills)

Put the **wenn**-clauses into the appropriate tenses of subjunctive II.

1. Wenn ich daran **denke** . . .
2. Wenn er hier geblieben **ist** . . .
3. Wenn ich es **übersetze** . . .
4. Wenn Sie mich verstanden **haben** . . .
5. Wenn er schneller **läuft** . . .

6. Wenn er dicker geworden **ist** . . .
7. Wenn ich es **finde** . . .
8. Wenn du es **tust** . . .
9. Wenn er es mir **bringt** . . .
10. Wenn sie auf uns gewartet **haben** . . .

Express in German (mixed drills)

1. If he had stayed here . . .
2. If she were to fly to Berlin . . .
3. If he had put on a new suit . . .
4. If I were to find it . . .
5. If you brought it to me . . .
6. If I had known that . . .
7. If he had called him up . . .
8. If he could do it . . .
9. If that hadn't happened . . .
10. If we'd been there . . .
11. If we'd thought of it . . .
12. If we had a car . . .
13. If he'd given it to me . . .
14. If he were to read it . . .
15. If you could do it . . .

LEVEL TWO

I. CONDITIONAL SENTENCES

Conditional sentences are based on an *if . . . then* (**wenn . . . dann**) pattern
in both English and German. In the first part of this chapter, focus was
on the *if*-clauses (**wenn**-clauses). In this section, your attention is directed
to the *then*-clauses (**dann**-clauses).

PRESENT INDICATIVE
If I have time, *(then) I will go to the movies.*
Wenn ich Zeit habe, **(dann) gehe ich ins Kino.**

PRESENT SUBJUNCTIVE II
If I had time, (*then*) *I would go to the movies.*
Wenn ich Zeit hätte, (dann) ginge ich ins Kino.
(dann) würde ich ins Kino gehen.

PAST SUBJUNCTIVE II
If I had had time, (*then*) *I would have gone to the movies.*
Wenn ich Zeit gehabt hätte, (dann) wäre ich ins Kino gegangen.

A. Present indicative

Wenn ich Zeit **habe,** (dann) **gehe** ich ins Kino.

NOTE: The *verb comes first in the* **dann-***clause.* Only the word **dann** can come before it. **Dann,** however, is often omitted:

Wenn . . . . habe, gehe . . . .

The inflected verbs of the two clauses are separated only by a comma.

B. Present subjunctive II (ginge = würde gehen)

Wenn ich Zeit **hätte,** (dann) **ginge** ich ins Kino.
(dann) **würde** ich ins Kino **gehen.**

1. **Würde** is the present subjunctive II form of **werden:**

Ich werde gehen.   (I will go.)
Ich **würde** gehen.   (I *would* go.)

2. **Ginge** and **würde . . . gehen** are alternate forms. They both correspond to the English *would go,* but

würde + *an infinitive* (e.g. **gehen**)

is more common than the one-word form (e.g. **ginge**) in the **dann**-clause. **Wenn**-clauses, on the other hand, tend to avoid the **würde**-construction.

EXCEPTIONS:

(hülfe)	= würde helfen	(brennte)	= würde brennen
(stünde)	= würde stehen	(kennte)	= würde kennen
(stürbe)	= würde sterben	(nennte)	= würde nennen
(würfe)	= würde werfen	(rennte)	= würde rennen

In these eight cases, German uses **würde** + *an infinitive* in the **wenn**-clause. These one-word subjunctive II forms (hülfe, etc.) are archaic.

Moreover, *conversational* German tends to replace many other subjunctive II forms of *strong* verbs by the **würde** + *an infinitive* construction. For example:

flöge = würde . . . fliegen
äße = würde . . . essen

Wenn er fliegen würde . . .
Wenn er mehr essen würde . . .

C. Past subjunctive II

Wenn ich Zeit **gehabt hätte,** (dann) **wäre** ich ins Kino **gegangen.**

The past tense of subjunctive II is a compound construction:

wäre gegangen   would have gone
hätte geholfen   would have helped

Past subjunctive II = **hätte** or **wäre** + *a past participle.*

II. MIXED TENSES IN CONDITIONAL SENTENCES

When the logic of a situation requires it, both English and German may mix tenses within the same sentence:

If X *had happened* in the *past,* Y *would be* the case *now.*

PAST SUBJUNCTIVE II	PRESENT SUBJUNCTIVE II
Wenn Sie später **gefrühstückt hätten,**	**wären** Sie jetzt nicht so hungrig.
	würden Sie jetzt nicht so hungrig **sein.**
(If you *had eaten* breakfast later,	you *wouldn't be* so hungry now.)
Wenn du früher **gekommen wärest,**	**hätten** wir jetzt weniger zu tun.
	würden wir jetzt weniger zu tun **haben.**
(If you *had come* earlier,	we *would have* less to do now.)

III. INVERSION IN CONDITIONAL SENTENCES

INDICATIVE Wir trinken den Kaffee nicht,
 wenn er zu heiß ist.

PRESENT SUBJUNCTIVE II Wir würden den Kaffee nicht trinken,
 wenn er zu heiß wäre.

PAST SUBJUNCTIVE II Wir hätten den Kaffee nicht getrunken,
 wenn er zu heiß gewesen wäre.

As you see, a conditional sentence may begin with the **dann**-clause. When this is the case:

1. The word **dann** is never used.

2. The **dann**-clause uses normal (declarative) word order.

IV. BEGINNING THE WENN-CLAUSE WITH A VERB

 Kommt er heute nicht, (dann) kommt er morgen.
 Wäre der Kaffee zu heiß, (dann) würde ich ihn nicht trinken.
 Hätte ich das gewußt, (dann) wäre ich zu Hause geblieben.

Wenn-clauses may be introduced by a verb—in that case **wenn** disappears —and the word **dann** may be replaced by **so**:

 Kommt er heute nicht, (so) kommt er morgen.

▣ DRILLS

Substitutions

Put the following indicative sentences into present subjunctive II and past subjunctive II.

 Example: Wenn ich Zeit habe, gehe ich ins Kino.
  Wenn ich Zeit hätte, ginge ich ins Kino.
    würde ich ins Kino gehen.
  Wenn ich Zeit gehabt hätte, wäre ich ins Kino gegangen.

1. Wenn er es weiß, sagt er es dir.
2. Wenn er in Mainz bleibt, kauft er sich ein Haus.
3. Wenn der Anzug nicht zu teuer ist, nehme ich ihn.
4. Wenn wir ins Restaurant gehen, verpassen wir den Zug.
5. Wenn der Mantel nicht zuviel kostet, kaufe ich ihn.
6. Wenn das Wetter schön ist, gehen wir schwimmen.
7. Wenn ich es kann, tue ich es.
8. Wenn er etwas früher kommt, haben wir genug Zeit.
9. Wenn ich in die Stadt muß, gehe ich zu Fuß.
10. Wenn er daran denkt, lädt er sie ein.

Synthetic exercises (dann-clauses)

Generate the suggested **dann**-clauses. These clauses must agree *logically*
with the **wenn**-clauses.

> Example: Wenn ich Zeit hätte, (ich / gehen / Kino).
> Wenn ich Zeit hätte, ginge ich ins Kino.
> würde ich ins Kino gehen.

1. Wenn der Anzug nicht zu teuer wäre, (ich / nehmen / ihn).
2. Wenn ihr so laut sprecht, (ihr / stören / andere Leser).
3. Wenn er schneller gefahren wäre, (er / ankommen / früher).
4. Wenn es etwas wärmer wäre, (ich / anziehen / Sommeranzug).
5. Wenn du mir einen guten Roman empfehlen könntest, (ich / sein / dir / sehr dankbar).
6. Wenn wir Zeit haben, (ich / einlösen / noch / Scheck).
7. Wenn ihr früher ins Bett ginget, (ihr / sein / nicht so müde).
8. Wenn Sie Ihre Arbeit gestern vorbereitet hätten, (Sie / haben / heute / weniger zu tun).
9. Wenn sie früher angekommen wäre, (sie / verpassen / Schiff / nicht).
10. Wenn ich mehr Geld gehabt hätte, (ich / bleiben / länger / Wien).
11. Wenn er in der Innenstadt wohnte, (er / brauchen / kein / Wagen).
12. Wenn der Film nicht so lange gedauert hätte, (wir / kommen / nicht so spät / nach Hause).
13. Wenn ich eine zweite Tasse Kaffe trinke, (ich / rauchen / noch / Zigarette).
14. Wenn ich ihre Adresse wüßte, (ich / schreiben / ihr / Brief).
15. Wenn ich es könnte, (ich / tun / es).
16. Wenn wir ins Restaurant gegangen wären, (wir / verpassen / Zug).

Synthetic exercises (**wenn**-clauses)

Generate the suggested **wenn**-clauses.

1. Wir würden schwimmen gehen, (wenn / Wetter / sein / schön).
2. Ich hätte dir gerne geholfen, (wenn / du / anrufen / mich).
3. Ich würde den Mantel kaufen, (wenn / er / kosten / nicht so viel).
4. Er hätte ein interessanteres Leben gehabt, (wenn / er / werden / Arzt).
5. Ihr wäret glücklicher, (wenn / ihr / streiten / weniger / miteinander).
6. Ich hätte nicht so viel geraucht, (wenn / ich / wissen // daß Zigarrenrauch dich stört).
7. Wir gingen öfter ins Konzert, (wenn / wir / können / verstehen / moderne Musik).
8. Ihr wäret nicht so müde, (wenn / ihr / gehen / früher / Bett).
9. Ich wäre jetzt schon in Berlin, (wenn / ich / fliegen).
10. Ich hätte dieses Buch bestellt, (wenn / ich / denken / daran).

Synthetic exercises (**wenn**-clauses and **dann**-clauses)

Generate the suggested conditional sentences.

> Example: Wenn / ich / haben / Zeit // ich / gehen / Kino
> (*present* and *past subjunctive II*)
> Wenn ich Zeit hätte, ginge ich ins Kino.
>   würde ich ins Kino gehen.
> Wenn ich Zeit gehabt hätte, wäre ich ins Kino gegangen.

1. Wenn / Anzug / sein / nicht zu teuer // ich / kaufen / ihn   (*present* and *past subjunctive II*)
2. Wenn / Hilde / wohnen / nicht so weit von hier // ich / besuchen / sie öfter   (*present* and *past subjunctive II*)
3. Wenn / er / fahren / nicht so schnell // er / haben / kein / Unfall (*past subjunctive II*)
4. Wenn / wir / haben / längere Ferien // wir / fahren / nach Europa (*indicative; present* and *past subjunctive II*)
5. Wenn / es / regnen // wir / bleiben / zu Hause   (*indicative; present* and *past subjunctive II*)
6. Wenn / wir / finden / Buch // wir / zurückgeben / es / Ihnen (*indicative; past subjunctive II*)

7. Wenn / ihr / einladen / mich // ich / kommen / gerne / zu euch
(*indicative; past subjunctive II*)
8. Wenn / wir / fliegen // wir / sein / jetzt schon in Berlin   (*subjunctive II, mixed tenses*)

Express in German

1. If I had time, I'd go to the movies.
2. I'd buy this suit if it didn't cost so much.
3. If the children were here, you'd know it.
4. If you can find it, give it to me.
5. If Hilda didn't live so far from here, I would visit her more often.
6. If the film hadn't lasted so long, we wouldn't have come home so late.
7. If I had flown, I would be in Berlin already.
8. I would have bought this book if I had thought of it.
9. If you went to bed earlier, you wouldn't be so tired.
10. If he had driven faster, he would have arrived earlier.
11. If I knew her address, I'd write her a letter.
12. If we had more money, we'd stay in Vienna longer.
13. He would have had a more interesting life if he had become a lawyer.
14. We'd go more often if we could understand modern music.
15. If we find the book, we'll give it back to you.
16. I would have come if you had invited me.
17. If it were warmer, I would put on a summer suit.
18. If you had prepared your work yesterday, you would have less to do today.

LEVEL THREE

I. CONDITIONAL SENTENCES WITH MODAL AUXILIARIES

A. Constructions with modals

INDICATIVE   Wenn du mit ihm **sprechen willst,**
                               kannst du ihn zu Hause **anrufen.**

PRESENT SUBJUNCTIVE II   Wenn du mit ihm **sprechen wolltest,**
                               könntest du ihn zu Hause **anrufen.**

PAST SUBJUNCTIVE II Wenn du mit ihm **hättest sprechen wollen,**
hättest du ihn zu Hause **anrufen können.**

1. Present Subjunctive II

The **würde-**construction should *not* be used with modal auxiliaries:

Wenn du mit ihm sprechen **wolltest,**
könntest du ihn zu Hause anrufen.

2. Past Subjunctive II

Wenn du mit ihm **hättest sprechen wollen,**
hättest du ihn zu Hause **anrufen können.**

1. sprechen wollen and anrufen können

These are *double-infinitive* constructions. (For a complete explanation,
see p. 145, "Compound Tenses of Modal Auxiliaries.")

2. . . . hättest sprechen wollen

When the auxiliary **(haben)** is forced to the end of the clause by the
subordinating conjunction **wenn** (word order in subordinate clauses), it
will *precede a double-infinitive construction.*

B. Contrastive grammar

Du **kannst** es tun.   (You *can do* it.)
Du **könntest** es tun.   (You *could do* it.)
Du **hättest** es **tun können.**   (You *could have done* it.)

Notice how differently German and English form the past tense of the
subjunctive with a modal auxiliary.

Du **hättest** es **tun können.**
(You *could   have done* it.)

NOTE: As the sentences above show, subjunctive II can be used in simple
sentences as well as in conditional sentences.

▣ DRILLS

Substitution

Put the following indicative sentences into the present and past subjunctive II.

> Example: Er kann es tun.
> Er könnte es tun.
> Er hätte es tun können.

1. Du sollst wirklich nach Hause fahren.
2. Dann müssen Sie es ihm sagen.
3. Wenn ich Ihnen helfen kann, tue ich es gern.
4. Wenn du kommen kannst, bin ich sehr froh.
5. Wenn ich das Geld habe, kann ich mir einen neuen Anzug kaufen.
6. Wenn wir Zeit haben, können wir noch ein Glas Wein trinken.
7. Wenn er Karten haben will, muß er rechtzeitig schreiben.
8. Wenn der Regen aufhört, können wir spazierengehen.

Synthetic exercises

Generate the suggested conditional sentences in both present and past subjunctive II.

1. Wenn / er / wollen / haben / Karten // er / müssen / schreiben / rechtzeitig
2. Wenn / wir / wissen / Adresse // wir / können / finden / Haus / leichter
3. Wenn / ich / dir / können / helfen // ich / tun / es / gern
4. Wenn / Hilde / wohnen / näher // wir / können / besuchen / sie / öfter
5. Es / sein / großartig // wenn / er / können / kommen
6. Wenn / er / nicht / wollen / lesen / Buch // er / können / sich aussuchen / ein anderes
7. Wenn / ihr / kommen / rechtzeitig // ich / müssen / anrufen / euch / nicht

Express in German

1. If I could help you, I would gladly do it.
2. If you had lived closer, I could have visited you more often.
3. If you had come on time, I wouldn't have had to call you up.

4. If we knew the address, we could find the house more easily.
5. We really should have driven home earlier.
6. It would be great if you could come.
7. Then you would have to tell him.
8. If I could have helped you, I'd have gladly done it.
9. If I had the money, I could buy a new suit.
10. If we had had time, we could have drunk another glass of wine.
11. If the rain stopped, we could take a walk.

LEVEL FOUR

I. OTHER USES OF SUBJUNCTIVE II

A. Wishes

> If he were only here!
> Wenn er nur hier wäre!
> Wäre er nur hier!

If he had only been here!
Wenn er nur hier gewesen wäre!
Wäre er nur hier gewesen!

> If he would only come!
> Wenn er nur käme!
> Käme er nur!
> Wenn er nur kommen würde!

If he had only come!
Wenn er nur gekommen wäre!
Wäre er nur gekommen!

To express a wish in German, simply insert the word **nur** into the **wenn**-clause:

Wenn er nur kommen würde!

As this sentence illustrates, **würde** may be used in a **wenn**-clause (present subjunctive II) to express a wish or even a suggestion. This is also true for a complete conditional sentence:

> Wenn er nur weniger rauchen würde, würde er sich besser fühlen.
> (If he would only smoke less, he'd feel better.)

NOTE: The **würde**-construction is *not* used with the modal auxiliaries or with **sein, haben,** or **wissen.**

> Wenn er nur hier **wäre!**
> Wenn ich nur kommen **könnte!**

Colloquial German tends to avoid many of the irregular present subjunctive II forms and to use instead the **würde**-construction as a conversational convenience, even when no wish or suggestion is implied. For example, instead of "wenn er flöge, . . ." one often hears "wenn er fliegen würde, . . ."

B. Polite forms

Can I come along?	Kann ich mitkommen?
Could I come along?	Könnte ich mitkommen?
Will you help me?	Werden Sie mir helfen?
Would you help me?	Würden Sie mir helfen?
May I disturb you?	Darf ich Sie stören?
Might I disturb you?	Dürfte ich Sie stören?
Are you against it?	Sind Sie dagegen?
Would you be against it?	Wären Sie dagegen?
Do you have time to help me?	Haben Sie Zeit, mir zu helfen?
Would you have time to help me?	Hätten Sie Zeit, mir zu helfen?

German, like English, uses the present tense of the subjunctive as a polite form. The use of the subjunctive makes a request or an observation more tentative, less restrictive, which is a courtesy.

NOTE: For all practical purposes, the polite forms are limited to the *modals* and **wäre, hätte,** and **würde.** For this reason, you will hear "Würden Sie mir helfen?" but never "Hülfen Sie mir?"

C. ALS OB (ALS WENN) = as if (as though)

Er tut, **als ob** (**als wenn**) er nichts Besseres zu tun hätte.
(He acts *as if* [*as though*] he had nothing better to do.)

Als ob ich das nicht wüßte!
(*As if* I didn't know that!)

Als ob- and **als wenn-**constructions ordinarily require the use of subjunctive II. They also require dependent word order (conjugated verb at the *end of the clause*).

▣ DRILLS

Subjunctive II (wishes)

Use the following elements to express wishes in both the present and past subjunctive II.

> Example: er / hier / sein / !
> Wenn er nur hier wäre!
> Wenn er nur hier gewesen wäre!

1. Wir / Zeit / haben / !
2. Du / laut / sprechen / !
3. Ich / das / wissen / !
4. Sie / nicht so schnell / fahren / !
5. Sie / zurückkommen / !
6. Du / ihn / fragen / !
7. Ich / es / tun / können / !

Express in German

1. If I'd only known that!
2. If only she would come back!
3. If I'd only sold it!
4. If I could only do it!
5. If you'd only speak louder!   Wenn du nur lauter sprech
6. If we only had time!   würdest.
7. If he just wouldn't say that!

Subjunctive II (polite forms)

Put the following indicative sentences into subjunctive II to stress politeness.

1. Ist es Ihnen recht?
2. Haben Sie fünf Minuten für mich?
3. Kann ich Ihnen eine Tasse Kaffee bringen?
4. Darf ich etwas sagen?
5. Können Sie länger bleiben?
6. Sie sind jetzt an der Reihe.
7. Wir haben eine große Bitte an Sie.
8. Werden Sie mir einen Gefallen tun?
9. Sind Sie dagegen?

[handwritten: 2. Dürfte ich etwas sagen?]

Express in German

1. Could I bring you a cup of coffee? *[handwritten: Könnte ich der eine Tasse Kaffee bringen?]*
2. Might I say something?
3. Would you do me a favor? *[handwritten: Würden Sie mir einen Gefallen tun]*
4. Would you come with me? *[handwritten: Würden Sie (mit mir) mitkommen?]*
5. Would you have time? *[handwritten: Würden Hätten Sie Zeit?]*
6. Would that be all right with you? *[handwritten: Wäre Ihnen das recht?]*
7. Could you stay longer? *[handwritten: Könnten Sie hier länger bleiben]*
8. Would you be against it? *[handwritten: Wären Sie dagegen?]*

Subjunctive II (*as if*-expressions)

Use the following elements to form subjunctive II sentences in the tenses indicated.

1. Als ob / ich / wissen / das / nicht / ! (*present* and *past*)
2. Als ob / wir / sehen / das / nicht / ! (*past*) *[handwritten: Als ob wir das nicht gesehen würde,]*
3. Er sah aus // als ob / er / schlafen / tagelang / nicht (*past*) *[handwritten: hätten]*
4. Als ob / ich / denken / daran / nicht / ! (*past*)
5. Es war // als ob / wir / sein / wieder / in Wien (*present*)

[handwritten: Es war, als ob wir wieder in Wien wären.]

Express in German

1. As if we didn't know that! *[handwritten: Als ob wir das nicht wüßten!]*
2. It was as though we'd never seen it before.
3. It was as if we were in Vienna again.

4. He looked as though he hadn't slept for days.
5. As if I hadn't thought *of that* (**daran**)!

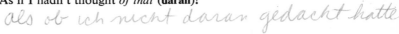

▣ MIXED DRILLS (all levels)

Synthetic exercises

Generate the suggested conditional sentences, wishes, etc., using the tense(s) indicated in brackets.

1. Wenn / ich / wissen / ihre Adresse // ich / schreiben / ihr / Brief   (*present subjunctive II*)
2. Wenn / ihr / kommen / rechtzeitig // ich / müssen / anrufen / euch / nicht   (*past subjunctive II*)
3. Wenn / ich / wissen / das / nur / !   (*past subjunctive II*)
4. Wenn / er / wollen / haben / Karten // er / müssen / schreiben / rechtzeitig   (*present indicative*)
5. Wenn / er / fahren / nicht so schnell // er / haben / kein / Unfall   (*past subjunctive II*)
6. Wenn / ich / können / tun / es nur / !   (*present* and *past subjunctive II*)
7. Ich / helfen / dir // wenn / du / anrufen / mich   (*past subjunctive II*)
8. Wenn / Regen / aufhören // wir / können / spazierengehen   (*present subjunctive II*)
9. Wenn / Karl / nur / sein / hier / !   (*past* and *present subjunctive II*)
10. Wenn / ich / haben / Geld // ich / können / kaufen / neu / Anzug   (*present subjunctive II*)
11. Wenn / ich / nur nicht / ausgeben / mein ganzes Geld / !   (*past subjunctive II*)
12. Ich / tun / es // wenn / ich / können / es   (*present subjunctive II*)
13. Wenn / du / können / kommen // ich / sein / sehr froh   (*present subjunctive II*)
14. Ich / kaufen / Karten / selbst // wenn / ich / denken / daran   (*past subjunctive II*)
15. Wenn / wir / haben / Zeit // wir / können / trinken / noch / Glas Wein   (*present subjunctive II*)
16. Wenn / es / sein / wärmer // ich / anziehen / Sommeranzug   *present subjunctive II*)
17. Wenn / ich / fliegen // ich / sein / jetzt schon / Berlin   (*subjunctive II, mixed tenses*)

18. Wenn / ich / haben / mehr Geld // ich / bleiben / länger / München
    (*present subjunctive II*)
19. Vielleicht / ich / können / helfen / dir // wenn / du / sagen / mir //
    was los ist   (*present subjunctive II*)
20. Wenn / du / wollen / tun / es / nicht // du / sollen / sagen / es /
    mir   (*past subjunctive II*)
21. Wenn / Film / dauern / nicht so lange // wir / kommen / nicht
    so spät / nach Hause   (*past subjunctive II*)
22. Wenn / Ferien / sein / nur / länger / !   (*present subjunctive II*)
23. Wenn / Hilde / wohnen / näher // wir / können / besuchen / sie
    öfter   (*present subjunctive II*)

Express in German *for 4-30*

1. If I had only known that! *Wenn ich das nun gewust hätte!*
2. If I had more money, I'd stay in Munich longer.
3. Could you help me?
4. If I knew her address, I'd write her a letter.
5. If he hadn't driven so fast, he wouldn't have had an accident.
6. Maybe I could find it if you'd tell me where it is.
7. If only I could have done it!
8. He speaks as if he'd never studied (**lernen**) German.
9. That would be a good idea.
10. If Hilda lived closer, we could visit her more often.
11. I would have bought the tickets myself if I had thought of it.
12. Would that be all right with you?
13. I'd do it if I could.
14. You wouldn't be so tired if you would go to bed earlier.
15. I would have bought the coat if it hadn't cost so much.
16. We should have visited him yesterday.
17. If we had a map (**der Stadtplan**), we could find the house more easily.
18. Would you do me a favor?
19. If it were warmer, I'd put on a summer suit.
20. If the film hadn't lasted so long, we wouldn't have come home so late.
21. As if I hadn't thought of that!
22. You should have told him. *Du hättest es ihm erzählen sollen.*
23. If we had time, we could drink another glass of wine.
24. If I had flown, I would be in Berlin already.

relative pronouns and relative clauses

chapter nine

LEVEL ONE

I. INTRODUCTION

Look at the following examples:

MAIN CLAUSE	RELATIVE CLAUSE
That's the man	*who bought our house.*
Here are the books	*that (which) you wanted.*

Each of the sentences above has two distinct parts. One part can meaning-fully stand alone (That's the man *and* Here are the books) and is called a *main clause*. The other part, however, is meaningful only when joined to a main clause; it is called a *subordinate clause* (who bought our house, that you wanted).

Subordinate clauses in English beginning with the pronouns *who, that,* and *which* are called *relative clauses.* The pronouns themselves are called *relative pronouns;* they *relate* the clause to the main clause by referring to one of its elements (*who* refers to *man* and *that* refers to *books* in the examples above). The element in the main clause to which the pronoun refers is called the *antecedent* of the pronoun (*man,* who; *books,* that).

A relative clause, therefore, always tells us something new about the antecedent: it defines or specifies it more fully.

> That's the man

is grammatically a complete sentence. Yet only a broader context can specify *which* man. The addition of a relative clause is one common way of creating such a context:

> That's the man *who bought our house.*

Relative pronouns and relative clauses may also be viewed another way:

> That's *the man.* He (*the man*) bought our house.
> That's the *man who* bought our house.

When two sentences have a common element, they may be combined to form a more complex sentence by making one of the sentences a relative clause. The common element appears as a noun in the main clause (e.g. *the man*) and as a relative pronoun in the relative clause (e.g. *who*).

II. GERMAN RELATIVE PRONOUNS

In English the antecedent determines whether the relative pronoun is a form of *who* (the person *who . . .*) or *that* (the thing *that . . .*). German, however, has a fully developed *gender* system for all nouns, things as well as persons. In German, therefore, the antecedent determines the gender and number of the relative pronoun. If the antecedent is masculine, the pronoun must also be masculine; if the antecedent is plural, the pronoun must also be plural, and so on. For this reason German has masculine, neuter, feminine, and plural relative pronouns.

Moreover, English has only a few forms (*whom, whose*) for the relative pronoun when it is not the subject of its clause. German, on the other hand, has a fully developed *case* system, so the case of the relative pronoun is also completely expressed.

German, therefore, has masculine, neuter, feminine, and plural relative pronouns in all four cases. These are very similar to the forms of the definite article:

	MASC.	NEUT.	FEM.	PLURAL
NOM.	der	das	die	die
ACC.	den	das	die	die
DAT.	dem	dem	der	**denen**
GEN.	**dessen**	**dessen**	**deren**	**deren**

NOTE 1: Pay particular attention to the *five forms in boldface;* they are *unlike* the definite article.

NOTE 2: *alternate forms*
In older works, forms of **welcher** (i.e. **welch–** and the appropriate strong adjective endings) were often used as relative pronouns. These forms are now archaic.

III. RULES

A. Word order

Relative clauses are *subordinate* clauses: they require subordinate word order. This means that the *inflected verb form is in the final position in the clause.*

> Das ist der Mann, der unser Haus gekauft **hat.**

B. Gender and number

The gender and number of a relative pronoun are the same as the gender and number of the noun to which the relative pronoun refers (its antecedent). If the antecedent is masculine singular, the pronoun must also be masculine singular; if it is plural, the pronoun must be plural, and so on.

> Das ist **der Mann, der** unser Haus gekauft hat.
> Das sind **die Leute, die** unser Haus gekauft haben.

C. Case

The case of a relative pronoun depends upon its use or *function in the relative clause.*

The following examples are all in the masculine singular:

NOM. Das ist der Mann, **der** unser Haus gekauft hat.
  (who bought our house.)

ACC. Das ist der Mann, **den** Sie gestern kennengelernt haben.
  (whom you met yesterday.)
  Das ist der Mann, an **den** ich gedacht hatte.
  (whom I was thinking of.)

DAT. Das ist der Mann, **dem** wir es gegeben haben.
  (to whom we gave it *or* whom we gave it to.)
  Das ist der Mann, **dem** du danken solltest.
  (whom you should thank.)
  Das ist der Mann, nach **dem** Sie gefragt haben.
  (about whom you were asking *or* whom you were asking about.)

GEN. Das ist der Mann, **dessen** Hilfe du brauchst.
  (whose help you need.)
  Das ist der Mann, auf **dessen** Rat ich warte.
  (whose advice I am waiting for *or* for whose advice I am waiting.)

As the examples show, a relative pronoun can have various functions within the relative clause. It can be:

1. a subject (nominative case): Der Mann, **der** unser Haus gekauft hat.
2. an accusative object of a verb: Der Mann, **den** Sie gestern kennengelernt haben.
3. an accusative object of a preposition: Der Mann, an **den** ich gedacht hatte.
4. an indirect object (dative case): Der Mann, **dem** Sie es gegeben haben.
5. a dative object of a verb: Der Mann, **dem** du danken solltest.
6. a dative object of a preposition: Der Mann, nach **dem** Sie gefragt haben.
7. a possessive (genitive case): Der Mann, **dessen** Hilfe du brauchst.

NOTE: **Dessen** and **deren** have the same gender and number as the person(s) or thing(s) *to which they refer.*

MASC. **Der** Mann, **dessen** Tochter . . .
NEUT. **Das** Land, **dessen** Grenze . . .
FEM. **Die** Stadt, **deren** Bürgermeister . . .
PLURAL **Die** Leute, **deren** Sohn . . .

D. Position and punctuation

> Der Mann, **den Sie suchen,** ist gerade ausgezogen.
> (The man whom you're looking for just moved out.)

1. A German relative clause comes immediately after the antecedent in the main clause.

2. German relative clauses are always set off by commas.

3. A German relative pronoun is normally the first element of a relative clause. The *only* exception to this rule occurs when the relative pronoun is the object of a preposition:

> Das ist der Mann, **an den** ich gedacht hatte.

E. No omission of German relative pronoun

It is often possible to omit a relative pronoun from an English sentence. However, *relative pronouns may never be omitted in German:*

> Der Film, **den** wir gestern abend gesehen haben, war großartig.
> (The movie [*that*] we saw last evening was great.)

When the progressive form (e.g. *is standing*) is used, English often omits both the relative pronoun and the form of *to be* (e.g. *is*). Such a construction is not possible in German:

> Der Mann, **der** da an der Ecke steht, will mit Ihnen sprechen.
> (The man [*who is*] standing on the corner there wants to talk to you.)

▣ DRILLS

Fill-ins

MASCULINE

1. Das ist der Herr, _____ mit Ihnen sprechen will.
   (who)

2. Das ist der Mann, _____ du danken solltest.
   (whom)

3. Kant ist ein Philosoph, _____ Ideen immer noch sehr
(whose)
wichtig sind.

4. Ist das der Wagen, _____ du vorige Woche verkauft hast?
(which)

5. Wo ist der Brief, auf _____ ich warte?
(which)

6. Der Mann, _____ Gepäck da steht, kommt gleich zurück.
(whose)

7. Hier ist ein Mantel, _____ Farbe mir gefällt.
(whose)

8. Wie heißt der Junge, mit _____ du gesprochen hast?
(whom)

9. Da kommt der Junge, _____ Schwester du so schön
(whose)
findest.

10. Ich zeige dir den Brief, _____ er uns geschrieben hat.
(which)

NEUTER

1. Hier ist ein Buch, _____ mich interessiert.
(which)

2. Das ist ein Land, _____ Außenpolitik mir gar nicht
(whose)
gefällt.

3. Ist das das Mädchen, _____ du so langweilig findest?
(whom)

4. Das Zimmer, in _____ ich jetzt wohne, ist viel zu klein.
(which)

5. Erinnern Sie sich an das Stück, _____ wir vorigen Monat
(which)
gesehen haben?

6. Siehst du das Kind, _____ da an der Ecke steht?
(who)

7. Das ist das Mädchen, für _____ Vater ich arbeite.
(whose)

8. Ich warte immer noch auf das Paket, _____ er mir
(which)
geschickt hat.

9. Das ist kein Haus, in _____ ich wohnen möchte.
(which)

10. Das Hemd, _____ ich kaufen wollte, war zu teuer.
(which)

FEMININE

1. Sehen Sie die Frau, _____ gerade aus dem Laden kommt?
   (who)

2. Vielen Dank für die Karte, _____ Sie uns geschickt haben.
   (which)

3. Wer war die Dame, mit _____ du da gesprochen hast?
   (whom)

4. Die Jacke, _____ Farbe mir gefiel, war mir zu teuer.
   (whose)

5. Ist das die Tasse, aus _____ ich getrunken habe?
   (which)

6. Die Suppe, _____ so gut war, steht nicht mehr auf der
   (which)
   Speisekarte.

7. Das ist die Frau, _____ ich es gegeben habe.
   (to whom)

8. Die Dame, _____ Pakete da liegen, kommt gleich zurück.
   (whose)

9. Die Lampe, _____ ich kaufen wollte, ist nicht mehr da.
   (which)

10. Die Familie, bei _____ ich wohne, spricht nur Deutsch.
    (whom)

PLURAL

1. Sehen Sie die zwei Mädchen, _____ vor dem Laden
   (who)
   stehen?

2. Die Leute, in _____ Haus wir wohnen, sind jetzt in
   (whose)
   Innsbruck.

3. Filme, _____ man im Fernsehen sieht, sind meistens sehr
   (which)
   alt.

4. Hier sind die Briefe, auf _____ du wartest.
   (which)

5. Das sind die Leute, _____ wir unser Haus verkauft
   (to whom)
   haben.

6. Was kosten die Zigarren, _____ Sie rauchen?
   (which)

7. Sind das die Bücher, _____ Sie meinen?
   (which)

8. Die Weine, _____ mir am besten gefallen, kommen aus
Frankreich. (which)

9. Sind das die Leute, mit _____ wir gestern gesprochen
haben? (whom)

10. Die Jungen, _____ Wagen vor dem Haus steht, kommen
gleich zurück. (whose)

Sentence combinations using relative clauses

NOMINATIVE

Example: Das ist der Herr. **Er** will mit Ihnen sprechen.
Das ist der Herr, **der** mit Ihnen sprechen will.

1. Hier ist ein Buch. **Es** interessiert mich.
2. Wir gaben es den Jungen. **Sie** waren gestern hier.
3. Hier ist ein Mantel. **Er** gefällt mir.
4. Sehen Sie die Frau? **Sie** geht in den Laden.
5. Wo ist der Mann? **Er** war gerade hier.
6. Das Buch liegt auf dem Tisch. **Er** steht in der Ecke.

ACCUSATIVE

1. Ich warte immer noch auf das Paket. Er hat **es** mir geschickt.
2. Was kosten die Zigarren? Er raucht **sie.**
3. War das die Nacht? Du hast an **sie** gedacht?
4. Erinnerst du dich an den Film? Wir haben **ihn** vorigen Monat gesehen.
5. Was hältst du von den Tassen? Ich habe **sie** gekauft.
6. Der Laden ist nicht weit von hier. Ich habe an **ihn** gedacht.

DATIVE

Example: Das sind die Leute. Wir haben gestern abend mit **ihnen**
gesprochen.
Das sind die Leute, mit **denen** wir gestern abend gesprochen haben.

1. Das ist der Mann. Du solltest **ihm** danken.
2. Ist das die Jacke? Sie haben nach **der** Jacke gefragt.
3. Wie heißt das Hotel? Wir haben in **dem** Hotel übernachtet.

4. Das sind die Leute. Ich habe bei **ihnen** gewohnt.
5. Das Zimmer ist zu klein. Ich wohne in **dem** Zimmer.
6. Wer war die Dame? Ihr habt mit **ihr** gesprochen.

GENITIVE

Example: Die Dame kommt gleich zurück. **Ihre** Handtasche liegt da.
Die Dame, **deren** Handtasche da liegt, kommt gleich zurück.

1. Die Leute sind in Innsbruck. Wir wohnen in **ihrem** Haus.
2. Kafka ist ein Dichter. **Sein** Name ist überall bekannt.
3. Das ist das Mädchen. Ich arbeite für **ihren** Vater.
4. Der Mantel war zu teuer. **Seine** Farbe gefiel mir.
5. Wo ist die Frau? Da liegt **ihr** Paket.
6. Die Häuser waren alle zu teuer. Er fragte nach **ihren** Preisen.

Express in German

1. That's the man I want to talk to.
2. Here's a book that interests me.
3. That's the girl whose father I work for.
4. Where do you buy the cigars that you smoke?
5. That's the man you should thank.
6. Do you see the two girls standing on the corner?
7. The lady whose package is lying there is coming right back.
8. Here's a coat whose color I like.
9. Many thanks for the card you sent us.
10. Is that the girl you find so boring?
11. The people whose house we're living in are in Innsbruck.
12. Is that the cup I was drinking out of?
13. I'll show you the letter he wrote us.
14. The room I'm living in is much too small.
15. Do you see the woman who is just coming out of the store?
16. Those are the people we sold our house to.
17. Who was that lady you were talking to?
18. What do you think of the cups I bought?
19. I am still waiting for the letter he sent me.
20. Those are the people I live with.
21. That's not a house I'd like to live in.
22. The family he's living with speaks only German.
23. The soup that was so good isn't on the menu any more.
24. The wines I like best come from France.

25. Is that the man you are waiting for?
26. Do you remember the film we saw last month?
27. Is that the night you were thinking of?
28. Is that the jacket you were asking about?
29. Movies one sees on television are usually rather old.
30. Where's the man who was just here?

LEVEL TWO

I. SPECIAL RELATIVE CONSTRUCTIONS

A. The relative adverb WO

> Er wohnt jetzt **in Wien** (in Deutschland).
> Es geht ihm **dort** sehr gut.

> Er wohnt jetzt **in Wien** (in Deutschland),
>   **wo** es ihm sehr gut geht.

Wo *must* be used, instead of a relative pronoun, when referring to place names (e.g. of cities, states, countries, continents).

NOTE 1: Like relative pronouns, the relative adverb **wo** requires subordinate word order: the inflected verb must be at the end of the clause.

NOTE 2: The relative adverb **wo** *may* be used when referring to other expressions of place. In such cases, it is an alternate form which *may* be used in place of a preposition and a relative pronoun:

> Ist das das Restaurant, **wo** du gearbeitet hast?
> (Is that the restaurant, *where* you worked?)

> or: Ist das das Restaurant, **in dem** du gearbeitet hast?
> (Is that the restaurant, *in which* you worked?
>   *that* you worked *in?*)

B. The relative pronoun WER
(unnamed antecedents with persons)

Look at the following sentences:

NOM.   Wissen Sie, **wer** das ist?
          (Do you know *who* that is?)

ACC.   Ich weiß nicht, **wen** Sie meinen.
(I don't know *whom* you mean.)

Ja, ich weiß ganz genau, **an wen** er gedacht hat.
(Yes, I know exactly *whom* he was thinking *of*.)

DAT.   Hast du gesehen, **wem** er es gegeben hat?
(Did you see *whom* he gave it to?)

Wissen Sie, **nach wem** er gefragt hat?
(Do you know *whom* he was asking about?)

GEN.   Ich bin nicht sicher, **wessen** Buch das ist.
(I'm not sure *whose* book that is.)

In none of these sentences is there an *antecedent* with which the pronoun can agree in gender and number. The antecedent (the *person* referred to) may be known to the speaker (e.g. Ich weiß ganz genau, an wen er gedacht hat.), *but it is not named in the sentence.* When the unnamed antecedent is a *person*, the appropriate form of the interrogative pronoun **wer** (**wen, wem, wessen**) must be used.

The relative pronoun **wer** is also used where the English language uses *whoever* (*he who*):

Wer zu spät kommt, wird den Zug verpassen.
(*Whoever* comes too late will miss the train.)

C. The relative pronoun WAS
(unnamed antecedents with things)

Look at the following sentences:

NOM.   Wissen Sie, **was** das ist?
(Do you know *what* that is?)

ACC.   Ich weiß nicht, **was** Sie meinen.
(I don't know *what* you mean.)

Ja, ich weiß ganz genau, **woran** er gedacht hat.
(Yes, I know exactly *what* he was thinking *of*.)

DAT.   Wissen Sie, **wonach** er gefragt hat?
(Do you know *what* he was asking about?)

As in the sentences with **wer,** these sentences have no expressed antecedent with which the relative pronoun can agree. Here, however, things, rather than persons, are being referred to. When the unnamed antecedent is a *thing*, the appropriate form of the interrogative pronoun **was** must be used.

NOTE: *prepositional usage with the relative pronouns* **wer** *and* **was:**

PERSONS	THINGS
Ich weiß, **an wen** er gedacht hat. Wissen Sie, **nach wem** er gefragt hat?	Ich weiß, **woran** er gedacht hat. Wissen Sie, **wonach** er gefragt hat?
With *persons* one uses: *preposition* + *appropriate form of* **wer**	With *things* one uses: **wo(r)**− + *preposition* **wor**− is used if the preposition begins with a vowel (e.g. **woran**). Otherwise, **wo**− is used (e.g. **wonach**).

The relative pronoun **was** also has the meaning *what*, in the sense of *that which:*

> **Was** er sagte, war sehr interessant.
> (*What* [*that which*] he said was very interesting.)

1. Special Uses of **was**

The relative pronoun **was** *must* be used when the antecedent is:

1. *a superlative adjective used as a noun*
   > Es war **das Beste, was** er tun konnte.
   > (It was *the best thing* [*that*] he could do.)

2. *a neuter pronoun indicating quantity*

alles	everything	**etwas**	something
vieles	much, many a thing	**wenig**	little
manches	much, many a thing	**nichts**	nothing

   > **Alles** (**vieles**, etc.), **was** er sagte, war interessant.
   > (*Everything* [*much*, etc.] that he said was interesting.)

3. *a clause*

Herr von Wiese geht jeden Tag spazieren, **was** ihm gar nicht schadet.
(Herr von Wiese goes walking every day, *which* doesn't hurt him at all.)

Karl will nicht mitkommen, **was** höchst ungewöhnlich ist.
(Karl doesn't want to come along, *which* is highly unusual.)

In these sentences the antecedent is not a single element in the main clause, but rather the entire clause itself. (What does not hurt Mr. von Wiese is *his act* of taking a walk every day. What is highly unusual is *the fact* that Karl does not want to come along.)

▣ DRILLS

Fill-ins

Supply the correct pronoun forms.

1. Ich weiß nicht, _____ heute abend kommt.
   (who)

2. Wissen Sie, _____ er machen will?
   (what)

3. Ich bin nicht sicher, _____ ich es gesagt habe.
   (to whom)

4. Ich habe nicht gehört, _____ er gefragt hat.
   (*what* he was asking *about*.)

5. Er sagte nicht, _____ er ins Kino geht.
   (with whom)

6. Das war das Interessanteste, _____ er sagte.
   (that)

7. _____ mitkommen will, muß fünf Mark zahlen.
   (Whoever)

8. Er hatte nichts, _____ uns interessierte.
   (that)

9. Ich habe nicht gesehen, _____ er getan hat.
   (what)

10. Weißt du, _____ sie meint?
    (whom)

11. Ich weiß nicht, _____ er gedacht hat.
    (*what* he was thinking *of*.)

12. _____ Sie da sagen, ist völlig falsch.
    (What)

13. Otto ist jetzt in der Schweiz, _____ er Freunde besucht.
    (where)

14. Es ist das Beste, _____ er geschrieben hat.
    (that)

15. Walter will nach Leipzig fahren, _____ ich nicht verstehen
    kann.   (which)

16. _____ das gesagt hat, muß ein kluger Mann sein.
    (Whoever)

17. Ich weiß nicht, _____ er meinte.
    (what)

18. Ich kann vieles, _____ er sagte, einfach nicht glauben.
    (that)

19. Wissen Sie, _____ er den Brief geschrieben hat?
    (to whom)

20. Ich möchte wissen, _____ Haus das ist.
    (whose)

21. Haben Sie gehört, _____ er gesprochen hat?
    (*what* he was talking *about?*)

22. Wissen Sie, _____ ich gedacht habe?
    (*of whom* I was thinking?)

23. Erzähle mir alles, _____ du gesehen hast!
    (that)

24. Wissen Sie, _____ er wartet?
    (*what* he's waiting *for?*)

25. Nein, ich weiß nicht, _____ Uhr das ist.
    (whose)

26. Wissen Sie, _____ er sich so sehr freut?
    (*what* he's so happy *about?*)

Express in German

1. That was the most interesting thing he said.
2. I don't know what he meant.
3. I'm not sure whom I gave it to.
4. Tell me everything he said.
5. I don't know who is coming tonight.
6. Do you know what he's so happy about?
7. Whoever said that must be a smart man.

8. I'd like to know whose house that is.
9. He didn't say whom he went to the movies with.
10. Do you know what he wants to do?
11. Otto is in Switzerland visiting friends.
12. Do you know whom he's thinking of?
13. I'm not sure what he's waiting for.
14. He didn't have anything that interested us.
15. It's the best thing I've seen.
16. Do you know whom she meant?
17. No, I don't know whose watch that is.
18. He goes walking every afternoon, which can't hurt him.
19. I don't know what he's thinking about.
20. What you're saying is completely wrong.
21. Did you hear what he was talking about?
22. Do you know whom he wrote the letter to?
23. Whoever wants to come along has to pay five marks.

◻ MIXED DRILLS (both levels)

✳ **Express in German** *für Montag 11-16*

1. That's the man you should thank.
2. I'm not sure what he's waiting for.
3. The room I'm living in is much too small.
4. Tell me everything he said.
5. What do you think of the cups I bought?
6. Where's the man who was just here?
7. I'd like to know whose house that is.
8. Those are the people I live with.
9. Do you know whom he wrote the letter to?
10. It's the best thing I've seen.
11. I'm still waiting for the letter he sent me.
12. Is that the jacket you were asking about?
13. Many thanks for the card you sent us.
14. He goes walking every afternoon, which can't hurt him.
15. I don't know what he meant.
16. The family he's living with speaks only German.
17. Whoever said that must be a smart man.
18. Is that the man you're waiting for?

19. Here's a book that interests me.
20. Did you hear what he was talking about?
21. Otto is in Switzerland visiting friends.
22. I'll show you the letter he wrote us.
23. Who was the lady you were talking to?
24. Do you know whom she meant?
25. Is that the night you were thinking of?
26. No, I don't know whose watch that is.
27. Do you know whom he's thinking of?
28. That's the girl whose father I work for.
29. That was the most interesting thing he said.
30. The wines I like best come from France.
31. I don't know what he's talking about.
32. Those are the people we sold our house to.
33. Do you know what he's so happy about?
34. Do you remember the film we saw last month?
35. Here's a coat whose color I like.
36. Movies one sees on TV are usually rather old.
37. He didn't have anything that interested us.
38. That's not a house I'd like to live in.
39. I'm not sure whom I gave it to.
40. He didn't say whom he went to the movies with.

conjunctions

chapter ten

LEVEL ONE

I. INTRODUCTION

Conjunctions—as the name implies—join units of language together: words to words, phrases to phrases, clauses to clauses, and so on.

WORDS	*Hans and I* are going swimming.
PHRASES	Are you going *by ship or by plane?*
CLAUSES	*I'm not going because I have too much to do.*

In both English and German, it is necessary to select the right conjunction to define the right relationship. This is a *lexical* problem, a matter of vocabulary. But when it comes to joining *clauses* to *clauses* or *sentences* to *sentences*, German presents a slight *structural* problem. Look at these two German sentences:

Ich gehe nicht ins Kino. Ich habe den Film schon gesehen.
(I'm not going to the movies.) (I've already seen the movie.)

Note what happens when these sentences are connected with two different conjunctions, **denn** and **weil**, both of which mean *because:*

Ich gehe nicht ins Kino, **denn** ich **habe** den Film schon gesehen.
Ich gehe nicht ins Kino, **weil** ich   den Film schon gesehen **habe.**

These two *compound sentences* mean the same thing, but **denn** has not affected the word order of the clause it introduces, whereas **weil** has.

GENERAL RULES

1. Some German conjunctions *do not* affect the word order of the clauses they introduce:

> Ich gehe nicht.   **Ich habe zu viel zu tun.**
> Ich gehe nicht, **denn ich habe zu viel zu tun.**
> (I'm not going *because* I have too much to do.)

> Zuerst wollen wir essen.   **Dann gehen wir spazieren.**
> Zuerst wollen wir essen, **und dann gehen wir spazieren.**
> (First we want to eat *and* then we are going for a walk.)

These are called *coordinating* conjunctions; they do not affect word order:

> . . . , denn ich **habe** viel zu tun.
> . . . , und dann **gehen** wir spazieren.

NOTE: The verbs appear to be in the third position rather than in the second. The word order of the clauses is thus behaving as if the coordinating conjunctions were not present. Coordinating conjunctions, then, may be considered to be structurally inert: they are not counted as clause elements.

2. Other conjunctions *do* affect the word order of the clauses they introduce:

> Ich gehe nicht.   Ich **habe** zuviel zu tun.
> Ich gehe nicht, **weil** ich   zuviel zu tun **habe.**

Das Essen ist nicht teuer.   Es **ist** ein weltbekanntes Restaurant.
Das Essen ist nicht teuer, **obwohl** es   ein weltbekanntes Restaurant **ist**.
(The food isn't expensive *although* it's a world famous restaurant.)

These are called *subordinating* conjunctions. As you can see from the two examples, their effect on the word order of the *subordinate clause* is very simple: the conjugated verb (**habe** or **ist**) merely moves to the *end of the clause.* The other elements of the clause remain in their original order.

3. Commas are always found between joined clauses.

II. COORDINATING CONJUNCTIONS

The coordinating conjunctions—**denn, oder, und, aber,** and **sondern**—*do not* affect word order.

1. **denn** *because, since, for* (causal)

Ich kann heute nicht in die Stadt, **denn** meine Frau hat den Wagen.
(I can't go downtown today *because* my wife has the car.)

2. **oder** *or*

Soll ich einkaufen gehen, **oder** gehst du?
(Shall I go shopping, *or* are you going?)

NOTE: **. . . , oder gehst du?**
The inert coordinating conjunction does not affect the word order of a question. For purposes of word order, **oder** is inert, and **gehst** is the first element of the clause.

3. **und** *and*

Ich machte die Tür auf, **und** da stand er.
(I opened the door, *and* there he stood.)

4. **aber** *but, however*

Ich habe ihn nicht gesehen, **aber** er ist bestimmt hier.
(I haven't seen him, *but* he's certainly here.)

5. **sondern** *but, rather, on the contrary*

Ich komme nicht zu dir, **sondern** du kommst zu mir.
(I'm not coming to your place, *rather* you're coming to mine.)

NOTE: **Sondern** is used (rather than **aber**) after a *negative* clause where the words *rather* or *on the contrary* can sensibly be used in the equivalent English sentence. (The word *but* in the sentence "I haven't seen him *but* I know where he is" could not logically be replaced by the phrase *on the contrary.*)

III. OMISSION OF REDUNDANT ELEMENTS: ELLIPSIS

Diesen Sommer bleibt er nicht in der Stadt, **sondern (er) fährt aufs Land.**
(This summer he's not staying in the city, *but [he's] going to the country.*)

Er war aufgestanden und (er war) ins Wohnzimmer gegangen.
(He had gotten up and [he had] gone to the living room.)

Wir tun es jetzt oder (wir tun es) gar nicht.
(We will do it now or (we will) not (do it) at all.

In German, as in English, elements common to both clauses of a compound sentence are often eliminated from the second clause. This is true for clauses introduced by **oder, sondern,** and **und.** However, ellipsis is *not* found after **denn** and the subordinating conjunctions and is rare after **aber.** In this, too, German is similar to English.

Er ist zu Hause geblieben, denn **er** hatte zuviel zu tun.
(He stayed home because *he* had too much to do.

The second **er** / *he* in these sentences cannot be omitted.

🔲 DRILLS

Sentence combinations using conjunctions

Combine the following sentences with the German conjunctions corresponding to the English in parentheses.

1. Ich weiß nicht, wo sie jetzt ist. Ich werde sie suchen.   (but)
2. Er raucht viel. Er ist sehr nervös.   (because)
3. Hier ist die Bibliothek. Dort drüben steht das Verwaltungsgebäude. (and)
4. Sie sind schon da. Sie kommen spätestens morgen.   (or)
5. Ich bin nicht ganz sicher. Ich glaube es schon.   (but)
6. Er geht nicht gern ins Theater. Er besucht lieber seine Freunde. (rather)
7. Er hat sich warm angezogen. Es ist kalt geworden.   (since)
8. Soll ich ihn abholen? Willst du das machen?   (or)

9. Sie können zuerst mit ihm sprechen. Ich kann eine Stunde später kommen. (and)
10. Ich habe ihm zugewinkt. Er hat mich nicht gesehen. (but)
11. Er grüßte mich nicht. Er ging stumm weiter. (rather)
12. Sie stand um zwei Uhr auf. Sie konnte nicht schlafen. (because)

LEVEL TWO

I. SUBORDINATING CONJUNCTIONS

The subordinating conjunctions *do* affect word order. Look at the following two groups of examples:

MAIN CLAUSE	SUBORDINATE CLAUSE

Ich gehe heute abend nicht ins Kino, **da** ich den Film schon gesehen **habe.**
Das Essen ist gar nicht teuer, **obwohl** es ein weltbekanntes Restaurant **ist.**

SUBORDINATE CLAUSE	MAIN CLAUSE

Da ich den Film schon gesehen **habe, gehe** ich heute abend nicht ins Kino.
Obwohl es ein weltbekanntes Restaurant **ist, ist** das Essen gar nicht teuer.

1. In clauses introduced by subordinating conjunctions, the conjugated verb is forced to the *end of the clause.*

2. A sentence may also begin with a subordinate clause. In this case the *main clause begins with a conjugated verb.*

NOTE: This is in keeping with the *normal word order* of the German declarative sentence that requires the conjugated verb to be the second element of the sentence. A subordinate clause functions as a single (although extended) element as far as word order is concerned. Thus a conjugated verb occurring just after a subordinate clause is, in fact, in the second (or verb) position.

A. Conjunctions presenting special problems

Some German subordinating conjunctions present a particular problem to English-speakers. The same English conjunction may serve in a number of situations where German would require several distinct ones. These German conjunctions—and other parts of speech with which they might be confused—are discussed below under their English equivalents.

1. When

als (subordinating conjunction used in expressions of *past* time)

wenn (subordinating conjunction used in expressions of the future and for *whenever* and *if*)

wann (question word and subordinating conjunction)

1. **Als** (*when*) may refer to a point in past time:

> *When* I found him . . .
> **Als** ich ihn fand . . .

or to an extended, uninterrupted period of past time:

> *When* I lived in Munich . . .
> **Als** ich in München wohnte . . .

NOTE: **Als** is also used in narrating past events using the present tense—a literary technique. With this exception, **als** may be used only with the *past* or *past perfect* tenses. It is rarely used with the present perfect tense.

2. **Wenn** corresponds to the English *when* in the sense of *whenever* (recurrence):

> *When*(*ever*) he comes . . . (he stays with us).
> **Wenn** er kommt . . .

It is also used to imply the *future:*

> *When* he comes . . . (he will stay with us).
> **Wenn** er kommt . . .

or to express the English word *if:*

> *If* he comes . . . (he will stay with us).
> **Wenn** er kommt . . .

NOTE: As you can see, the clause **Wenn er kommt . . .** is dependent upon its broader context to indicate whether it refers to the *future* or means *if* or *whenever*.

3. **Wann** is a question word:

When is he coming?
Wann kommt er?

Wann is also used when a question is part of a larger syntactical unit:

Ich weiß, **wann** er kommt.
(I know *when* he's coming.)

Ich fragte ihn, **wann** er kommt.
(I asked him *when* he's coming.)

NOTE: In such cases, **wann** functions as a subordinating conjunction. For this reason, the conjugated verb is at the end of the subordinate clause. (This is the case whenever a question word introduces a subordinate clause.)

Express in German

1. I don't know when I'll do it.
2. When I was young, I lived in Stuttgart.
3. When we go to Berlin, we always stay in a good hotel.
4. I'll give it to him when I see him.
5. He was very tired when he arrived.
6. Whenever the weather was good, we took a walk.
7. When did you have time?

2. After / afterwards

1. **Nachdem** is a subordinating conjunction (it introduces a subordinate clause):

Ich komme zu dir, **nachdem** ich gegessen **habe.**
(I'll come to your place *after* I have eaten.)

Nachdem may be used only with the present perfect and past perfect tenses.

2. **Nach** is a preposition (it introduces prepositional phrases):

Ich komme **nach dem Essen** zu dir.
(I'll come to your place *after dinner*.)

3. **Nachher** is an adverb of time (like **heute, morgen,** etc.):

> Ich komme **nachher** zu dir.
> (I'll come to your place *afterwards.*)

Express in German

1. After this program (**die Sendung**) I'm going to bed.
2. After that I'm going home.
3. After we visit friends in Munich, we're going to Berlin. (*first clause: present perfect*)
4. After such a hot summer I'm *looking forward to* (**sich freuen auf** + *acc.*) cold weather.
5. After she had sung the same song three times, I left.
6. We can eat afterwards.

3. Before / before (that)

1. **Bevor** / **ehe** (**ehe** is less common) are subordinating conjunctions:

> **Bevor** (**ehe**) er **wegging,** gab er mir den Schlüssel.
> (*Before* he left he gave me his key.)

2. **Vor** is a preposition. It can mean *before:*

> Er geht **vor elf Uhr** ins Bett.
> (He goes to bed *before eleven o'clock.*)

or *ago:*

> Das war **vor zwei Jahren.**
> (That was *two years ago.*)

3. **Vorher** is an adverb:

> Das hast du mir schon **vorher** gesagt.
> (You told me that *before.*)

Express in German

1. Come before dinner!
   Before I've eaten?
   Yes, certainly, before.
2. Call me up before you leave.

3. I'm going to Germany this summer, but before that I'll have to learn some German.
4. He moved out three weeks ago.

NOTE: All of the following are subordinating conjunctions, except where otherwise noted.

4. Since, ever since, because, as long as

1. Seitdem (*since, ever since*) refers to a *period of time:*

> Haben Sie ihn gesehen, **seitdem** er zurückgekommen **ist?**
> (Have you seen him *since* he returned?)

Choice of tenses with **seitdem:**
When *since* refers to a continuing or repeated action, German uses:

seitdem + *present*

. . . *since* he's been smoking less.
. . . **seitdem** er weniger **raucht.**

. . . *since* he's been living here.
. . . **seitdem** er hier **wohnt.**

When *since* refers to a one-time past action, German uses:

seitdem + *present perfect*

. . . *since* she went away.
. . . **seitdem** sie **weggegangen ist.**

. . . *since* we sold our house.
. . . **seitdem** wir unser Haus **verkauft haben.**

Various combinations of continuing and one-time actions are, of course, possible:

ONE-TIME ACTIONS	CONTINUING ACTIONS

Seitdem sie **weggegangen ist, rauche** ich weniger.
Seitdem wir unser Haus **verkauft haben, wohnen** wir in einem Hotel.

Seitdem is also an adverb that means *since then:*

CONTINUING ACTION (present)   *Since then* he's been living in a hotel.
                                     Seitdem wohnt er in einem Hotel.

ONE-TIME ACTION (present perfect)   I've only seen him once *since then.*
Seitdem habe ich ihn nur einmal **gesehen.**

2. **Solange** is used to indicate length of time only:

Ich bleibe, **solange** du **willst.**
(I'll stay *as long as* you want.)

3. **Weil** (*because*, since) indicates strong causal connection:

Ich mag das Haus, **weil** es schön gelegen **ist.**
(I like the house *because* it's in a good location.)

4. **Da** (*since*, because) indicates a less strong causal connection or no strict causal connection at all.

NOTE: The choice of **weil** or **da** depends on how strong a causal connection the speaker wishes to convey:

weil   If he considers his reasons for an action or an attitude *absolutely compelling*, he uses **weil** (not **da**):
Ich esse, **weil** ich sehr hungrig bin.
Ich arbeite, **weil** ich Geld verdienen **muß.**

weil / **da**   If he considers his reasons *good* and *adequate* (but not absolutely compelling), he uses either **weil** or **da**:
Ich ging heute schwimmen, **weil** es so schön war.
Da es heute so schön war, ging ich schwimmen.

da   If the reason is—in his eyes at least—*not at all compelling or forcing,* the speaker uses **da** (not **weil**):
Da ich noch zehn Minuten hatte, trank ich noch eine Tasse Kaffee.
Da ich **sowieso** nach München fahre, werde ich Tante Elvira besuchen.*

Express in German

1. Since I'm going to the library, I'll take your books back.
2. I haven't talked to him since he's come back from Berlin.

---

*__Sowieso__ (*anyway*) often accompanies **da** in such cases. In the last example, the visit to Aunt Elvira and the going to Munich are obviously not connected in any compelling causal way. As a matter of fact, Aunt Elvira would be insulted if she heard the word **sowieso.**

3. I couldn't see the movie very well because I had forgotten my glasses.
4. Since it's such a nice day, we can go swimming.
5. He can live at our place as long as he wants.
6. He looks much better since he's been working in the country.
7. I couldn't go shopping because I didn't have any money.

B. Other subordinating conjunctions

The following subordinating conjunctions, in contrast to the preceding ones, present few problems to English speakers because essentially they bear a one-to-one relationship to their English counterparts.

1. **Ob** expresses *whether* and *if* in the sense of *whether:*

> Ich weiß nicht, **ob** er heute **kommt.**
> (I don't know *if* [*whether*] he's coming today.)

2. **Daß** means *that:*

> Er zeigte uns, **daß** er es **konnte.**
> (He showed us *that* he was able to do it.)

3. **Damit (so daß)** is a subordinating conjunction meaning *so that:*

> Ich sage es dir noch einmal, **damit** du es nicht **vergißt.**
> (I'll tell you again *so that* you won't forget it.)

4. **Obwohl (obgleich, obschon)** is a subordinating conjunction meaning *although, even though:*

Obwohl es ein weltbekanntes Restaurant **ist,** ist das Essen nicht sehr teuer.
(*Although* it is a world famous restaurant, the food is not very expensive.)

5. **Während** is both a subordinating conjunction meaning *while:*

> **Während** Sie in Berlin **waren,** kam ein Paket für Sie an.
> (*While* you were in Berlin a package arrived for you.)

and a preposition (*during*) that requires the genitive case:

> **Während der Ferien** kam ein Paket für Sie an.
> (*During the vacation* a package arrived for you.)

6. **Bis** is both a subordinating conjunction meaning *until:*

Warten Sie, **bis** ich **zurückkomme!**
(Wait *until* I come back.)

and a preposition (*until*) that requires the accusative case:

Warten Sie **bis ein Uhr!**
(Wait *until* one o'clock.)

7. **Sobald,** meaning *as soon as,* refers to a point in time:

Wir fahren ab, **sobald** der Zug hier **ankommt.**
(We're leaving *as soon as* the train arrives here.)

8. **Sooft,** meaning *as often as, every time that,* refers to a series of points in time (recurrence):

Sooft ich daran **denke,** werde ich böse.
(*Every time* I think of that I get mad.)

9. **Indem** means *by* (do)*ing* (something).

Look at the English equivalent carefully:

Indem er das Problem **löste,** zeigte er, daß er ein guter Physiker war.
(*By* solv*ing* the problem, he showed that he was a good physicist.)

▣ DRILLS

Sentence combinations using conjunctions

Combine the following sentences, using the suggested conjunctions. Note that both *coordinating* and *subordinating* conjunctions are involved. Be sure to use correct word order.

1. Ich weiß nicht. (when)   Ich sehe ihn.
2. Hören Sie auf. (before)   Es ist zu spät.
3. Sprechen Sie lauter. (so that)   Ich kann Sie verstehen.
4. (After)   Ich hatte den Film dreimal gesehen. Ich habe ihn endlich verstanden.
5. (Although)   Er ist siebzig Jahre alt. Er geht jeden Tag ins Büro.
6. (Since)   Ich fuhr sowieso durch Heidelberg. Ich habe Onkel Max besucht.

7. (Whenever) Er verläßt das Büro. Er macht die Fenster zu.
8. Ich muß mich beeilen. (because) Unsere Gäste werden bald hier sein.
9. Ich weiß nicht, wo sie jetzt ist. (but) Ich werde sie suchen.
10. Er sieht besser aus. (since) Er arbeitet weniger.
11. (When) Ich war jung. Ich wohnte in Stuttgart.
12. Wir können heute abend Karten spielen. (or) Wir können ins Kino gehen, wenn Sie wollen.
13. Ich werde warten. (until) Er kommt morgen.
14. Wissen Sie? (if) Er hat es gefunden.
15. Rufen Sie mich an. (as soon as) Er kommt an.
16. Sie können zuerst mit ihm sprechen. (and) Ich kann eine Stunde später kommen.
17. Ich trank eine Tasse Kaffee. (while) Ich wartete auf Sie.
18. (Every time) Ich denke daran. Ich muß lachen.
19. Ich weiß. (that) Er liest gern.
20. Sie grüßte mich nicht. (but, rather) Sie ging stumm weiter.
21. (When) Ich hörte seine Stimme. Ich erkannte ihn gleich.
22. (Since) Wir haben noch Zeit. Ich trinke noch eine Tasse Kaffee.
23. Machen Sie das Licht aus. (before) Sie gehen nach Hause.
24. (By . . . ing) Ich rauche nicht mehr. Ich spare viel Geld.
25. Der Mantel ist sehr hübsch. (but) Ich finde ihn zu teuer.
26. Ich konnte nicht einkaufen gehen. (because) Ich hatte kein Geld.
27. Ich weiß nicht. (if) Sie ist heute zu Hause.
28. (Since) Wir haben das Haus verkauft. Wir wohnen in einem Hotel.
29. Er kennt diese Stadt nicht besonders gut. (although) Er wohnt sechs Jahre hier.
30. (While) Ich war in Hamburg. Ich bin jede Woche in die Oper gegangen.
31. (If) Er fragt Sie nach meiner Adresse. Geben Sie sie ihm.
32. Ich kann ihn abholen. (or) Willst du das machen?
33. Ich lernte ihn kennen. (when) Ich war an der Universität.
34. Ich sage es dir. (so that) Du bist vorbereitet.
35. Es ist möglich. (that) Er ist im Büro.
36. Sie stand um zwei Uhr auf. (because) Sie konnte nicht mehr schlafen.
37. (Every time) Wir sehen ihn. Er sieht müde aus.

Synthetic exercises

Use *all* of the elements to make a complete compound sentence. Be careful to reorder the elements should this be necessary.

Example: **Obwohl** / Restaurant / sein / weltbekannt // das Essen /
sein / gar nicht teuer
Obwohl das Restaurant weltbekannt ist, ist das Essen gar nicht
teuer.

1. Ich / sein / noch / sehr jung // **als** / ich / wohnen / Stuttgart
2. Wissen / du // **ob** / du / können / kommen / heute/?
3. **Da** / ich / gehen / Bibliothek // ich / zurückbringen / deine
Bücher
4. Karl / haben / vor zwei Jahren / Unfall // **und** / er / fahren /
seitdem / nicht mehr
5. Monika / aufstehen / zwei Uhr // **weil** / sie / können / schlafen /
nicht mehr
6. Ich / wollen / waschen / mir / Hände // **bevor** / wir / essen
7. Paul / kennen / Stadt / nicht gut // **obwohl** / er / wohnen /
seit Jahren / hier
8. Ich / gerade / hören // **daß** / Hilde / sein / krank
9. Ich / zuwinken / ihm // **aber** / er / nicht / sehen / mich
10. **Wenn** / er / verlassen / Büro // er / zumachen / Fenster
11. Er / nicht / grüßen / mich // **sondern** / weitergehen / stumm
12. **Obwohl** / er / sein / siebzig Jahre alt // er / gehen / jeden Tag
/ ins Büro
13. **Solange** / er / spielen / Tennis // er / werden / nicht / dick
14. Ich / verstehen / den Film // **nachdem** / ich / sehen / ihn / dreimal.
(*first clause: present perfect, second clause: past perfect*)
15. Ich / sagen / es / dir // **damit** / du / sein / vorbereitet
16. **Als** / ich / hören / seine Stimme // ich / erkennen / ihn / sofort
17. Ich / nicht / sprechen / mit ihm // **seitdem** / er / zurückkommen /
aus den Ferien
18. Ich / trinken / Tasse Kaffee // **während** / ich / warten / auf dich
19. Er / sich / warm / anziehen // **da** / es / kalt / werden
20. Ich / sparen / viel Geld // **indem** / ich / rauchen / nicht mehr

Express in German

Most of these sentences contain conjunctions. A few of them, however,
contain adverbs or prepositions that can be confused with conjunctions.

1. It's a pretty coat, but I think (**finden**) it's too expensive.
2. We went to the opera every week while we were in Hamburg.
3. If he asks you for my address, give it to him.

4. I'll stay here until you come back.
5. We can play cards this evening, or we can go to a movie if you want to.
6. Every time I think of it, I have to laugh.
7. When will you have time?
8. He looks much better since he's been working less.
9. My wife couldn't go shopping because she didn't have any money.
10. He showed us that he could do it.
11. Albrecht hasn't lived here since August.
12. I'm not sure, but I think he's in his office.
13. Do you know if she's home?
14. Call me up as soon as you arrive.
15. Two years ago he had an accident and since then he hasn't driven any more.
16. Stop it before it's too late.
17. Speak louder so that I can hear you better.

18. Since I'm going to the library anyway, I'll take your books back.
19. After we had visited our friends in Munich, we went to Berlin.
20. When they go to Berlin, they always stay in a good hotel.
21. I want to wash my hands before we eat.
22. Although he's seventy years old, he goes to the office every day.
23. Ever since they sold their house they have been living in a hotel.
24. I met him when I was at the university.
25. After she had seen the film three times, she finally understood it.
26. I save a lot of money by not smoking.
27. He doesn't know the city very well although he's lived here for six years.
28. Turn off the light before you go home.
29. I haven't spoken to him since he returned.
30. As soon as he speaks you'll notice (**merken**) he's an American.
31. I'm just telling you so that you'll be prepared.
32. Since we were driving through Heidelberg anyway, we visited Uncle Max.
33. I waved (**zuwinken**) to him, but he didn't see me.
34. Do you know if he's found it?
35. I'd heard that she was sick.
36. Since then he has been feeling (**sich fühlen**) much better.
37. Can't you wait until we are home?
38. I am only reading this book because I have to.
39. I drank a cup of coffee while I was waiting for you.
40. He read for two hours, and after that he went to bed.
41. When will you know if he's coming?

42. Every time we see him he looks tired.
43. Stay here as long as you want.
44. I have to hurry (**sich beeilen**) because our guests will be here soon.
45. When I heard his voice, I recognized him immediately. ——> *gleich*
46. Why don't you come to my place (**zu mir**) after the concert?
47. It never snows before the first of December.
48. I'll help you if I can.
49. Whenever he leaves the office, he closes the windows.
50. I gave him a book because I know that he likes to read.
51. I don't know where she is, but I'll look for her.
52. You can come by boat, or you can fly.

subjunctive I: indirect speech

chapter eleven

I. INTRODUCTION

There are essentially two ways of reporting what another person has said or written. The easier way is to use a direct quotation:

Die Münchener sagen: „Unser Bier ist das beste."
(People from Munich say, "Our beer is best.")

De Gaulle sagte: „Frankreich ist das bedeutendste Land Europas."
(De Gaulle said, "France is the most important country in Europe.")

As you can see, German and English treat direct quotations in basically the same manner: the speaker's exact words are reproduced and enclosed in quotation marks. The introductory statement that identifies the speaker **(Die Münchener sagen, De Gaulle sagte)** is separated from the quotation by a colon in German, by a comma in English.

It is much more common, however, to use *indirect quotation*. Indirect quotation reproduces what the speaker says, but not necessarily in the speaker's exact words.

DIRECT QUOTATION   De Gaulle said, "France is the most important country in Europe."

INDIRECT QUOTATION   De Gaulle said (that) France is the most important country in Europe.

DIRECT QUOTATION   People from Munich say, "Our beer is best."

INDIRECT QUOTATION   People from Munich say (that) their beer is best.

Indirect quotation is essentially the same in German—with one exception. When quoting indirectly, the German speaker can choose one of three verb forms (or moods), depending on his *attitude* toward the original quotation. The three forms are:

> subjunctive I
> indicative
> subjunctive II

A. Subjunctive I

Subjunctive I is used in formal, impartial reporting:

> De Gaulle sagte, daß Frankreich das bedeutendste Land Europas **sei.**

Sei is the subjunctive I counterpart of **ist.** By choosing this form of the verb, the reporter (person reporting) shows that he is maintaining an objective distance from de Gaulle's words. He is neither agreeing nor disagreeing with them, but merely attributing the statement to its source.

B. Indicative

If the same person were to write:

> De Gaulle sagte, daß Frankreich das bedeutendste Land Europas **ist.**

one might infer that the reporter is positively disposed toward de Gaulle's statement. **Ist** is in the indicative mood; it implies a statement of fact.

C. Subjunctive II

> De Gaulle sagte, daß Frankreich das bedeutendste Land Europas **wäre.**

The use of the subjunctive II form **wäre** implies a certain skepticism on the reporter's part. Essentially he is implying that de Gaulle's statement is open to question and is using subjunctive II (a form used with contrary-to-fact statements) to indicate this.

These three distinctions, while real and important, are nevertheless quite subtle and are usually reserved to carefully written German—newspaper articles, magazines, prepared speeches, books, essays, term papers (!). In everyday conversation the tendency is to avoid subjunctive I and to choose instead between the indicative and subjunctive II.

II. FORMS OF SUBJUNCTIVE I

A. Present tense

The present tense of subjunctive I is derived from the present tense of the indicative and is formed by adding the following subjunctive endings to the stem of the verb:

−e	−en
−est	−et
−e	−en

Note that subjunctive I verb forms never have the stem-vowel change found in their present indicative counterparts.

PRESENT INDICATIVE	SUBJUNC-TIVE I	PRESENT INDICA-TIVE	SUBJUNC-TIVE I	PRESENT INDICA-TIVE	SUBJUNC-TIVE I
ich sehe	sehe	kann	könne	werde	werde
du siehst	sehest	kannst	könnest	wirst	werdest
er sieht	sehe	kann	könne	wird	werde
wir sehen	sehen	können	können	werden	werden
ihr seht	sehet	könnt	könnet	werdet	werdet
sie sehen	sehen	können	können	werden	werden

The only exception is the verb **sein,** which has no endings in the 1st and 3rd persons singular:

ich	**sei**	wir	seien
du	seiest	ihr	seiet
er	**sei**	sie	seien

B. Past tense

The past tense of subjunctive I is derived from the present perfect tense of the indicative:

PRESENT PERFECT INDICATIVE	PAST SUBJUNCTIVE I
Er ist gekommen.	Er **sei** gekommen.
Er hat es gemacht.	Er **habe** es gemacht.

RULE: The past tense of subjunctive I is composed of:

> **sei** or **habe** + *a past participle*

C. Future tense

The future tense of subjunctive I is analogous to the future tense of the indicative. The only difference is that the auxiliary **werden** *uses subjunctive I forms.*

ich werde	wir werden
du werdest	ihr werdet
er werde	sie werden

D. Tense usage

In general the tense used in an indirect quotation is dependent upon the tense used in the direct quotation that underlies it.

1. If the direct quotation is in the present tense indicative, the indirect quotation must be in the present tense of subjunctive I:

PRESENT INDICATIVE	PRESENT SUBJUNCTIVE I
„Es **ist** notwendig."	Er sagte, es **sei** notwendig.

2. If the direct quotation is in any tense referring to *past time*, the indirect quotation is in the past tense of subjunctive I:

PAST TIME INDICATIVE	PAST SUBJUNCTIVE I
„Es **war** notwendig."	
„Es **ist** notwendig gewesen."	Er sagte, es **sei** notwendig **gewesen.**
„Es **war** notwendig gewesen."	

NOTE: Whereas the indicative has three tenses to use in referring to past time (past, present perfect, and past perfect), *subjunctive I has only one.*

3. If the direct quotation is in the future tense, the auxiliary **werden** is put into the present tense of subjunctive I:

FUTURE INDICATIVE   „Ippendorf **wird** eines Tages berühmt **sein.**"
PRESENT SUBJUNCTIVE I   Er sagte, Ippendorf **werde** eines Tages berühmt **sein.**

E. Mandatory substitution of subjunctive II for subjunctive I

In certain instances subjunctive I forms and indicative forms are identical. Whenever this is the case, *subjunctive II forms must be used.* (They must be used even though the subjunctive II forms may be identical with those of the past tense of the indicative.)

„Wir haben etwas gefunden."
Sie behaupten, sie (~~haben~~) hätten etwas gefunden.

F. Subjunctive II stays subjunctive II

If the original quotation is in subjunctive II, the indirect quotation will also be in subjunctive II:

„Ich wäre damit zufrieden."
("I'd be satisfied with that.")

Er sagt, er wäre damit zufrieden.

„Man könnte das auch anders machen."
("One could do that another way.")

Er sagte, man könnte das auch anders machen.

⊡ DRILLS

Direct to indirect statements

Put the following sentences into subjunctive I.

Example: Ich habe nichts davon gehört.
           Er sagt, er **habe nichts davon gehört.**

1. Der Mercedes ist der beste Wagen.
   Herr Benz meint, der Mercedes . . .

2. Wir haben zuviel zu tun.
Alle Studenten behaupten, sie . . .
3. Er ist daran schuld.
Man sagt, er . . .
4. Er hat nichts gegen unseren Plan.
Er versicherte uns, er . . .
5. Wir haben etwas gefunden.
Sie riefen, daß . . .
6. Herr Stern war immer ein vorsichtiger Fahrer.
Im Bericht stand, daß . . .
7. Ich habe mich geirrt.
Herr Hausmann behauptet, daß er . . .
8. Wir waren da, aber wir konnten nichts finden.
Sie sagen, sie . . .
9. Es geht mir in Wien sehr gut.
Er schreibt, es . . .
10. England könnte wieder eine Weltmacht werden.
Der Minister meinte, England . . .
11. Ich habe vor, ein Buch darüber zu schreiben.
Herr Karst sagt, er . . .
12. Er wurde ermordet.
Man sagt, er . . .
13. Die Königin hat sich erkältet.
Es wurde berichtet, daß die Königin . . .
14. Herr Schmidt ist nicht im Büro.
Die Sekretärin sagt, Herr Schmidt . . .
15. Ich kenne keinen besseren Wagen.
Er hat gesagt, daß er . . .
16. Wir sind nie in Amsterdam gewesen.
Sie behaupten, sie . . .
17. Ein Krieg mit China käme nicht in Frage.
Diesem Artikel nach, . . .

Direct to indirect reports

Put the following sentences into subjunctive I.

1. Ein Hubschrauber der französischen Armee ist in der Nähe von Augsburg abgestürzt. Alle fünf Insassen kamen mit dem Leben davon.
Aus München wurde heute berichtet, daß . . .

2. Die Hausmusik ist heute so rar, weil die Eltern fehlen, die die Energie besitzen, ihre Kinder zum Musikunterricht zu zwingen.
Ein Kritiker behauptet . . .

(2)   sei   fehlten (fehlen wurden)
besäßen (besitzen wurden)

3. Marseilles wurde am Dienstag von der Polizei „abgeriegelt“. An allen größeren Straßen hätten die Beamten Sperren errichtet. Sie kontrollierten alle vorbeigehenden Wagen. Mehrere Personen wurden festgenommen, aber die Gesuchten waren nicht dabei. Es handelte sich um die Männer, die in der vorigen Woche einen Geldtransport überfallen und 450.000 Franc erbeutet hatten.

   Unser Korrespondent berichtete, daß . . .

4. In den USA ist etwas Undenkbares geschehen: ein Minister entschuldigte sich bei einem Journalisten für eine Taktlosigkeit. Nachdem ein Korrespondent eine etwas scharfe Frage an Verteidigungsminister McNamara gestellt hatte, verlor der Minister seine Beherrschung. Er gestikulierte wild, schlug mit der Faust auf den Tisch und rief: „Ich habe die Nase voll von diesen Andeutungen.“ Einen Tag später bat McNamara den Reporter in sein Büro und entschuldigte sich für seinen Wutanfall.

   Man sagt, daß in den USA . . .

5. Mit Tränengas und Schlagstöcken ging die Bonner Polizei gegen Studenten vor, die beim Sommerfest der Universität zwei Feuer entzündet hatten. Die Feuerwehr ist von Randalierern behindert worden. Beamte, die man darauf eingesetzt hat, sind mit Flaschen beworfen worden.

   Folgendes wurde uns Dienstag mitgeteilt: . . .

Reconstruction of indirect discourse

In Adalbert Stifter's "Brigitta," the narrator presents the following information as indirect quotation. Reconstruct Stifter's original text by putting the two excerpts into subjunctive I.

Der Major ist nicht in der Gegend geboren. Er stammt von einer sehr reichen Familie. Er ist seit seiner Jugend fast immer auf Reisen gewesen, man weiß eigentlich nicht recht wo, so wie man auch nicht weiß, in welchen Diensten er sich den Majorsrang verdient hat.

. . .

(Brigitta) hält ihre Dienerschaft zusammen, ist tätig und wirtschaftet vom Morgen bis in die Nacht. Man kann hier sehen, was unausgesetzte Arbeit vermag. (Der Major) ist, als er sie kennenlernte, ihr Nachahmer geworden und hat ihre Art und Weise auf seiner Besitzung eingeführt. Bis jetzt hat er es nie bereut. Er . . . ist mehrere Jahre nicht zu ihr hinübergekommen. Dann wurde sie einmal todkrank: da ist er zu ihr über die Heide geritten und hat sie gesund gemacht.

special problems

chapter twelve

I. BASIC WORD ORDER

A. Order of direct and indirect objects

1. Introduction

Many German and English verbs can take both a *direct object* (D.O.) and an *indirect object* (I.O.):

	I.O.	D.O.
Ich schicke	**dem Chef**	**eine Karte.**
(I'm sending	*the boss*	*a postcard.*)
Ich kaufe	**dem Jungen**	**einen Mantel.**
(I'm buying	*the boy*	*a coat.*)

The *direct object* is the person or thing immediately acted upon. In our examples it designates:

> *what* is being sent (a postcard)
> and: *what* is being bought (a coat)

The *indirect object* indicates the "destination" of the direct object. Since the indirect object is almost always a person, it tells us *whom* the direct object is intended for. In our examples:

D.O.   I.O.
The postcard is intended for *the boss.*
The coat   is intended for *the boy.*

2. Order of Noun and Pronoun Objects

Ich schicke dem Chef die Liste.

In the example above, both the direct object and the indirect object are *nouns.* But either one—or both—can be replaced by personal pronouns. German arranges these pronoun objects in a certain order, depending on whether the *direct* object is a noun or a pronoun.

RULES:
1. *If the direct object is a noun, it follows the indirect object.*

I.O.   D.O.
Ich schicke dem Chef **die Liste.**
Ich schicke ihm   **die Liste.**

2. *If the direct object is a personal pronoun, it precedes the indirect object.*

D.O.   I.O.
Ich schicke **sie** dem Chef.
Ich schicke **sie** ihm.

NOTE: It is the *direct* object that determines the order. Whether the indirect object is a noun or a pronoun has no effect on the order of objects.

3. Indefinite Pronouns

Words like **nichts, alles,** and **etwas** are called *indefinite pronouns.* As far as word order is concerned, *they behave like nouns.* This means that they must follow an indirect object.

I.O.   D.O.
Ich schicke dem Chef **etwas.**
Ich schicke ihm   **etwas.**

4. *Agreement of Nouns and Pronouns*

If a personal pronoun is substituted for a noun, it must agree with the noun it replaces. That is, it must reflect the same gender, number, and case. The following table shows the agreement of nouns and of 3rd person pronouns.

		Singular	
	MASCULINE	NEUTER	FEMININE
NOM.	der Mann, der Tisch: **er**	das Kind, das Buch: **es**	die Dame, die Zeitung: **sie**
ACC.	den Mann, den Tisch: **ihn**	das Kind, das Buch: **es**	die Dame, die Zeitung: **sie**
DAT.	dem Mann, dem Tisch: **ihm**	dem Kind, dem Buch: **ihm**	der Dame, der Zeitung: **ihr**
		Plural ALL GENDERS	
NOM.	die Männer, Tische, Kinder, Bücher, Damen, Zeitungen: **sie**		
ACC.	die Männer, etc.		**sie**
DAT.	den Männern, etc.		**ihnen**

The 1st and 2nd person pronouns are as follows:

NOM.	ich	du	wir	ihr	Sie
ACC.	mich	dich	uns	euch	Sie
DAT.	mir	dir	uns	euch	Ihnen

▣ DRILLS

Pronoun replacement of noun indirect objects

Replace the noun indirect object with a personal pronoun.

> Example: Fräulein Sutter bringt dem Chef die Post.
> Fräulein Sutter bringt **ihm** die Post.

1. Herr Lange bringt den Gästen den Rotwein.
2. Er gibt der Katze den Goldfisch.
3. Wir zeigen Herrn Jantz das Haus.
4. Er zeigt den Kindern das Pferd.
5. Wir bringen der Dame Blumen.
6. Ich kaufe den Jungen etwas.
7. Eva sagt der Mutter alles.
8. Bringt ihr dem Lehrer ein Geschenk?
9. Ich schicke Inge einen Brief.

Pronoun replacement of noun direct objects

Replace the noun direct object with a personal pronoun.

> Example: Fräulein Sutter bringt dem Chef die Post.
> Fräulein Sutter bringt **sie** dem Chef.

1. Wir zeigen den Kindern das Pferd.
2. Ich bringe der Dame Blumen.
3. Eva sagt der Mutter die Adresse.
4. Er gibt der Katze den Fisch.
5. Bringt ihr dem Lehrer das Geschenk?
6. Ich zeige Herrn Jantz den Garten.
7. Bringen Sie den Gästen den Wein?

Pronoun replacement of noun direct and indirect objects

Answer the following questions in the form suggested, *replacing all nouns with pronouns.*

> Example: „Bringen Sie dem Chef die Post?"
> „Ja, ich bringe **sie ihm.**"

1. „Gibst du Helga den Schlüssel?"
   „Ja, ich gebe . . . "
2. „Zeigt er uns das Haus?"
   „Ja, er zeigt . . . "
3. „Gibt er Felix den Wagen?"
   „Ja, er gibt . . . "
4. „Zeigen Sie der Dame das Kleid?"
   „Ja, ich zeige . . . "

5. „Sagt sie uns die Adresse?“
   „Ja, sie sagt . . . “
6. „Kaufen wir Vater das Buch?“
   „Ja, wir kaufen . . . “
7. „Wirfst du Karl den Ball?“
   „Ja, ich werfe . . . “
8. „Bringt er Mutter die Blumen?“
   „Ja, er bringt . . . “
9. „Gibst du ihm das Geld?“
   „Ja, ich gebe . . . “
10. „Zeigen Sie ihnen den Brief?“
    „Ja, ich zeige . . . “
11. „Schicken Sie Inge die Karte?“
    „Ja, ich schicke . . . “
12. „Gibt sie Franz das Paket?“
    „Ja, sie gibt . . . “
13. „Gibt er uns die Telefonnummer?“
    „Ja, er gibt . . . “
14. „Kaufst du Peter das Geschenk?“
    „Ja, ich kaufe . . . “
15. „Erklären Sie ihnen das Problem?“
    „Ja, ich erkläre . . . “

B. Order of adverbs

When a German sentence contains two or more adverbial expressions,
they occur in the following order:

TIME **wann** / *when*	MANNER **wie** / *how*	PLACE **wo** / *where*

	WANN	WIE	WO
Ich fahre	immer	langsam.	
Ich fahre	sehr oft		nach Berlin.
Ich fahre		schnell	nach Hause.
Ich fahre	in zwei Wochen		nach Deutschland.

NOTE: As you can see from the prepositional phrases **nach Berlin, nach
Hause, in zwei Wochen,** and **nach Deutschland,** entire phrases can function
as adverbs.

◻ DRILLS

Word order with adverbial expressions

Put the adverbial expressions into their proper order. (This drill does *not* require the use of case endings.)

1. Ich fahre   (nach Stuttgart
                   morgen).
2. Er arbeitet   (immer
                   zu Hause).
3. Er bleibt   (hier
                   zehn Tage).
4. Ich gehe   (nach Hause
                   sehr selten).
5. Wir sind   (da
                   bald).
6. Machst du das   (immer
                   so)?
7. Wir bleiben   (in Amerika
                   zwei Jahre).
8. Ich gehe   (zu Hans
                   später).
9. Sie singt   (meistens
                   zu laut).
10. Man ißt   (in Frankreich
                   sehr gut).

Express in German

1. He's staying here ten days.
2. One eats very well in France.
3. We'll be there soon.
4. I'm going to Hans' later.
5. He always works at home.
6. I'm going to Stuttgart tomorrow.
7. We're staying there two years.
8. Do you always do it that way?
9. He usually sings too loud.
10. I very rarely go home.

Word order with adverbial expressions

(This drill *requires* the use of case endings.)

1. Wir gehen   (ins Theater
          am Freitag).
2. Wir kommen   (morgen
          zu euch).
3. Er fährt   (auf das Land
          im Juli).
4. Ich arbeite   (im Büro
          ganz allein).
5. Er bleibt   (bei uns
          zwei Wochen).
6. Sie gehen   (ins Restaurant
          nach dem Konzert).
7. Ich fahre   (nach Deutschland
          nächstes Jahr).
8. Hans fährt   (mit dem Wagen
          in die Stadt).
9. Er kommt   (mit dem Zug
          morgen).
10. Ich fahre   (nach Mainz
          am siebzehnten [17.] August).

Express in German

1. We're going to the country in July.
2. I'm going to the theater on Friday.
3. I'm going to Germany next year.
4. He's working alone in his office.
5. He's staying at his place for two weeks.
6. He's coming on the train tomorrow.
7. I'm going to Mainz in August.
8. We're going home after the concert.

C. Position of NICHT (and NIE) in the simple sentence

In a simple sentence **nicht** comes

after subject, verb, + all objects:

Ich gebe es ihm **nicht.**
Gibst du es mir **nicht?**

before everything else:

Ich sehe ihn **nicht** oft.   (before time expression)
Er ist **nicht** zu Hause.   (before expression of place)
Er läuft **nicht** schnell.   (before expression of manner)
Das ist **nicht** schön.   (before predicate adjective)
Sie geht **nicht** weg.   (before separable prefix)
Er will **nicht** bleiben.   (before infinitive)
Wir haben ihn **nicht** gesehen.   (before past participle)

EXCEPTIONS:
1. *specific time expressions*

Ich arbeite **heute (diese Woche)** nicht.

Nicht comes *after specific* time expressions, but *before general* time expressions (e.g. Ich sehe ihn nicht **oft.**).

2. *special stress*

Nicht can come before an object that is being given special emphasis:

Ich gab es nicht Karl (sondern Hans).

This implies a contrast, e.g. *not* to Karl *but rather* to Hans.

▣ DRILLS

Introductory drills on negative constructions

Negate the following statements and questions.

1. Siehst du ihn?
2. Ich verstehe ihn.
3. Bleibt er hier?
4. Ich finde das Buch sehr interessant.
5. Er ist immer hier.
6. Gehst du heute abend nach Hause?
7. Arbeitet er zu Hause?
8. Singt sie zu laut?
9. Machst du das immer so?
10. Ich sehe ihn sehr oft.
11. Er ist jetzt da.

12. Ich komme aus Berlin.
13. Werden Sie müde?
14. Ich sag's dir.

Express in German

1. I don't understand him.
2. Aren't you going home this evening?
3. He isn't there now.
4. Aren't you getting tired?
5. Don't you see him?
6. I don't find that book very interesting.
7. Isn't she singing too loud?
8. I don't come from Berlin.
9. Doesn't he work at home?
10. Don't you always do it that way?
11. I don't see him very often.
12. He isn't always here.
13. I won't tell you.
14. Isn't he staying here?

Advanced drills on negative constructions

Negate the following statements and questions.

1. Warum fährst du mit dem Zug?
2. Sie arbeitet allein im Büro.
3. Alwin ist heute in die Stadt gegangen.
4. Kurt ist gestern gekommen.
5. Können Sie das für mich machen?
6. Er ist heute vorbeigekommen.
7. Das ist sehr interessant.
8. Das Hotel liegt neben dem Bahnhof.
9. Laufen Sie gern Ski?
10. Das ist leicht zu machen.
11. Ich kann es heute machen.
12. Er hat uns sehr gut unterhalten.

Express in German

1. I can't do it today.
2. Kurt didn't come yesterday.

3. That isn't very interesting.
4. Why didn't you take the train?
5. Don't you like to ski?
6. She isn't working at the office.
7. That isn't easy to do.
8. Can't you do that for me?
9. Alwin didn't go downtown today.
10. He didn't come by yesterday.
11. He didn't entertain us very well.
12. The hotel isn't next to the railroad station.

Wed.
10-28-81

II. SETZEN / SITZEN, LEGEN / LIEGEN, HÄNGEN / HÄNGEN

German and English have three pairs of look-alike verbs that are also related in meaning:

setzen / **sitzen**	to set / to sit
legen / **liegen**	to lay / to lie
hängen / **hängen**	to hang / to hang

1. **Setzen, legen,** and **hängen** are *transitive* (i.e. can take a direct object):

SUBJECT	VERB	D.O.	ADVERB PHRASE
Die Gäste	legen	ihre Mäntel	aufs Bett.

Sitzen, liegen, and **hängen** are *intransitive* (i.e. cannot take a direct object):

SUBJECT	VERB	ADVERB PHRASE
Die Mäntel	liegen	auf dem Bett.

No direct object is possible.

2. When *adverbs of place* are used with the *transitive* verbs **setzen, legen,** and **hängen,** they answer the question **wohin** / *where* (*to*).

Adverbs of place used with the *intransitive* verbs **sitzen, liegen,** and **hängen** answer the question **wo** / *where.*

Thus: Die Gäste legen ihre Mäntel **auf das** Bett.   (**wohin**)
but: Die Mäntel liegen **auf dem** Bett.   (**wo**)*

---

*For a discussion of the distinction between **wo** and **wohin,** see p. 102, "Two-way Prepositions."

3. **Setzen, legen, hängen** (*action*) are *weak* (regular) verbs.
Sitzen, liegen, hängen (*condition*) are *strong* (irregular) verbs.

The following table compares the principal parts of these verbs with those of their English counterparts:

Comparison of Principal Parts

Transitive			Intransitive		
INFINITIVE	PAST	PRESENT PERFECT	INFINITIVE	PAST	PRESENT PERFECT
setzen to set	**setzte** set	**hat gesetzt** has set	**sitzen** to sit	**saß** sat	**hat gesessen** has sat
legen to lay	**legte** laid	**hat gelegt** has laid	**liegen** to lie	**lag** lay	**hat gelegen** has lain
hängen to hang	**hängte** hung	**hat gehängt** has hung*	**hängen** to hang	**hing** hung	**hat gehangen** has hung

stellen stellte hat gestellt stehen stand ist gestanden

☐ DRILLS
to put
to place   *to stand*

Substitution drills (past and present perfect tenses)

Put the following present tense sentences into the past tense and the present perfect tense.

1. Er hängt die Jacke an den Haken.
2. Die Jacke hängt an dem Haken.
3. Die Frau setzt das Kind auf den Stuhl.
4. Das Kind sitzt auf dem Stuhl.
5. Man legt die Karten auf den Tisch.
6. Seine Karten liegen auf dem Tisch.

Synthetic exercises

Make complete sentences in the present tense, past tense, and present perfect tense.

1. Wir / sitzen / an / Fenster   *Wir sitzen am Fenster*
2. Erich / hängen / Jacke / an / Haken   *Erich hängt die Jacke*

an die Haken

---

*English has a regular transitive verb: *to hang   hanged   has hanged*, but it is reserved for the specific case of *to execute by hanging*.

Warum liegst du solange im Bett

3. Warum / liegen / du / solange / in / Bett/?
4. Frau / setzen / Paket / auf / Stuhl   *Die Frau setzt das Paket auf den Stuhl*
5. Wir hängen / das Schild / über / Tür
6. Zeitung / liegen / auf / Tisch
7. Schlüssel / hängen / an / Tür
8. Vater / legen / Zeitung / auf / Stuhl
9. Kinder / sitzen / auf / Sofa
10. Bild / hängen / über / Bett
11. Ich / legen / Mäntel / auf / Bett
12. Mutter / setzen / Tassen / auf / Tisch

5. Wir hängen das Schild über die Tür.

Express in German   *6. Die Zeitung liegt auf dem Tisch.*

1. Mother set the cups on the table. *(12)*
2. We were sitting at the window. *Wir saßen am Fenster*
3. I laid the coats on the bed. *Ich legte die Mäntel auf das Bett*
4. Erich has hung his jacket on the hook. *Erich hat seinen Mantel an die Haken gehängt.*
5. The picture hangs over the bed.
6. Why did you lie in bed so long?   *6. Warum hast du in dem Bett solange gelegen?*
7. The children were sitting on the sofa.
8. The woman set her package on the chair.
9. Father laid his newspaper on the chair.   *Die Kinder saßen auf dem Sofa*
10. We've hung the sign over the door.
11. The keys are hanging on the door.
12. The newspaper is lying on the table.

10. Wir haben das Schild über die Tür gehängt.

5. Das Bild hängt über dem Bett.

9. Der Vater legte seine Zeitung auf den Stuhl

III. ADJECTIVAL NOUNS

A. Introduction   *11. Die Schlüssel hängen an der Tür.*

Look at the following two sentences:

> Hans is a German exchange student.
> Hans is a German.

In the first sentence, *German* is an adjective: it modifies the noun *student*.
In the second sentence, however, *German* is a noun.

Adjectives can also function as nouns in German. In fact, this is far more common in German than it is in English.

B. General rules

1. *Capitalization*

Adjectives functioning as nouns are capitalized (as are all German nouns):

> der Deutsche

2. *Adjective Endings*

German adjectives take the same adjective endings when they function as nouns as they do when functioning as adjectives:

> Er ist ein junger deutscher Student.
> Er ist ein junger Deutscher.

Similarly:

> Sie ist eine junge deutsche Studentin.
> Sie ist eine junge Deutsche.

with **der**-words	MASCULINE		FEMININE		PLURAL	
NOM.	der	Deutsche	die	Deutsche	die	Deutschen
ACC.	den	Deutschen	die	Deutsche	die	Deutschen
DAT.	dem	Deutschen	der	Deutschen	den	Deutschen
GEN.	des	Deutschen	der	Deutschen	der	Deutschen
with **ein**-words						
NOM.	ein	Deutscher	eine	Deutsche	keine	Deutschen
ACC.	einen	Deutschen	eine	Deutsche	keine	Deutschen
DAT.	einem	Deutschen	einer	Deutschen	keinen	Deutschen
GEN.	eines	Deutschen	einer	Deutschen	keiner	Deutschen

after **wenige, einige, andere, mehrere, viele**	
NOM.	viele Deutsche
ACC.	viele Deutsche
DAT.	vielen Deutschen
GEN.	vieler Deutscher

> when not preceded by a limiting word
>
> Er ist Deutscher.
> Sie ist Deutsche.
> Sie sind Deutsche.

a. Common adjectival nouns

der Bekannte	acquaintance, friend
der Verwandte	relative
der Fremde	stranger
der Angestellte	employee
der Beamte	official (governmental employee)
(but: die Beamtin, which is a normal noun)	

der Alte	old man
der Blinde	blind man
der Kranke	sick man
der Tote	dead man
der Arme	poor man
der Reiche	rich man
der Dumme	stupid man
der Kluge	smart, clever man
die Blonde	blond girl or woman

3. Gender

1. *Masculine* and *feminine* adjectival nouns usually refer to people:

der Kranke	sick *man* or *boy*
die Kranke	sick *woman* or *girl*

2. *Neuter* adjectival nouns refer to things, qualities, or characteristics:

Das ist **das Gute (Schlechte, Dumme)** daran.
(That's *the good thing* [*bad thing, stupid thing*] about it.)

Neuter adjectival nouns are commonly found after **etwas, nichts, viel, wenig,** and **alles:**

Er hat **nichts Interessantes** gesagt.
(He didn't say anything interesting.)

Er will Ihnen **etwas Wichtiges** sagen.
(He wants to tell you something important.)

Adjectives following **etwas, nichts, viel,** and **wenig** take *strong* endings.

etwas anderes*
nichts Besonderes
viel Gutes (much that is good)
wenig Neues (little that is new)

Adjectives following **alles** take *weak* endings.

alles mögliche*

⊡ DRILLS

Adjectival nouns (masculine and feminine)

Supply the correct endings.

1. Wer ist d____ Blond____ (*feminine*) da drüben?
2. Er ist doch kein Fremd____ (*masculine*).
3. Viel____ Deutsch____ wohnen im Mittelwesten.
4. Er muß ein____ Krank____ (*masculine*) besuchen.
5. D____ Arm____ (*plural*) klagen immer über d____ Reich____ (*plural*).
6. Der Brief ist von mein____ Verwandt____ (*plural*).
7. Ach, Siegfried. Du Arm____!
8. Er ist ein alt____ Bekannt____.
9. Ich kenne einig____ Angestellt____ bei Mercedes-Benz.
10. Er darf nie ohne sein____ Alt____ (*feminine*) ausgehen.
11. Sein____ Verwandt____ wohnen alle in Leipzig.
12. Ist er Beamt____?
13. Sehen Sie d____ arm____ Blind____ (*masculine*) da drüben?
14. Haben Sie viel____ alt____ Bekannt____ in dieser Stadt?
15. Wir können d____ Arm____ (*feminine*) nicht helfen.
16. Gehen Sie zu d____ Beamt____ (*masculine*) da vorne (up front)!
17. Er hat ein____ Tot____ (*masculine*) in der Badewanne gefunden.
18. Ist sie dein____ Verwandt____?
19. Viel____ Fremd____ besuchen diese Stadt.
20. Ich muß ein____ Bekannt____ (*masculine*) helfen.

*Note that andere(s) and mögliche(s) are *not* capitalized.

Adjectival nouns (neuter)

Supply the correct endings.

1. Das ist nichts Wichtig____.
2. Haben Sie etwas Neu____ gehört?
3. Er hat nichts Interessant____ gesagt.
4. Haben Sie je etwas Ähnlich____ gesehen?
5. Er tut alles möglich____.
6. Das Theaterstück hatte wenig Gut____.
7. Das ist nichts Besonder____.
8. Das Schlecht____ daran ist, daß ich mehr arbeiten muß.
9. Alles Gut____! (*a wish:* "All the best to you!")
10. Das Nett____ daran ist, daß Eva da sein wird.
11. Alles ander____ muß bis Freitag fertig sein.
12. „Im Westen nichts Neu____" ("All Quiet on the Western Front").
13. Das ist das Dumm____ daran.
14. Ich möchte etwas Einfach____ kaufen.
15. Können Sie mir etwas ander____ zeigen?

Adjectival nouns (mixed drills)

Supply the correct endings.

1. Ist sie ein____ Verwandt____ von dir?
2. Das ist nichts Besonder____.
3. Wer ist d____ Schön____ (*feminine*) da drüben?
4. Er ist ein alt____ Bekannt____ von mir.
5. Das ist das Dumm____ daran.
6. Viel____ Fremd____ besuchen diese Stadt.
7. Er hat nichts Interessant____ gesagt.
8. Wir können d____ Arm____ (*masculine*) nicht helfen.
9. Ist sie Beamt____?
10. Sie tut alles möglich____.
11. Alles ander____ muß bis Freitag fertig sein.
12. Viel____ Blind____ führen ein fast normales Leben.
13. Kann der Arzt d____ Krank____ (*masculine*) helfen?
14. Diese Firma hat nur wenig____ Angestellt____.
15. Haben Sie nichts Ähnlich____?
16. Alles Gut____!
17. Ein Kleid, bitte! Etwas Einfach____.
18. Viel____ Deutsch____ wohnen in dieser Stadt.
19. Haben Sie etwas Neu____ gehört?

20. Es ist nichts Wichtig____.
21. Er hat nur wenig____ Bekannt____ in dieser Stadt.
22. Das ist das Schlecht____ daran.
23. Ist der Brief von dein____ Verwandt____ (*plural*) in Berlin?
24. Können Sie mir etwas ander____ zeigen?
25. Das Nett____ daran ist, daß Eva da sein wird.

Express in German   *10-14-81*

1. Who is the pretty girl over there? *Wer ist die Hübscher dadrüben*
2. He didn't say anything interesting. *Er hat nichts Interessantes gesagt*
3. Can you show me something different? *etwas anderes*
4. A lot of Germans live in Princeton. *Viele Deutsche*
5. Is he a relative of yours? *Ist er ein Verwandte von dir*
6. It's nothing important.
7. This firm only has a few employees. *nur wenige Angestellte*
8. That's the stupid thing about it. *Das ist das Dumme daran*
9. The letter is from my relatives in Berlin.
10. Don't you have anything like it (similar)?
11. He's an old friend (acquaintance) of mine.
12. He's a high official. *Er ist ein   Beamter*
13. All the best! *Alles gute!*
14. It was nothing special. *Es war nichts Besonderes*
15. He only has (a) few friends (acquaintances) in this city. *einige Freunde*
16. Many blind people lead an almost normal life.
17. His relatives live in Leipzig.
18. Have you heard anything new?
19. The poor always complain about the rich. *Die Armen klagen immer*
20. We're doing everything possible. *über die Reichen*
21. Were many strangers there?
22. The nice thing about it is that Eva will be there.

Das Nette daran ist, daß Eva dort sein wird

alles Möglicher

IV. THE PRESENT PARTICIPLE

A. Formation

infinitive + **d**	
kochend	boiling
führend	leading

The German present participle is formed by adding the ending **–d** to the infinitive form of the verb.

B. Usage

German present participles usually function as *adjectives* and take the usual adjective endings:

> kochendes Wasser   boiling water
> die führenden Kritiker   the leading critics

Occasionally, one finds them in other environments:

„In die Hütte **tretend** hatte er den Todgeweihten beim Abendessen am Tisch **sitzend** vorgefunden, in Hemdsärmeln mit beiden Backen **kauend.**"

> *Bertolt Brecht* „Der Augsburger Kreidekreis"

(*Stepping* into the cottage he had found the doomed man at dinner, *sitting* at the table in his sleeves, *chewing* with both cheeks.)

Such constructions are rare, however, and almost never occur in *spoken* German.

C. Contrastive usage

The German present participle should never be confused with progressive forms of English verbs.

> Er **sitzt** am Tisch.   He *is sitting* at the table.
> Er **saß** am Tisch.   He *was sitting* at the table.

German has *no* progressive verb forms.

▣ DRILLS

Present participles

Change the infinitives into present participles, and supply the correct adjective endings.

1. Kein denken____ Mensch tut so etwas.
2. Das ist ein brennen____ Problem.
3. Aber er ist doch ein zahlen____ Gast.
4. Ich möchte ein Zimmer mit fließen____ Wasser.

5. In kommen____ Jahren machen wir das anders.
6. Das war eine überraschen____ Antwort.
7. Er sagte es mit ein____ wohlwollen____ Lächeln. *(11)*
8. Das ist ein____ wachsen____ Firma.
9. Vorsicht vor d__em__ fahren__en__ Zug! *(dative)*
10. Das ist ein stören____ Lärm.
11. Es war ein____ erschrecken____ Erlebnis.
12. Sie sagte es mit zittern____ Stimme.
13. Ja, Heidi, es gibt doch fliegen____ Untertassen.
14. Das ist kein überzeugen____ Argument.
15. Er ist ein hervorragend____ Physiker.

Express in German   *10-14-81*

1. That was a surprising answer.
2. That's a burning problem.
3. But he's a paying guest.   *mit*
4. She said it with (a) trembling voice.   *zitternder Stimme*
5. That's a disturbing noise.   *störendes Geräusch*
6. He's an outstanding physicist.
7. I'd like a room with running water.   *Ich möchte ein Zimmer mit*
8. That's not a convincing argument.   *Fließendem Wasser*
9. It was a frightening experience.   *kein überzeugendes*
10. It's a growing firm.   *wach*
11. He said it with a well-meaning smile.
12. In coming years we'll do that differently. *(5)*
13. Yes, Heidi, there really are flying saucers. *(13)*
14. Watch out for (**Vorsicht vor**) the moving train. *(9)*
15. No thinking person does something like that. *(1)*

V. INFINITIVAL CONSTRUCTIONS

A. Basic pattern: the infinitival clause

English and German treat infinitival clauses in essentially the same manner:

> Er bat mich, ihm **zu helfen.**
> (He asked me *to help* him.)

> Es ist zu spät, ins Kino **zu gehen.**
> (It's too late *to go* to the movies.)

The basic difference is that the *German infinitive must stand at the end of its clause*. It is always immediately preceded by the preposition **zu**:

> ..., ihm **zu helfen.**   (... *to help* him.)
> ..., ins Kino **zu gehen.**   (... *to go* to the movies.)

In both English and German the infinitive may take an object (**ihm** zu helfen), or it may be found with prepositional phrases or expressions of time, manner, and place (e.g. **ins Kino** zu gehen).

NOTE: Er fing sehr früh an **zu arbeiten.**
Er fing sehr früh **zu arbeiten** an.

When the construction consists *only* of an infinitive and the preposition **zu** (zu arbeiten), it is no longer strictly treated as a clause. For this reason it may be incorporated into the main clause (er fing sehr früh **zu arbeiten** an), or it may appear after the main clause (er fing sehr früh an **zu arbeiten**). Unlike German clauses it is *not* separated from the main clause by a comma. As soon as another element is added, however, the infinitival construction becomes a clause and must be separated from the main clause by a comma:

> Er fing sehr früh an, an seiner Dissertation zu arbeiten.

B. Contrastive grammar   *sehr, sehr wichtig!*

Under certain conditions German may *not* use infinitival constructions—even though English commonly uses them in these same environments. Note carefully the three points where English and German go radically separate ways:

1. *when the subordinate clause is introduced by a question word*

I don't know *when* to come.	Ich weiß nicht, **wann** ich kommen soll.
what to say.	**was** ich sagen soll.
who to see.	**wen** ich sehen soll.
where to go.	**wohin** ich gehen soll.

In these instances English has a choice between two constructions:

> I don't know *when to come*
> and: I don't know *when I'm supposed to come.*

German has no such choice. It *must* use a construction similar to the second English example, that is, a construction with a *subject* and a *conjugated verb:*

> Ich weiß nicht, **wann** ich kommen **soll.**

2. *when* **sagen** *is used as the conjugated verb in the main clause*

He *told* me *to do it.*

He *told* me *that I should do it.*   Er **sagte** mir, **daß ich es tun soll.**

Here again English has a choice, whereas German does not. After **sagen** German requires a full clause with a subject and a conjugated verb form (normally a form of **sollen**).

However, when another verb is substituted for **sagen,** an infinitival clause is used:

> Er befahl mir, das **zu tun.**
> (He ordered me *to do* it.)

3. *with modal auxiliaries,* **helfen** *and* **lassen,** *and the verbs of the senses**

He *wants to* (*would like to*) come along.   Er **will (möchte)** mitkommen.

German never uses **zu** before infinitives in modal expressions, whereas the English equivalents often require the preposition *to* (e.g. he wants *to* come along).

In the case of **wollen** and **möchten,** however, there is an even more radical difference between English and German structure:

> He wants (would like) <u>her</u> *to come along.*
> Er will (möchte), **daß** <u>sie</u> **mitkommt.**

In the English sentence *wants to* and *would like to* can take an object. The object (in this case: *her*) also functions as the subject of the infinitive (i.e. *she* is to come along). Such a construction is impossible in German. Once again, German requires a clause containing a *subject* and a *conjugated verb form* (e.g. daß **sie mitkommt**).

NOTE: **Er will es tun.**

In this example, **es** is the object of **tun** (to do *it*), not of **wollen.** It is the modal (**wollen, möchten**) that cannot take an object in such a construction, not the dependent infinitive (**tun**).

---

*See also p. 137, "Omission of **zu** with Infinitives in Modal Expressions."

C. UM . . . ZU, OHNE . . . ZU, (AN)STATT . . . ZU

The prepositions **um, ohne,** and **(an)statt** may introduce infinitival clauses:

> um
> ohne   . . . zu + *infinitive*
> (an)statt

Um . . . zu: Er kam, **um** das Buch abzuholen.
  (He came [*in order*] *to* pick up the book.)

Ohne . . . zu: Sie sagte es, **ohne** mich anzusehen.
  (She said it, *without* look*ing* at me.)

(An)statt . . . zu: Statt hier **zu** sitzen, sollten wir ihn suchen.
  (*Instead of* sitt*ing* here, we should look for him.)

1. **Um . . . zu** is used to indicate purpose. It must be used (instead of just **zu**) when one can sensibly use *in order to* in the equivalent English sentence.

2. **Ohne . . . zu** and **(an)statt . . . zu** are used in conjunction with *infinitives*. However, the English equivalents require a present participle:

  . . . , ohne mich **anzusehen.** (without *looking* at me.)
  Statt hier **zu sitzen, . . .** (Instead of *sitting* here, . . .)

D. SEIN + ZU + infinitive

Look at the following examples:

> Das **ist** leicht **zu machen.**
> (That *is* easy *to do*.)

> So etwas **ist** nicht leicht **zu finden.**
> (Something like that *isn*'t easy *to find*.)

Both English and German have the same pattern, but it is far more common in German than it is in English:

> Das **ist** nicht **zu machen.**
> (That can't be done.)

> Das **ist** in jedem Laden **zu finden.**
> (That can be found in any store.)

When the pattern cannot be used sensibly in English, one usually finds *can + a passive infinitive* (passive infinitive = *be + past participle*, e.g. *be bought*).

▣ DRILLS

Synthetic exercises (infinitive clauses)

1. Er bat mich // helfen / ihm
2. Es ist zu spät // gehen / heute abend / Kino
3. Es hörte auf // regnen
4. Ich finde es sehr schwer // verstehen / Film
5. Wir haben vor // fahren / nächstes Jahr / Wien
6. Es ist Zeit // gehen / nach Hause
7. Ich habe keine Lust // werden / Arzt
8. Es ist immer nett // bekommen / Brief / von dir
9. Darf ich Sie bitten // nehmen / Platz / ?
10. Es ist fast unmöglich // kriegen / jetzt / Karten

Express in German

1. It's time to go home. Es ist Zeit n
2. He asked me to help him.
3. It stopped raining. Es hört auf zu reghen
4. We plan to go to Vienna next year.
5. It's too late to go to the movies tonight.
6. May I ask you to take a seat?
7. It's always nice to get a letter from you.
8. I have no desire to become a doctor.
9. I find it very hard to understand this movie.
10. It's almost impossible to get tickets now.

Synthetic exercises (subordinate clauses)

1. Ich wußte nicht // was / ich / sollen / sagen
2. Erich sagte uns // daß / wir / sollen / bleiben / hier
3. Er will nicht // daß / ich / helfen / ihm
4. Wissen Sie // wohin / Sie / müssen / gehen / ?
5. Ich will // daß / Anna / mitkommen
6. Kannst du mir sagen // wie / man / machen / das / ?
7. Ich sagte dir // daß / du / sollen / warten

8. Er zeigte uns // wo / wir / sollen / parken / Wagen
9. Willst du nicht // daß / ich / einladen / Hans / ?
10. Wir wissen nicht // mit wem / wir / sollen / sprechen
11. Ich sage dir // wen / du / sollen / anrufen

Express in German   *10-23*

1. He doesn't want me to help him. *3*
2. I didn't know what to say. *1*
3. Erich told us to stay here.
4. We don't know whom to talk to. *10*
5. He showed us where to park the car. *8*
6. I want Anna to come along. *5*
7. I told you to wait. *7*
8. Do you know where to go? *4*
9. Can you tell me how to do that? *6*
10. Hanna doesn't want me to invite Kurt. *Hanna will nicht, daß ich Kurt einladen.*
11. I'll tell you whom to call. *11*

Synthetic exercises (prepositions with infinitive clauses)

1. Oft nimmt er den Wagen // ohne / fragen / Vater
2. Karl arbeitet nachts // um / verdienen / mehr Geld
3. Anstatt / fliegen / nach Wien // blieben wir eine zweite Woche in München
4. Ich ging in die Stadt // um / kaufen / neue / Platte
5. Anstatt / essen / zu Hause // gehen wir lieber ins Restaurant
6. Barbara ging weg // ohne / geben / mir / Adresse

Express in German

1. I went into town to buy a new record. *4*
2. Instead of eating at home, let's go to a restaurant. *5*
3. Karl works nights to earn more money. *2*
4. Barbara went away without giving me her address. *6*
5. Instead of flying to Vienna we stayed a second week in Munich. *3*
6. He often takes the car without asking his father. *1*

Synthetic exercises (**zu** + infinitives)

Example: Das / sein / leicht / sagen
Das ist leicht zu sagen.

1. Das / sein / schwer / sagen
2. Dieser Wein / sein / kaum / trinken
3. Bergmanns Filme / sein / schwer / verstehen
4. Volkswagen / sein / leicht / fahren
5. Herr Rey / sein / nicht / finden
6. Das / sein / kaum / glauben
7. Solche Bücher / sein / überall / kaufen
8. So etwas / sein / eigentlich / erwarten

Express in German

1. That's hard to believe. Das ist schwer zu glauben.
2. Mr. Rey couldn't be found. 5
3. Bergmann's films are hard to understand. 3
4. Volkswagens are easy to drive. 4
5. That's hard to say. 1
6. This wine is scarcely to be drunk. 2
7. Books like that can be found everywhere. 7
8. Something of the sort was to be expected. 8

Synthetic exercises (mixed drills)

1. Er bat mich // helfen / ihm
2. Ich sage dir // wen / du / sollen / anrufen
3. Oft nimmt er den Wagen // ohne / fragen / Vater
4. Es hörte auf // regnen
5. Wir wissen nicht // wen / wir / sollen / sprechen
6. Das / sein / schwer / sagen
7. Es ist zu spät // gehen / heute abend / Kino
8. Willst du nicht // ich / einladen / Hans / ?
9. Karl arbeitet nachts // um / verdienen / mehr Geld
10. Wir haben vor // fahren / nächstes Jahr / Wien
11. Er zeigte uns // wo / wir / sollen / parken / Wagen
12. Dieser Wein / sein / kaum / trinken
13. Ich finde es sehr schwer // verstehen / Film
14. Ich sagte dir // du / sollen / warten
15. Anstatt / fliegen / nach Wien // blieben wir eine zweite Woche in München
16. Ich habe keine Lust // werden / Arzt
17. Kannst du mir sagen // wie / man / machen / das / ?
18. Bergmanns Filme / sein / schwer / verstehen

19. Es ist Zeit // gehen / nach Hause
20. Ich will // Anna / mitkommen
21. Ich ging in die Stadt // um / kaufen / neue Platte
22. Es ist immer nett // bekommen / Briefe / von dir
23. Wissen Sie // wohin / Sie / sollen / gehen / ?
24. Volkswagen / sein / leicht / fahren
25. Darf ich Sie bitten // nehmen / Platz / ?
26. Er will nicht // ich / helfen / ihm
27. Anstatt / essen / zu Hause // gehen wir lieber ins Restaurant
28. Es ist fast unmöglich // kriegen / jetzt / Karten
29. Erich sagte uns // wir / sollen / bleiben / hier
30. Das / sein / kaum / glauben
31. Ich wußte nicht // was / ich / sollen / sagen
32. Barbara ging weg // ohne / geben / mir / Adresse
33. So etwas / sein / eigentlich / erwarten

Express in German

1. He doesn't want me to help him.
2. It's time to go home.
3. That's hard to believe.
4. I didn't know what to say.
5. He asked me to help him.
6. I went into town to buy a record.
7. Erich told us to stay here.
8. It stopped raining.
9. Bergmann's films are hard to understand.
10. We didn't know whom to talk to.
11. We plan to go to Vienna next year.
12. Instead of eating at home, let's go to a restaurant.
13. He showed us where to park the car.
14. It's too late to go to the movies tonight.
15. Volkswagens are easy to drive.
16. I want Anna to come along.
17. May I ask you to take a seat?
18. Karl works nights to earn more money.
19. I told you to wait.
20. It's always nice to get a letter from you.
21. That's hard to say.
22. Do you know where to go?

23. I have no desire to become a doctor.
24. Barbara went away without giving me her address.
25. Can you tell me how to do that?
26. I find it very hard to understand this movie.
27. This wine is scarcely to be drunk.
28. Hanna doesn't want me to invite Kurt.
29. It's almost impossible to get tickets now.
30. Instead of flying to Vienna, we stayed a second week in Munich.
31. I'll tell you whom to call.
32. Something of the sort was to be expected.
33. He often takes the car without asking his father.

VI. REFLEXIVE PRONOUNS AND VERBS

A. Introduction

A verb is said to be *reflexive* when its subject and object are the same person or thing: *I* hurt *myself.*

I and *myself* obviously refer to the same person. *Myself* in the sentence *I hurt myself* is called a reflexive pronoun. An object is *always* a reflexive pronoun when it is identical with the subject. When an object is *not identical* with the subject, nouns or personal (not reflexive) pronouns are used.

REFLEXIVE	I hurt myself.
	He hurt himself.
NON-REFLEXIVE	I hurt him (the dog, etc.).
	He hurt me (his brother, etc.).

B. Reflexive pronouns

English uses the suffixes –*self* or –*selves* (e.g. myself, himself, ourselves, themselves) in forming reflexive pronouns.

German, on the other hand, has reflexive pronouns that are identical with the personal pronouns in all but the 3rd person singular and plural:

	PERSONAL PRONOUNS			REFLEXIVE PRONOUNS	
ACC.		mich		mich	ACC.
DAT.		mir		mir	DAT.
		dich		dich	
		dir		dir	
	ihn	es	sie	**sich**	
	ihm	ihm	ihr	**sich**	
		uns		uns	
		uns		uns	
		euch		euch	
		euch		euch	
		sie, Sie		**sich**	
		ihnen, Ihnen		**sich**	

NOTE: The polite form of the reflexive pronoun is *not* capitalized, e.g. Setzen Sie sich!

USAGE: Reflexive pronouns must be used when an *object* (*any* object) is identical with the subject of a sentence, which means that a reflexive pronoun can be:

1. *the direct object*

REFLEXIVE	NON-REFLEXIVE
Er erschoß **sich.**	Er erschoß es (das Reh).
(He shot himself.)	(He shot it [the deer].)

2. *the indirect object*

REFLEXIVE	NON-REFLEXIVE
Er kaufte **sich** eine Krawatte.	Er kaufte **ihm (seinem Bruder)** eine Krawatte.
(He bought himself a tie.)	(He bought him [his brother] a tie.)
Er bestellte **sich** ein Glas Wein.	Er bestellte **ihr** ein Glas Wein.
(He ordered himself a glass of wine.)	(He ordered her a glass of wine.)

Such indirect objects are *datives of reference*, i.e. the dative case is used to indicate who is to "receive" the direct object:

a tie *for himself* (*for his brother*)
a glass of wine *for himself* (*for her*)

3. *the object of a preposition*

Er hat kein Geld bei **sich.**
(He hasn't got any money on him [on his person].)

C. Reflexive verbs with direct objects

A reflexive verb is one that uses a reflexive pronoun to complete its meaning.

1. Verbs That Are Both Reflexive and Non-reflexive

A number of verbs may be used either reflexively or non-reflexively.

NON-REFLEXIVE	REFLEXIVE
Er machte es fertig.	**Er** machte **sich** fertig.
(He got it ready.)	(He got ready.)

NOTE: English often omits the reflexive pronoun. Rather than saying "He got *himself* ready," one more commonly says "He got ready." Such an omission of a reflexive pronoun is not possible in German.

a. Further examples

	NON-REFLEXIVE	REFLEXIVE
waschen	Er wäscht den Wagen.	Er wäscht **sich.**
	(He's washing the car.)	(He's washing.)
rasieren	Er rasiert einen Kunden.	Er rasiert **sich.**
	(He's shaving a customer.)	(He's shaving.)
√**beugen**	Er beugte seinen Kopf über den Tisch.	Er beugte **sich** über den Tisch.
	(He bent his head over the table.)	(He bent over the table.)
fürchten	Er fürchtet Hunde.	Er fürchtet **sich.**
	(He's afraid of dogs.)	(He's afraid.)
setzen	Er setzte es aufs Sofa.	Er setzte **sich** aufs Sofa.
	(He set it on the sofa.)	(He sat down on the sofa; *literally:* He set himself onto the sofa.)

bedienen	Bedienen Sie den Kunden da drüben! (Serve the customer over there!)	Bedienen Sie **sich**! (Serve or help yourself!)
an·ziehen	Er zog den Mantel an. (He put on the coat.)	Er zog **sich** an. (He got dressed.)
aus·ziehen	Er zog den Mantel aus. (He took off the coat.)	Er zog **sich** aus. (He got undressed.)
wundern	Das wunderte ihn. (That surprised him.)	Er wunderte **sich**. (He was surprised.)
erinnern	Das erinnerte ihn daran. (That reminded him of it.)	Er erinnerte **sich** daran. (He remembered it.)
interessieren	Das interessiert ihn. (That interests him.)	Er interessiert **sich** dafür. (He's interested in it.)

NOTE: There may be differences in translation and meaning depending upon whether a verb is used reflexively or non-reflexively. For example, **an·ziehen** means *to put on* (e.g. a coat) and **sich an·ziehen** means *to dress;* **erinnern** means *to remind* and **sich erinnern** means *to remember.*

2. Verbs That Are Only Reflexive

sich amüsieren (to have a good time)	Haben Sie **sich** gut amüsiert?
sich beeilen (to hurry)	Er mußte **sich** beeilen.
sich entschließen (to decide)	Hat er **sich** schon entschlossen?
sich erkälten (to catch cold)	Ich habe **mich** erkältet.
sich freuen auf + *acc.* (to look forward to)	Er freut **sich** auf die Ferien.
sich freuen über + *acc.* (to be happy about)	Er freute **sich** wirklich darüber.
sich gewöhnen an + *acc.* (to get used to)	Ich kann **mich** nicht an das heiße Wetter gewöhnen.

sich interessieren

sich irren (to be mistaken)	Sie irren **sich**.
sich schämen über + *acc.* (to be ashamed of)	Schämte sie **sich** nicht?
sich genieren (to be embarrassed)	Genieren Sie **sich** nicht!

D. Verbs with reflexive indirect objects

Reflexive indirect objects fall into three basic groups.

1. Datives of Reference

> Er kaufte **sich (ihm, seinem Bruder)** eine Krawatte.
> Er bestellte **sich (ihm, seinem Bruder)** eine Tasse Kaffee.

In these sentences the reflexive pronouns may be replaced by nouns or personal pronouns. Moreover, such sentences are complete even if one omits the dative expressions:

> Er kaufte eine Krawatte.
> Er bestellte eine Tasse Kaffee.

The addition of a dative object tells us who is going to receive the direct object:

> a tie *for himself* (*his brother*, etc.)

but it does not affect the basic meaning of the verb in any way.

2. Purely Reflexive Indirect Objects

Compare the meanings of the verbs in the following pairs:

merken (to notice)	Ich merke nichts. (I don't notice anything)
sich etwas merken (to keep in mind, make a mental note of, remember)	Ich werde es **mir** merken. (I'll keep it in mind.)
an·sehen (to look at)	Ich sah ihn lange an. (I looked at him for a long time.)

sich etwas an·sehen (to take a look at, look over, inspect)	Ich will **mir** das Haus ansehen. (I want to take a look at the house [look it over].)
denken an + *acc.* (to think)	Haben Sie an etwas anderes gedacht? (Were you thinking of something else?)
sich etwas denken (to imagine)	Das kann ich **mir** denken. (I can imagine that.)
vor·stellen (to introduce)	Stellen Sie ihn mir vor! (Introduce him to me.)
(sich) vor·stellen (to introduce [oneself])	Darf ich **mich** vorstellen? (May I introduce myself?)
sich etwas vor·stellen (to imagine, picture to oneself)	Ich kann es **mir** gut vorstellen. (I can just imagine it.)

In these cases the addition of the indirect object has a profound effect on the basic meaning of the verb. Moreover, the pronouns must always be reflexive; i.e. they may not be replaced by personal pronouns.

3. *Reflexive Usage When Referring to Parts of the Body*

Compare the following German sentences with their English equivalents:

Er hat **sich den** Arm gebrochen.	(He broke *his* arm.)
Ich wasche **mir die** Hände.	(I'm washing *my* hands.)
Er muß **sich die** Zähne putzen.	(He has to brush *his* teeth.)

Unlike English, German does not use possessive pronouns when referring to parts of the body. Instead it uses a definite article that is usually preceded by a dative reflexive pronoun (e.g. **sich die** Hände waschen).

▣ DRILLS

Form drills

Restate these sentences using the suggested subjects.

1. Wir müssen uns beeilen.   (ich, er, ihr)
2. Sie irren sich.   (du, ihr).

3. Ich freue mich auf die Ferien. (er, wir, sie)
4. Zieht euch schnell an! (du, Sie)
5. Ich will mir das Haus ansehen. (er, wir, sie)
6. Setzen Sie sich! (du, ihr)
7. Er hat sich gestern erkältet. (ich, wir)
8. Interessiert sie sich dafür? (du, er, ihr)
9. Er hat sich den Arm gebrochen. (ich)
10. Er kann sich nicht an das heiße Wetter gewöhnen. (ich, wir, sie)
11. Ich will mir die Hände waschen. (er, wir, sie)
12. Das muß ich mir merken. (du, er, wir, sie)
13. Erinnerst du dich an den Film? (er, ihr, Sie)
14. Ich habe mich entschlossen. (er, wir, sie)
15. Fürchten Sie sich? (du, er, ihr)
16. Kannst du es dir vorstellen? (ihr, Sie)
17. Er hat sich warm angezogen. (ich, wir)

Fill-ins

Supply the correct *reflexive* pronoun.

1. Mußt du _____ beeilen?
2. Fürchten Sie _____ nicht!
3. Hat er _____ schon rasiert?
4. Das muß ich _____ merken.
5. Ich muß _____ schnell fertigmachen.
6. Willst du _____ die Hände waschen?
7. Sie freut _____ nicht darüber.
8. Erinnerst du _____ an den Film?
9. Ich habe _____ gut amüsiert.
10. Ich will _____ das Haus ansehen.
11. Kannst du _____ nicht an das heiße Wetter gewöhnen?
12. Bediene _____!
13. Ich schäme _____ gar nicht.
14. Johann! Du mußt _____ die Zähne putzen.
15. Darf ich _____ vorstellen?
16. Die Jungen müssen _____ waschen.
17. Das kann ich _____ denken.
18. Geniert ihr _____ nicht?
19. Der alte Mann beugte _____ über den Tisch und sah nicht auf.
20. Hast du _____ erkältet?

21. Ich habe _____ den Arm gebrochen.
22. Ich interessiere _____ nicht für Kandinsky.

Synthetic exercises

These exercises include both reflexive and non-reflexive sentences.

Examples: Er / setzen / Buch / Tisch
Er setzt das Buch auf den Tisch.

Er / setzen / Sofa (*past*)
Er setzte sich aufs Sofa.

1. Er / müssen / beeilen
2. Er / beugen / über / Tisch
3. Hilda / fürchten / Hunde   *Hilda fürchtet sich vor den Hund.*
4. Freuen / Sie / auf / Ferien /? *die*
5. Ich / müssen / waschen / Hände   *Ich muss mir die Hände wasc...*
6. Interessieren / du / für / Film /?
7. Friseur / rasieren / Kunde   *Der*
8. Ich / erkälten (*present perfect*)
9. Er / beugen / über / Teller
10. Kurt / können / gewöhnen / nicht / an / Hitze   *die*
11. Ich / entschließen / schon   (*present perfect*)
12. Erinnern / Sie / nicht / an / Film /?
13. Anziehen / Sie / Mantel /?
14. Ich / müssen / putzen / Zähne
15. Genieren / du / nicht /?
16. Ich / irren / nicht   *Ich irre mich nicht*
17. Er / müssen / waschen / Wagen
18. Amüsieren / du / gut /? (*present perfect*)
19. Er / setzen / an / Tisch
20. Wir / müssen / fertigmachen / schnell

Express in German

1. He has to hurry.   *Er muss sich beeilen*
2. I have to get ready now.
3. She's afraid.   *Sie*
4. Sit down.
5. You're wrong.
6. I have to wash my hands.
   Ich muss die Hände waschen.
      mir

7. Aren't you ashamed?
8. He's washing the car.
9. I'm looking forward to the vacation.
10. I'm not interested in Kandinsky.
11. Are you afraid of dogs, Anna?
12. Have you already decided?
13. I want to take a look at the house.
14. Set it on the table.
15. Is he shaving?
16. Weren't you embarrassed?
17. Help (serve) yourself!
18. I'll have to keep that in mind.
19. She caught cold.
20. I have to brush my teeth.
21. He bent over the table.
22. May I introduce myself?
23. Did you have a good time?
24. He's shaving a customer.
25. I can imagine that.
26. Heinz broke his arm.
27. I can't get used to the hot weather.
28. Do you remember that movie?
29. He reminded me of it.
30. The children got dressed.

VII. FUTURE PERFECT

A. Formation

The future perfect, like the future, consists of **werden** + *infinitive*. The only difference is that the infinitive in this case is a so-called *perfect infinitive*.

The perfect infinitive consists of the *past participle of a verb* followed by the *infinitive of its perfect auxiliary* (i.e. **haben** or **sein**).

REGULAR INFINITIVE	PRESENT PERFECT	PERFECT INFINITIVE
rauchen	**hat** geraucht	**geraucht** <u>haben</u>
(to smoke)	(has smoked)	(to have smoked)

nehmen	**hat** genommen	genommen **haben**
(to take)	(has taken)	(to have taken)
sein	**ist** gewesen	gewesen **sein**
(to be)	(has been)	(to have been)
gehen	**ist** gegangen	gegangen **sein**
(to go)	(has gone)	(to have gone)
werden	**ist** geworden	geworden **sein**
(to become)	(has become)	(to have become)

Note that the perfect auxiliary can be either **sein** or **haben** depending upon the verb in question and that consequently the *perfect infinitive* will end in either **sein** or **haben.**

B. Comparison

		INFINITIVE	
FUTURE	Ich **werde** es	**nehmen.**	
	I *will*	*take*	it.

		PERFECT INFINITIVE	
FUTURE PERFECT	Ich **werde** es	**genommen haben.**	
	I *will*	*have taken*	it.

		INFINITIVE
FUTURE	Er **wird**	**gehen.**
	He *will*	*go.*

		PERFECT INFINITIVE
FUTURE PERFECT	Er **wird**	**gegangen sein.**
	He *will*	*have gone.*

As in all compound tenses, only the auxiliary (**werden** in this instance) can change; the infinitive is a constant:

	AUXILIARY	INFINITIVE
Ich	werde	gegangen sein.
Du	wirst	gegangen sein.
Er, sie es	wird	gegangen sein.

C. Usage

The future perfect (like the future) has both a literal and a figurative meaning.

1. Literal Meaning

The future perfect deals with the future as if it were already past time. This tense is to the future tense what the present perfect is to the present.

PRESENT	He's doing it (now).
PRESENT PERFECT	He *has done* it (by now).
FUTURE	He will do it (tomorrow).
FUTURE PERFECT	He *will have done* it (by tomorrow).

Both the present perfect and the future perfect imply that an action is *finished* (i.e. past) as of a certain point in time. In one instance that point is *now* (i.e. the present instant); in the other, the point is sometime in the future, e.g. *tomorrow*.

2. Figurative Meaning: Probability

In English as well as German, the future and the future perfect can be used to imply probability. The *future* connotes *present* probability. The *future perfect* connotes *past* probability. For example, if you hear a door slam, you might say:

> „Das wird Rudi sein." (future tense)
> ("That *will be* Rudi" *or* "That *is probably* Rudi.")

If you heard a door slam last night, you might now say:

> „Das wird Rudi gewesen sein." (future perfect)
> ("That *will have been* Rudi" *or* "That *was probably* Rudi.")

▣ DRILLS

Substitutions

Put the following *present perfect* sentences into the *future perfect*.

> Example: Das **ist** Rudi **gewesen.**
> Das **wird** Rudi **gewesen sein.**

1. Anna ist wohl zu Hause geblieben.
2. Er hat den Brief schon geschrieben.
3. Onkel Franz ist längst eingeschlafen.
4. Bald haben wir unser ganzes Geld ausgegeben.
5. Bis Montag habe ich die letzte Seminararbeit eingereicht.
6. Bis Freitag sind wir eine ganze Woche hier gewesen.
7. Bis morgen hast du seinen Namen vergessen.
8. Sie ist wohl nach Mitternacht angekommen.
9. Dieser Mantel hat über 200 Mark gekostet.
10. Bis nächstes Jahr sind die Kinder alle viel größer geworden.

Fill-ins

1. Er wird den Brief schon _____.
   (have written)
2. Bis morgen wirst du seinen Namen _____.
   (have forgotten)
3. Bis Freitag werden wir eine ganze Woche hier _____.
   (have been)
4. Bald werden wir unser ganzes Geld _____.
   (have spent)
5. Bis nächstes Jahr werden die Kinder alle viel größer _____.
   (have become)
6. Bis Montag werde ich die letzte Seminararbeit _____.
   (have handed in)

Synthetic exercises

Make complete sentences in the future perfect.

> Example: Das / sein / wohl / Rudi
>   Das wird wohl Rudi gewesen sein.

1. Er / schreiben / schon / Brief
2. Bis Freitag / sein / wir / ganze Woche / hier
3. Sie / ankommen / wohl / nach Mitternacht
4. Bis nächstes Jahr / werden / Kinder / alle / viel größer
5. Dieser Mantel / kosten / über 200 Mark
6. Bald / ausgeben / wir / unser ganzes Geld
7. Anna / bleiben / wohl / zu Hause

8. Bis morgen / vergessen / du / seinen Namen
9. Onkel Franz / einschlafen / längst
10. Bis Montag / einreichen / ich / letzte Seminararbeit

X Express in German

Use the future perfect.

Bis Montag
1. By Monday I'll have handed in my last seminar paper.
2. He has probably written the letter already.
3. By tomorrow you'll have forgotten his name.
4. Uncle Franz has probably long since fallen asleep. *sein*
5. By next year the children will all have gotten much bigger.
6. This coat probably cost over two hundred marks.
7. By Friday we'll have been here a whole week.
8. They probably arrived after midnight.
9. Soon we'll have spent all of our money.
10. Anna probably stayed home.

7. *Bis Freitag werden wir eine ganze Woche hier gewesen sein*

10. *Anna wird wohl zu Hause geblieben sein.*

strong and irregular verbs

INFINITIVE (3rd sing. pres.)	PAST (3rd sing. pres. subj. II)	PAST PARTICIPLE	MEANING
backen (bäckt)	**buk** *or* **backte** (büke *or* backte)	**gebacken**	to bake
befehlen (befiehlt)	**befahl** (beföhle)	**befohlen**	to command
beginnen	**begann** (begänne)	**begonnen**	to begin
beißen	**biß**	**gebissen**	to bite
bergen (birgt)	**barg** (bärge)	**geborgen**	to hide

bersten	**barst**	ist **geborsten**	to burst
(birst)	(bärste)		
bewegen	**bewog**	**bewogen**	to induce[1]
	(bewöge)		
biegen	**bog**	**gebogen**	to bend
	(böge)		
bieten	**bot**	**geboten**	to offer
	(böte)		
binden	**band**	**gebunden**	to bind
	(bände)		
bitten	**bat**	**gebeten**	to request
	(bäte)		
blasen	**blies**	**geblasen**	to blow
(bläst)			
bleiben	**blieb**	ist **geblieben**	to remain
braten	**briet**	**gebraten**	to roast
(brät *or*			
bratet)			
brechen	**brach**	**gebrochen**	to break
(bricht)	(bräche)		
brennen	**brannte**	**gebrannt**	to burn
	(brennte)		
bringen	**brachte**	**gebracht**	to bring
	(brächte)		
denken	**dachte**	**gedacht**	to think
	(dächte)		
dingen	**dingte** *or* **dang**	**gedungen**	to engage,
	(dänge)		hire
dringen	**drang**	ist, hat **gedrungen**	to press
	(dränge)		
dünken	**dünkte** *or* **deuchte**	**gedünkt** *or*	to seem
(*impers.*)		**gedeucht**	
(dünkt *or*			
deucht)			
dürfen	**durfte**	**gedurft**	to be allowed
(darf)	(dürfte)		
einladen	**lud . . . ein** *or*	**eingeladen**	to invite
	ladete . . . ein		
	(lüde . . . ein *or*		
	ladete . . . ein)		

---

[1] **Bewegen** meaning *to move* is weak.

empfehlen (empfiehlt)	empfahl (empfähle)	empfohlen	to recommend
erbleichen	erblich	ist erblichen	to grow pale
erlöschen (erlischt)	erlosch (erlösche)	erloschen	to go out (*of light*)
erschrecken[1] (erschrickt)	erschrak (erschräke)	ist erschrocken	to become frightened
essen (ißt)	aß (äße)	gegessen	to eat (*of people*)
fahren (fährt)	fuhr (führe)	ist, hat gefahren	to drive
fallen (fällt)	fiel	ist gefallen	to fall
fangen (fängt)	fing	gefangen	to catch
fechten (ficht)	focht (föchte)	gefochten	to fight
finden	fand (fände)	gefunden	to find
flechten (flicht)	flocht (flöchte)	geflochten	to braid
fliegen	flog (flöge)	ist, hat geflogen	to fly
fliehen	floh (flöhe)	ist geflohen	to flee
fließen	floß (flösse)	ist geflossen	to flow
fressen (frißt)	fraß (fräße)	gefressen	to eat (*of animals*)
frieren	fror (fröre)	gefroren	to freeze
gebären (gebiert *or* gebärt)	gebar (gebäre)	geboren	to bear
geben (gibt)	gab (gäbe)	gegeben	to give
gedeihen	gedieh	gediehen	to thrive
gehen	ging	ist gegangen	to go
gelingen	gelang (gelänge)	ist gelungen	to succeed

[1] **Erschrecken** used transitively is weak.

gelten	**galt**	**gegolten**	to be worth
(gilt)	(gälte)		
genesen	**genas**	ist **genesen**	to recover
	(genäse)		
genießen	**genoß**	**genossen**	to enjoy
	(genösse)		
geschehen	**geschah**	ist **geschehen**	to happen
(*impers.*)	(geschähe)		
(geschieht)			
gewinnen	**gewann**	**gewonnen**	to win
	(gewönne)		
gießen	**goß**	**gegossen**	to pour
	(gösse)		
gleichen	**glich**	**geglichen**	to resemble
gleiten	**glitt**	ist **geglitten**	to glide
glimmen	**glomm** *or* **glimmte**	**geglommen** *or*	to gleam
	(glömme)	**geglimmt**	
graben	**grub**	**gegraben**	to dig
(gräbt)	(grübe)		
greifen	**griff**	**gegriffen**	to seize
haben	**hatte**	**gehabt**	to have
(du hast,	(hätte)		
er hat)			
halten	**hielt**	**gehalten**	to hold
(hält)			
hängen	**hing**	**gehangen**	to hang
			(*intrans.*)
heben	**hob**	**gehoben**	to lift
	(höbe)		
heißen	**hieß**	**geheißen**	to be called
helfen	**half**	**geholfen**	to help
(hilft)	(hülfe)		
kennen	**kannte**	**gekannt**	to know
	(kennte)		
klimmen	**klomm**	ist **geklommen**	to climb
	(klömme)		
klingen	**klang**	**geklungen**	to sound
	(klänge)		
kneifen	**kniff**	**gekniffen**	to pinch
kommen	**kam**	ist **gekommen**	to come
	(käme)		

können	**konnte**	**gekonnt**	to be able
(kann)	(könnte)		
kriechen	**kroch**	ist **gekrochen**	to creep
	(kröche)		
laden	**lud**	**geladen**	to load; invite
(lädt)	(lüde)		
lassen	**ließ**	**gelassen**	to let
(läßt)			
laufen	**lief**	ist **gelaufen**	to run
(läuft)			
leiden	**litt**	**gelitten**	to suffer
leihen	**lieh**	**geliehen**	to lend
lesen	**las**	**gelesen**	to read
(liest)	(läse)		
liegen	**lag**	**gelegen**	to lie, recline
	(läge)		
lügen	**log**	**gelogen**	to (tell a) lie
	(löge)		
mahlen	**mahlte**	**gemahlen**	to grind
meiden	**mied**	**gemieden**	to avoid
melken	**molk** or **melkte**	**gemolken**	to milk
(melkt)	(mölke)	or **gemelkt**	
messen	**maß**	**gemessen**	to measure
(mißt)	(mäße)		
mögen	**mochte**	**gemocht**	to like; may
(mag)	(möchte)		
müssen	**mußte**	**gemußt**	must
(muß)	(müßte)		
nehmen	**nahm**	**genommen**	to take
(nimmt)	(nähme)		
nennen	**nannte**	**genannt**	to name
	(nennte)		
pfeifen	**pfiff**	**gepfiffen**	to whistle
preisen	**pries**	**gepriesen**	to praise
quellen	**quoll**	ist **gequollen**	to gush
(quillt)	(quölle)		
raten	**riet**	**geraten**	to advise
(rät)			
reiben	**rieb**	**gerieben**	to rub
reißen	**riß**	ist, hat **gerissen**	to rip
reiten	**ritt**	ist, hat **geritten**	to ride

rennen	**rannte** (rennte)	ist **gerannt**	to run
riechen	**roch** (röche)	**gerochen**	to smell
ringen	**rang** (ränge)	**gerungen**	to struggle, wrestle; wring
rinnen	**rann** (ränne)	ist **geronnen**	to run
rufen	**rief**	**gerufen**	to call
salzen	**salzte**	**gesalzen**	to salt
saufen (säuft)	**soff** (söffe)	**gesoffen**	to drink (*of* *animals*)
saugen	**sog** (söge)	**gesogen**	to suck
schaffen[1]	**schuf** (schüfe)	**geschaffen**	to create
scheiden	**schied**	ist **geschieden**	to separate
scheinen	**schien**	**geschienen**	to seem; shine
schelten (schilt)	**schalt** (schälte)	**gescholten**	to scold
schieben	**schob** (schöbe)	**geschoben**	to shove
schießen	**schoß** (schösse)	**geschossen**	to shoot
schlafen (schläft)	**schlief**	**geschlafen**	to sleep
schlagen (schlägt)	**schlug** (schlüge)	**geschlagen**	to strike
schleichen	**schlich**	ist **geschlichen**	to sneak
schließen	**schloß** (schlösse)	**geschlossen**	to close
schmeißen	**schmiß**	**geschmissen**	to fling, throw
schmelzen (schmilzt)	**schmolz** (schmölze)	ist, hat **geschmolzen**	to melt (*intrans.*)
schneiden	**schnitt**	**geschnitten**	to cut
schreiben	**schrieb**	**geschrieben**	to write
schreien	**schrie**	**geschrieen**	to cry

---

[1] **Schaffen** meaning *to work, to be busy* is weak.

schreiten	schritt	ist geschritten	to stride
schweigen	schwieg	geschwiegen	to be silent
schwellen	schwoll	ist geschwollen	to swell
(schwillt)	(schwölle)		(*intrans.*)
schwimmen	schwamm	ist, hat geschwommen	to swim
	(schwämme)		
schwinden	schwand	ist geschwunden	to disappear
	(schwände)		
schwingen	schwang	geschwungen	to swing
	(schwänge)		
schwören	schwor	geschworen	to swear
	(schwüre)		
sehen	sah	gesehen	to see
(sieht)	(sähe)		
sein	war	ist gewesen	to be
(ist)	(wäre)		
senden	sandte *or* sendete	gesandt	to send
	(sendete)	*or* gesendet	
sieden	sott	ist, hat gesotten	to boil
	(sötte)		
singen	sang	gesungen	to sing
	(sänge)		
sinken	sank	ist gesunken	to sink
	(sänke)		
sinnen	sann	gesonnen	to think
	(sänne)		
sitzen	saß	gesessen	to sit
	(säße)		
sollen	sollte	gesollt	shall
(soll)			
speien	spie	gespieen	to spit
spinnen	spann	gesponnen	to spin
	(spänne)		
sprechen	sprach	gesprochen	to speak
(spricht)	(spräche)		
sprießen	sproß	ist gesprossen	to sprout
	(sprösse)		
springen	sprang	ist gesprungen	to spring
	(spränge)		
stechen	stach	gestochen	to prick
(sticht)	(stäche)		

stecken	stak (stäke)	gesteckt	to stick (*intrans.*)
stehen	stand (stünde)	gestanden	to stand
stehlen (stiehlt)	stahl (stähle)	gestohlen	to steal
steigen	stieg	ist gestiegen	to ascend
sterben (stirbt)	starb (stürbe)	ist gestorben	to die
stieben	stob (stöbe)	ist gestoben	to scatter
stinken	stank (stänke)	gestunken	to stink
stoßen (stößt)	stieß	gestossen	to push
streichen	strich	ist, hat gestrichen	to stroke
streiten	stritt	gestritten	to argue
tragen (trägt)	trug (trüge)	getragen	to carry
treffen (trifft)	traf (träfe)	getroffen	to meet; hit
treiben	trieb	getrieben	to drive
treten (tritt)	trat (träte)	ist, hat getreten	to step
triefen	troff (tröffe)	getroffen	to drip
trinken	trank (tränke)	getrunken	to drink
trügen	trog (tröge)	getrogen	to deceive
tun (tut)	tat (täte)	getan	to do
verderben (verdirbt)	verdarb (verdürbe)	ist, hat verdorben	to spoil
verdrießen	verdroß (verdrösse)	verdrossen	to annoy
vergessen (vergißt)	vergaß (vergäße)	vergessen	to forget
verlieren	verlor (verlöre)	verloren	to lose ·

verlöschen (verlischt)	verlosch (verlösche)	ist verloschen	to extinguish
verschlingen	verschlang (verschlänge)	verschlungen	to wind; devour
verschwinden	verschwand (verschwände)	ist verschwunden	to disappear
verzeihen	verzieh (verziehe)	verziehen	to pardon
wachsen (wächst)	wuchs (wüchse)	ist gewachsen	to grow
wägen	wog (wöge)	gewogen	to weigh (*fig.*)
waschen (wäscht)	wusch (wüsche)	gewaschen	to wash
weichen	wich	ist gewichen	to yield
weisen	wies	gewiesen	to show
wenden	wandte *or* wendete	gewandt *or* gewendet	to turn
werben (wirbt)	warb (würbe)	geworben	to apply (for)
werden (wird)	wurde (würde)	ist geworden	to become
werfen (wirft)	warf (würfe)	geworfen	to throw
wiegen	wog (wöge)	gewogen	to weigh (*lit.*)
winden	wand (wände)	gewunden	to wind
wissen (weiß)	wußte (wüßte)	gewußt	to know
wollen (will)	wollte	gewollt	will
wringen	wrang (wränge)	gewrungen	to wring
ziehen	zog (zöge)	ist, hat gezogen	to pull, move
zwingen	zwang (zwänge)	gezwungen	to force

vocabulary

Nominative singular and plural forms are indicated; unusual genitive singular endings are also supplied. Principal parts, as well as the 3rd person singular present tense form, of strong and irregular verbs are given; weak verbs appear in the infinitive form only. The following symbols are used:

        * strong verb
        · separable prefix
      (s) verb with auxiliary **sein**

der **Abend, –e** evening
  aber but
  ***ab·fahren** to leave
    (fährt . . . ab), fuhr . . . ab,
    ist abgefahren
  ab·holen to pick up

  ab·riegeln to cordon off
  ab·schicken to send off
  ab·stürzen (s) to crash (*airplane*)
  acht eight
die **Adresse, –n** address

der **Agent,** –en, –en   agent
ähnlich   similar
alle   all
allein   alone
alles   everything
als   when; than
als ob   as though, as if
alt, älter, ältest–   old
der **Amerikaner,** —   American
amerikanisch (*adj.*)   American
sich **amüsieren**   to have a good time
an (*two-way prep.*)   on (*with vertical surfaces*), at, to
ander–   other
ändern   to change
anders   otherwise, another way
die **Andeutung,** –en   allusion, insinuation
der **Anfang,** –e   beginning
***an·fangen**   to begin (fängt . . . an), fing . . . an, angefangen
der **Angestellte,** –n (*adj. noun*)   employee
***an·kommen**   to arrive (kommt . . . an), kam . . . an, ist angekommen
***an·rufen**   to call up (ruft . . . an), rief . . . an, angerufen
***an·sehen**   to look at (sieht . . . an), sah . . . an, angesehen
sich etwas ***an·sehen**   to take a look at, look over
anstatt   instead of
antworten + *dat.*   to answer (*with people*)

antworten (auf + *acc.*)   to answer (*with things*)
***an·ziehen**   to put on (zieht . . . an), zog . . . an, angezogen
sich ***an·ziehen**   to get dressed
der **Anzug,** –e   suit
der **Apfel,** –   apple
der **April**   April
die **Arbeit,** –en   work
arbeiten (an + *dat.*)   to work (on)
das **Argument,** –e   argument
arm, ärmer, ärmst–   poor
der **Arm,** –e   arm
die **Armee,** –n   army
der **Artikel,** —   article
die **Art und Weise**   way, way of doing things
der **Arzt,** –e   doctor
der **Atem**   breath
auf (*two-way prep.*)   on (*with horizontal surfaces*)
***auf·halten**   to hold up (hält . . . auf), hielt . . . auf, aufgehalten
auf·hören   to stop, cease
auf·machen   to open
auf·räumen   to clean up, straighten up
der **Aufsatz,** –e   essay, paper
***auf·stehen**   to get up; stand up (steht . . . auf), stand . . . auf, ist aufgestanden
auf und ab   back and forth; up and down
auf·wachen (s)   to wake up
das **Auge,** –n   eye
der **August**   August
aus (+ *dat.*)   from; out of

*aus·geben to spend
(gibt . . . aus), gab . . . aus,
ausgegeben
*aus·gehen to go out
(geht . . . aus), ging . . . aus,
ist ausgegangen
aus·machen to turn out
*aus·sehen to look (*appearance*)
(sieht . . . aus), sah . . . aus,
ausgesehen
die Außenpolitik foreign policy
außer (+ *dat.*) besides
*aus·steigen to get out, climb
out
(steigt . . . aus), stieg . . . aus,
ist ausgestiegen
aus·suchen to select
ausverkauft sold out
*aus·ziehen to take off; move
out
(zieht . . . aus), zog . . .
aus, hat, ist ausgezogen
sich *aus·ziehen to get undressed
das Auto, –s car
der Automat, –en, –en coin-operated machine
der Autor, –en author
der Autoschlosser, — automobile mechanic

die Backe, –n cheek
die Badewanne, –n bathtub
der Bahnhof, ⸚e railroad station
bald soon
der Ball, ⸚e ball
die Banane, –n banana
der Bart, ⸚e beard
bauen to build
der Baum, ⸚e tree

Bayern Bavaria
bayrisch Bavarian
der Beamte, –n (*adj. noun*) official, government employee
die Beamtin, –nen official, government employee (*female*)
bedeutend significant, important
bedienen to serve
sich bedienen to serve oneself
sich beeilen to hurry
*befehlen to order
(befiehlt), befahl, befohlen
begegnen (s) + *dat.* to meet, run into
*beginnen to begin
(beginnt), begann, begonnen
*begraben to bury
(begräbt), begrub, begraben
behandeln to treat
behaupten to assert, maintain, say
die Beherrschung control
behindern to obstruct, hinder
bei (+ *dat.*) near; at (a person's house)
beiseite aside, to the side
das Beispiel, –e example
bekannt known, well-known
der Bekannte, –n (*adj. noun*) acquaintance, friend
*bekommen to get, receive
(bekommt), bekam, bekommen
belegen to occupy
beleidigen to insult
das Benzin gasoline

beobachten   to observe
bequem   comfortable
bereuen   to regret
der **Berg, –e**   mountain
der **Bericht, –e**   report
berichten   to report
berühmt   famous
besichtigen   to look at (*sight-seeing*)
die **Besitzung, –en**   estate
besonder– (*adj.*)   special
besonders   especially
*besprechen**   to discuss
(bespricht), besprach, besprochen
besser   better
bestellen   to order (food, etc.)
am besten   best
bestimmt   certainly, for certain, for sure
der **Besuch, –e**   visit
besuchen   to visit
außer Betrieb   out of order
das **Bett, –en**   bed
beugen   to bend
sich **beugen (über + acc.)**   to bend (over)
bevor (*conj.*)   before
beworfen   thrown, plastered
(**Sie wurden mit Flaschen beworfen.** Bottles were thrown at them.)
bezahlen   to pay (for)
die **Bibliothek, –en**   library
das **Bier, –e**   beer
das **Bild, –er**   picture
billig   cheap
die **Birne, –n**   pear
bis (*conj.*)   until

(*prep.* + *acc.*)   until; as far as; to; by
bitte   please
die **Bitte, –n**   request
*bitten (um + acc.)**   to ask (for)
(bittet), bat, gebeten
*bleiben**   to stay, remain
(bleibt), blieb, ist geblieben
der **Bleistift, –e**   pencil
die **Blume, –n**   flower
die **Bombe, –n**   bomb
böse   angry, mad
brauchen   to need; use
braun   brown
*brechen**   to break
(bricht), brach, gebrochen
*brennen**   to burn
(brennt), brannte, gebrannt
der **Brief, –e**   letter
die **Briefmarke, –n**   postage stamp
die **Brille, –n**   (eye)glasses
*bringen**   to bring, take
(bringt), brachte, gebracht
das **Brot**   bread
die **Brücke, –n**   bridge
der **Bruder, ÷**   brother
das **Buch, ÷er**   book
der **Bürgermeister, —**   mayor
das **Büro, –s**   office
der **Bus, –se**   bus

der **Chef, –s**   boss
(das) **China**   China

da (*adv.*)   there
(*conj.*)   since, because

dabei *sein to be there, be present
da drüben over there
dagegen against it
die **Dame, –n** lady
damit so that
dankbar grateful
danken to thank
dann then
daß that
dauern to last
die **Decke, –n** blanket
decken to set (a table)
dein your (*familiar singular*)
sich **etwas *denken** to imagine (denkt), dachte, gedacht
***denken (an + *acc.*)** to think (about)
denn (*conj.*) for, because
derselbe, dasselbe, diesselbe the same
deutsch German
der **Deutsche, –n** (*adj. noun*) German
(das) **Deutschland** Germany
der **Dezember** December
der **Dialekt, –e** dialect
der **Dichter, —** poet; writer
dick fat
die **Dienerschaft, –en** staff (of servants)
der **Dienst, –e** service
der **Dienstag, –e** Tuesday
dieser, dieses, diese this
das **Ding, –e** thing
direkt direct(ly)
der **Direktor, –en** director
doch but
der **Donnerstag, –e** Thursday
drei three

dritt– third
drohen (+ *dat.*) to threaten
dumm, dümmer, dümmst– stupid
dunkel, dunkler, dunkelst– dark
durch (+ *acc.*) through
durchsuchen to search
***dürfen** may, to be allowed to (darf), durfte, gedurft

die **Ecke, –n** corner
die **Ehe, –n** marriage
ehrlich honest, honorable
eigentlich actually, really
einfach simple, simply
der **Einfluß, ⸚sse** influence
ein·führen to introduce
einige some, several
Einkäufe machen to do (some) shopping
ein·kaufen to shop
ein·kaufen gehen to go shopping
das **Einkommen** income
***ein·laden** to invite (lädt . . . ein), lud . . . ein, eingeladen
ein·lösen to cash (a check)
einmal once
ein·reichen to hand in
***ein·schlafen** to fall asleep (schläft . . . ein), schlief . . . ein, ist eingeschlafen
ein·setzen to put into action
***ein·steigen** to get in, climb in (steigt . . . ein), stieg . . . ein, ist eingestiegen
die **Eltern** (*pl.*) parents

*empfehlen   to recommend
(empfiehlt), empfahl,
empfohlen

das Ende, –n   end

endlich   at last, finally

die Energie   energy

(das) England   England

das Enkelkind, –er   grandchild

entdecken   to discover

sich *entschließen   to decide
(entschließt), entschloß,
entschlossen

sich entschuldigen (bei + dat.)   to
apologize (to)

entzünden   to ignite, light

erinnern   to remind

sich erinnern   to remember

sich erinnern an (+ acc.)   to remember

sich erkälten   to catch cold

*erkennen   to recognize
(erkennt), erkannte,
erkannt

erklären   to explain

das Erlebnis, –se   experience

erledigen   to take care of

ermorden   to murder

die Ernte, –n   harvest

*erschrecken   to become
frightened
(erschrickt), erschrak, ist
erschrocken

erst–   first

erwarten   to expect

erzählen   to tell, relate

*essen   to eat
(ißt), aß, gegessen

das Essen, —   meal

etwas   something

etwas langsamer   a little
slower

euer   your (familiar plural)

(das) Europa   Europe

europäisch   European

das Experiment, –e   experiment

*fahren   to drive
(fährt), fuhr, ist gefahren

der Fahrer, —   driver

der Fahrplan, ⁼e   timetable

*fallen   to fall
(fällt), fiel, ist gefallen

die Familie, –n   family

*fangen   to catch
(fängt), fing, gefangen

die Farbe, –n   color

fast   almost

die Faust, ⁼e   fist

der Februar   February

fehlen   to be missing, absent,
or lacking

der Fehler, —   mistake

das Fenster, —   window

die Ferien (pl.)   vacation

das Fernsehen   television

im Fernsehen   on T.V.

fertig   ready; finished

sich fertig·machen   to get
ready

*fest·nehmen   to detain, arrest
(nimmt ... fest), nahm ...
fest, festgenommen

das Feuer, —   fire

die Feuerwehr   fire depart-
ment

der Film, –e   film

*finden   to find
(findet), fand, gefunden

die Firma, die Firmen   firm,
company

der Fisch, –e   fish

flach flat
die **Flasche, –n** bottle
***fliegen** to fly
(fliegt), flog, ist geflogen
***fließen** to flow
(fließt), floß, ist geflossen
der **Flughafen, —** airport
der **Fluß, ⸚sse** river
folgen (+ *dat.*) to follow
Folgendes the following
das **Foto, –s** photo
die **Frage, –n** question
fragen (nach + *dat.*) to ask
(about)
der **Franc, —** franc
(das) **Frankreich** France
französisch French
die **Frau, –en** woman; wife;
Mrs.
der **Freitag, –e** Friday
der **Fremde, –n** (*adj. noun*)
stranger
sich **freuen (auf** + *acc.*) to look
forward to
(**über** + *acc.*)‚ to be
happy about
der **Freund, –e** friend
frisch fresh
der **Friseur, –e** barber
froh happy, glad
fröhlich merry
früh, früher, frühst– early
der **Frühling, –e** spring
das **Frühstück, –e** breakfast
frühstücken to breakfast,
eat breakfast
sich **fühlen** to feel
führen to lead
fünf five
fünfzig fifty
für (+ *acc.*) for

die **Furcht** fear
fürchten (+ *dir. obj.*) to be
afraid of
sich **fürchten (vor** + *dat.*) to be
afraid (of)
der **Fuß, ⸚e** foot

ganz whole, entire, all, com-
plete(ly)
die **Garage, –n** garage
gar nicht not at all
der **Garten, ⸚** garden
der **Gast, ⸚e** guest
das **Gebäude, —** building
***geben** to give
(gibt), gab, gegeben
geboren (+ **sein**) (to be)
born
gebrauchen to use; need
der **Geburtstag, –e** birthday
die **Gefahr, –en** danger
***gefallen** (+ *dat.*) to please
(gefällt), gefiel, gefallen
(**Es gefällt mir.** I like it;
lit.: It pleases me.)
der **Gefallen, —** favor
gegen (+ *acc.*) against,
into
die **Gegend, –en** area, neighbor-
hood, region
gegenüber (+ *dat.*) opposite, across from
***gehen** to go
(geht), ging, ist gegangen
gehören (+ *dat.*) to belong
(to)
das **Geld, –er** money
der **Geldtransport, –e** a
"Brink's" truck
gelegen situated

gemeinsam common, mutual
genau exact(ly)
der **Generaldirektor, –en** director (of a firm)
sich **genieren** to be embarrassed
genug enough
das **Gepäck** luggage
gerade just; right now
geradeaus straight ahead
gern, lieber, am liebsten gladly, willingly
etwas gern (lieber, am liebsten) tun to like (prefer, like best) to do something
der **Geruch, –̈e** smell
das **Geschäft, –e** business
*__geschehen__ to happen (geschieht), geschah, ist geschehen
das **Geschenk, –e** present
die **Geschichte, –n** story; history
geschlossen closed
geschult schooled, trained
gestern yesterday
gestikulieren to gesticulate
der **Gesuchte, –n** (*adj. noun*) person being hunted for
gesund healthy
sich **gewöhnen (an + *acc*.)** to get used (to)
die **Gewohnheit, –en** habit
gewöhnlich usual(ly)
das **Glas, –̈er** glass
glauben (+ *acc. with things*) (+ *dat. with persons*) to believe
gleich right now, immediately

glücklich happy; lucky
das **Gold** gold
der **Goldfisch, –e** goldfish
das **Gras** grass
gratulieren (+ *dat*.) to congratulate
die **Grenze, –n** border, edge
grob, gröber, gröbst– coarse, crude
groß, größer, größt– large
großartig great (*colloquial*)
der **Großvater, –̈** grandfather
grün green
der **Grund, –̈e** reason, cause
grüßen to greet
gut, besser, best– good, well

das **Haar, –e** hair
*__haben__ to have (hat), hatte, gehabt
der **Haken, —** hook
halb half
*__halten__ to hold (hält), hielt, gehalten
*__halten von__ (+ *dat*.) to think of (*opinion*)
der **Hammer, –̈** hammer
die **Hand, –̈e** hand
sich **handeln um** to concern, deal with, be a matter of
der **Handschuh, –e** glove
die **Handtasche, –n** purse
hängen (*trans*.) to hang (hängt), hängte, gehängt
*__hängen__ (*intrans*.) to hang (hängt), hing, ist gehangen
hart, härter, härtest– hard; severe
häßlich ugly

die **Hauptstraße, –n** main street
das **Haus, ⁼er** house
  nach Hause home (*motion towards*)
  zu Hause at home
die **Hausmusik** music in the home
die **Heide, –n** heather; heath
  heiß hot
  *****heißen** to be called (heißt), hieß, geheißen
  *****helfen** (+ *dat.*) to help (hilft), half, geholfen
das **Hemd, –en** shirt
der **Hemdsärmel, —** shirt sleeve
  *****heraus·geben** to publish (gibt . . . heraus), gab . . . heraus, herausgegeben
der **Herbst** fall, autumn
  *****herein·kommen** to come in (kommt . . . herein), kam . . . herein, ist hereingekommen
der **Herr, –n, –en** Mr.; gentleman
  *****her·sehen** to look (here) (sieht . . . her), sah . . . her, hergesehen
  (Sieh mal her! Look here!)
  her·stellen to manufacture
  *****herum·laufen** to run around (läuft . . . herum), lief . . . herum, ist herumgelaufen
  hervorragend outstanding
das **Heu** hay
  heute today
  heute abend this evening
  hier here (*location*)
  hierher here (*destination*)
die **Hilfe** help

  hin·stellen to put, put down
  hinter (*two-way prep.*) behind
die **Hitze** heat
  hoch, höher, höchst– high
  höchst highly
  hoffen (auf + *acc.*) to hope (for)
  hoh– high
  holen to fetch, get
das **Holz** wood
  hören to hear
das **Hörspiel, –e** radio play
die **Hose, –n** pants
das **Hotel, –s** hotel
  hübsch pretty
der **Hubschrauber, —** helicopter
der **Hund, –e** dog
  hundert hundred
  hungrig hungry
die **Hütte, –n** hut

die **Idee, –n** idea
  ihr her, their
  Ihr your (*polite form*)
  immer always
  in (*two-way prep.*) in; into, to
  immer noch still
  indem (*conj.*) in that; by (do)ing (something); while
die **Innenstadt** inner city
  intelligent intelligent
  interessant interesting
  interessieren to interest
sich **interessieren (für** + *acc.*) to be interested (in)
sich **irren** to be mistaken, be wrong
(das) **Italien** Italy
  italienisch Italian

die **Jacke, –n** jacket
das **Jahr, –e** year
jahrelang for years
die **Jahrhundertwende** turn of
the century
der **Januar** January
jeder, jedes, jede each, every
je ... desto the ... the
je mehr desto besser the
more the better
jetzt now
der **Journalist, –en, –en** journalist
die **Jugend** youth
der **Juli** July
jung, jünger, jüngst– young
der **Junge, –n, –n** boy
der **Juni** June

der **Kaffee** coffee
kalt, kälter, kältest– cold
das **Kammerorchester, —**
chamber orchestra
die **Karte, –en** ticket; postcard;
map; card(s)
die **Katze, –n** cat
kauen to chew
kaufen to buy
kaum hardly, scarcely
kein none, not any
der **Kellner, —** waiter
kennen to know, be ac-
quainted with
kennen·lernen to meet,
make the acquaintance
of
das **Kind, –er** child
das **Kino, –s** movie theater
die **Kirche, –n** church

klagen (über + acc.) to
complain about
klar clear
klassisch classical
das **Klavier, –e** piano
das **Kleid, –er** dress
klein small
klopfen to knock
klug, klüger, klügst– clever,
smart
kochen to cook; boil
der **Koffer, —** suitcase
(das) **Köln** Cologne
*__kommen__ to come
(kommt), kam, ist gekom-
men
die **Königin, –nen** queen
*__können__ can, to be able to
(kann) konnte, gekonnt
kontrollieren to check,
inspect
das **Konzert, –e** concert
der **Kopf, ∺e** head
der **Korrespondent, –en, –en**
correspondent
der **Korridor, –e** corridor
kosten to cost
kräftig powerful(ly), with
force
das **Krankenhaus, ∺er** hospital
die **Krawatte, –n** tie
der **Kreidekreis** chalk circle
der **Kreis, –e** circle
der **Krieg, –e** war
kriegen to get
der **Kritiker, —** critic
die **Kuh, ∺e** cow
der **Kunde, –n, –n** customer
der **Kurs, –e** course
kurz, kürzer, kürzest– short

das **Labyrinth, –e** labyrinth
lächeln to smile
lachen to laugh
*__laden__ to load; invite
(lädt), lud, geladen
der **Laden, ÷** store, shop
die **Lampe, –n** lamp
das **Land, ÷er** country; land
lang, länger, längst– long
langsam slow
langweilig boring
der **Lärm** noise
*__lassen__ to let, allow; have
something done
(läßt), ließ, gelassen
der **Lastwagen, —** truck
*__laufen__ to run
(läuft), lief, ist gelaufen
laut, lauter, lautest– loud
leben to live
das **Leder, —** leather
legen to lay
der **Lehrer, —** teacher
leicht easy, easily; light
leise soft(ly)
lernen to learn, study
*__lesen__ to read
(liest), las, gelesen
letzt– last
die **Leute** (*pl.*) people
das **Licht, –er** light
die **Liebe, –n** love
lieben to love
lieber preferably
der **Liebhaber, —** lover
das **Lied, –er** song
*__liegen__ to lie, recline
(liegt), lag, gelegen
die **Liste, –n** list
lösen to solve

*__los·lassen__ to let loose
(läßt . . . los), ließ . . . los,
losgelassen
die **Lust, ÷e** desire

machen to make, do, take
(e.g. a trip)
das **Mädchen, —** girl
der **Mai** May
der **Major, –e** major
der **Majorsrang** rank of major
mal ever; just
das **Mal, –e** time, occasion
däs erste Mal the first time
man one
manch– many a
der **Mann, ÷er** man
der **Mantel, ÷** coat
die **Mappe, –n** bookbag, briefcase
die **Mark, —** mark (*currency*)
der **März** March
die **Maus, ÷e** mouse
das **Meer, –e** sea, ocean
mehr more
mehrere several
mein my
meinen to think, be of the
opinion; mean
meinetwegen for my sake;
for all I care
meistens usually
der **Mensch, –en** man, human
being
merken to notice
sich **merken** to keep in mind
das **Messer, —** knife
die **Methode, –n** method
die **Milch** milk

die **Milchflasche, –n**   milk bottle
der **Minister, —**   minister
die **Minute, –n**   minute
*miß**verstehen**   to misunderstand
   (mißversteht), mißverstand,
   mißverstanden
mit (+ *dat.*)   with
*mit·**bringen**   to bring along
   (bringt ... mit), brachte ...
   mit, mitgebracht
miteinander   with each other
*mit·**kommen**   to come along
   (kommt ... mit), kam ...
   mit, ist mitgekommen
das **Mitleid**   sympathy
der **Mittag, –e**   noon
das **Mittagessen, —**   lunch
mit·teilen   to transmit, communicate
die **Mitternacht**   midnight
der **Mittwoch, –e**   Wednesday
möchte   would like
modern   modern
*m**ögen**   to like; may
   (mag), mochte, gemocht
möglich   possible
der **Monat, –e**   month
monatelang   for months
der **Mond, –e**   moon
der **Montag, –e**   Monday
morgen   tomorrow
der **Morgen, —**   morning
morgen früh   tomorrow
   morning
die **Mücke, –n**   gnat, bug
müde   tired
die **Mühe, –n**   effort
München   Munich
die **Musik**   music
der **Musikfreund, –e**   music lover

der **Musikunterricht**   music
   lessons
*m**üssen**   must, to have to
   (muß), mußte, gemußt
die **Mutter, –̈**   mother
Mutti   Mom

nach (+ *dat.*)   to; after
der **Nachahmer, —**   imitator
nachdem (*conj.*)   after
nachher (*adv.*)   afterwards
der **Nachmittag, –e**   afternoon
nachmittags   in the afternoon
*nach·**laufen**   to run after
   (läuft ... nach), lief ...
   nach, ist nachgelaufen
nächst–   next
die **Nacht, –̈e**   night
nachts   nights, at night
der **Nachttisch, –e**   night table
nah(e), näher, nächst–   near,
   close
die **Nähe**   vicinity
der **Name, –n, –n**   name
die **Nase, –n**   nose
die **Nase voll haben**   to have a
   belly full
der **Nebel, —**   fog
neben (*two-way prep.*)   next
   to, beside
*n**ehmen**   to take
   (nimmt), nahm, genommen
nein   no
*n**ennen**   to call, name
   (nennt), nannte, genannt
nervös   nervous
nett   nice
neu   new
nicht   not
nichts   nothing

nicht wahr   isn't it, aren't
they, etc.
nie   never
niemand   no one
noch   still
immer noch   still
noch nicht   not yet
norwegisch   Norwegian
notwendig   necessary
die Novelle, –n   novella
der November   November
nur   only

ob   whether
oben   on top, up there
obwohl   although, even
though
oder   or
öffnen   to open
oft, öfter, öftest–   often
öfters   often, frequently
ohne (+ acc.)   without
der Oktober   October
der Onkel, —   uncle
die Oper, –n   opera
operieren   to operate on
die Orange, –n   orange
das Orchester, —   orchestra
das Ostern   Easter

das Paket, –e   package
der Park, –s   park
parken   to park
der Pfadfinder, —   Boy Scout
der Pfennig, –e   cent (*1/100th
of a mark*)
das Pferd, –e   horse
das Pfingsten   Pentecost
pflanzen   to plant

der Philosoph, –en, –en   philoso-
pher
der Physiker, —   physicist
die Pistole, –n   pistol
der Plan, ∺e   plan
die Platte, –n (Schallplatte)
record
der Plattenspieler, —   record
player
der Platz, ∺e   seat; place
plaudern   to chat
pleite   broke (*financially*)
die Polizei   police
die Post   mail; post office
der Präsident, –en, –en   president
der Preis, –e   price
das Problem, –e   problem
der Professor, –en   professor
die Prüfung, –en   test, exam
putzen   to polish, clean
die Putzfrau, –en   cleaning
woman

das Radio, –s   radio
der Rand, ∺er   edge, border
der Randalierer, —   rowdy
rar   rare
rasch   quick
rasieren   to shave
sich rasieren   to shave (oneself)
der Rat   advice
raten (+ acc. with things)
(+ dat. with people)
to advise
(rät), riet, geraten
das Rathaus, ∺er   city hall
rauchen   to smoke
die Rechnung, –en   bill
recht   right
recht *haben   to be right

rechts to the right
einem recht *sein to be all right with someone
rechtzeitig on time
der **Redner, —** speaker
der **Regen, —** rain
die **Regierung, –en** government
regnen to rain
reich rich
die **Reihe, –n** row
an der Reihe*sein to be one's turn
die **Reise, –n** trip
reisen to travel
*****reiten** to ride (a horse) (reitet), ritt, ist, hat geritten
*****rennen** to run (rennt), rannte, ist gerannt
reparieren to repair
reservieren to reserve
das **Restaurant, –s** restaurant
das **Resultat, –e** result
der **Ring, –e** ring
roh coarse; raw
die **Rolle, –n** role
rollen to roll
der **Roman, –e** novel
die **Romantik** Romanticism
rot red
der **Rotwein, –e** red wine
*****rufen** to call (ruft), rief, gerufen
ruhig quiet
der **Rundfunk** radio station

die **Sache, –n** thing, affair
sagen to say, tell
sammeln to gather, collect
der **Samstag, –e** Saturday

samstags Saturdays
der **Satz, ⸚e** sentence
sauber·machen to clean, clean up
*****saufen** to drink (of animals); booze (säuft), soff, gesoffen
schaden (+ dat.) to hurt, damage
sich **schämen (über + acc.)** to be ashamed (of)
scharf, schärfer, schärfst– sharp
der **Schauspieler, —** actor
der **Scheck, –s** check
schenken to give (a present)
schicken to send
*****schieben** to shove, push (schiebt), schob, geschoben
das **Schiff, –e** ship
das **Schild, –er** sign
*****schlafen** to sleep (schläft), schlief, geschlafen
*****schlagen** to hit, beat (schlägt), schlug, geschlagen
der **Schlagstock, ⸚e** night stick, billy
schlank slender
schlecht bad
*****schließen** to close (schließt), schloß, geschlossen
der **Schluß, ⸚sse** conclusion, end
der **Schlüssel, —** key
schmuggeln to smuggle
schnell, schneller, schnellst– fast
das **Schnitzel, —** cutlet
die **Schokolade** chocolate

schon already
schön beautiful
***schreiben** to write
(schreibt), schrieb,
geschrieben
der **Schreibtisch, –e** desk
das **Schreibwarengeschäft, –e**
stationery store
der **Schritt, –e** step
der **Schuh, –e** shoe
schuld an (+ *dat.*) guilty of,
responsible for
die **Schule, –n** school
**schwach, schwächer,
schwächst–** weak
schwarz black
das **Schwarzbrot** black bread
die **Schweiz** Switzerland
schwer heavy; difficult
die **Schwester, –n** sister
***schwimmen** to swim
(schwimmt), schwamm,
geschwommen
der **See, die Seen** lake
die **See, –n** sea
***sehen** to see
(sieht), sah, gesehen
sehr very
sein his, its
***sein** to be
(ist), war, ist gewesen
seit (+ *dat.*) since
seitdem (*adv.*) since then
(*conj.*) (ever) since
die **Seite, –n** side
die **Sekretärin, –nen** secretary
selten (*adj.*) rare
(*adv.*) seldom
das **Semester, —** semester
die **Seminararbeit, –en** term
paper (*for a seminar*)

die **Sendung, –en** program
(*radio or T.V.*)
der **September** September
servieren to serve
die **Serviette, –n** napkin
setzen to set
sich **(hin)setzen** to sit down
sicher certain(ly), sure(ly)
siebzig seventy
das **Silber** silver
silbergrau silver-gray
***singen** to sing
(singt), sang, gesungen
***sitzen** to sit
(sitzt), saß, gesessen
***ski·laufen** to ski
(läuft . . . ski), lief . . .
ski, ist skigelaufen
so so, that way
sobald as soon as
so ein such a
das **Sofa, –s** couch, sofa
sofort immediately
der **Sohn, ¨e** son
solange as long as
solch– such
***sollen** to be supposed to,
be said to; ought to,
should
der **Sommer, —** summer
der **Sommeranzug, ¨e** summer
suit
das **Sommerfest, –e** summer
festival
das **Sommerhaus, ¨er** summer
house
sondern but (but rather)
der **Sonntag, –e** Sunday
sooft as often as
der **Sopran, –e** soprano
sowieso anyway, anyhow

sparen to save (money)
spät, später, spätest– late
spätestens at the latest
spazieren to stroll, walk
die Speisekarte, –n menu
die Sperre, –n barrier, road-
block
das Spiel, –e game
spielen to play
der Sportfilm, –e sport film
die Sprache, –n language
*sprechen (über + acc.) to
speak (about)
(spricht), sprach,
gesprochen
*springen to jump
(springt), sprang, ist
gesprungen
die Staatsuniversität, –en gov-
ernment-supported uni-
versity
die Stadt, ⁼e city
in die Stadt *gehen to go
downtown
stark, stärker, stärkst–
strong
statt (+ gen.) instead of
stattdessen instead of that
*stehen to stand
(steht), stand, gestanden
*stehlen to steal
(stiehlt), stahl, gestohlen
*steigen to climb
(steigt), stieg, ist gestiegen
der Stein, –e stone
stellen to put, place
eine Frage stellen to pose or
ask a question
*sterben to die
(stirbt), starb, ist gestorben
die Stimme, –n voice

der Stock, ⁼e stick; story
(building)
stolz proud
stören to disturb
*stoßen (gegen + acc.) to
hit, run into
(stößt), stieß, gestoßen
der Strand, –e beach
die Straße, –en street
die Straßenbahn, –en streetcar
die Straßenlaterne, –n street
light
*streiten to quarrel, argue
(streitet), stritt, gestritten
das Stück, –e piece; play
(Theaterstück)
der Student, –en, –en student
studieren to study
der Stuhl, ⁼e chair
stumm silently, without a
word
die Stunde, –en hour
suchen to hunt for
die Suppe, –n soup

die Tafel, –n blackboard
der Tag, –e day
tagelang for days
tagsüber during the day
die Taktlosigkeit, –en tactless-
ness, breach of tact
die Tankstelle, –n gas station
Tante Elvira Aunt Elvira
tanzen to dance
tapfer brave
die Tasse, –n cup
tätig active
der Tee tea
die Telefonnummer, –n phone
number

der **Teller,** — plate
das **Tennis** tennis
der **Tennisplatz,** ⁼e tennis court
der **Tenor,** –e tenor
teuer expensive
das **Theater,** — theater
das **Theaterstück,** –e play
das **Tier,** –e animal
die **Tinte,** –n ink
der **Tisch,** –e table
die **Tochter,** ⁼ daughter
der **Todgeweihte,** –n (*adj. noun*)
  doomed man
todkrank deathly ill
toll crazy
die **Tomate,** –n tomato
*****tragen** to carry; wear
  (trägt), trug, getragen
das **Tränengas** tear gas
trauen (+ *dat.*) to trust
*****treffen** to meet
  (trifft), traf, getroffen
*****treten** to step
  (tritt), trat, getreten
treu true, faithful
*****trinken** to drink
  (trinkt), trank, getrunken
trocken dry
trotz (+ *gen.*) in spite of
trotzdem nevertheless
die **Tschechoslowakei** Czechoslovakia
*****tun** to do
  (tut), tat, getan
der **Tunnel,** — tunnel
die **Tür,** –en door
die **Türkei** Turkey

die **U-Bahn (Untergrundbahn),**
  –en subway

über (*two-way prep.*) over,
  above; across
überall everywhere
überholen to overtake;
  repair
übernachten to spend the
  night, stay overnight
überraschen to surprise
übersetzen to translate
überzeugen to convince
die **Übung,** –en exercise, drill
die **Uhr,** –en watch, clock;
  o'clock
um (+ *acc.*) around; at
*****um·kommen** to die
  (kommt um), kam um, ist
  umgekommen
um ... zu in order to
unausgesetzt continual,
  uninterrupted
und and
etwas Undenkbares something unthinkable
unerwartet unexpected
der **Unfall,** ⁼e accident
ungewöhnlich unusual
die **Universität,** –en university
UNO United Nations Orga-
  nization
unrecht *haben to be
  wrong
unser our
der **Unsinn** nonsense
unten below
unter (*two-way prep.*) under,
  beneath
*****unterhalten** to entertain
  (unterhält), unterhielt,
  unterhalten
sich *****unterhalten** to entertain
  oneself; converse

*unternehmen to undertake
(unternimmt) unternahm,
unternommen
*unterschreiben to sign
(unterschreibt), unter-
schrieb, unterschrieben
unterstützen to support
die Untertasse, –n saucer

der Vater, ÷ father
*verbringen to spend (time)
(verbringt), verbrachte,
verbracht
verdienen to earn, deserve
der Verfasser, — author
*vergessen to forget
(vergißt), vergaß, vergessen
verkaufen to sell
*verkommen to go to ruin
(verkommt), verkam, ist
verkommen
*verlassen to leave
(verläßt), verließ, verlassen
verletzen to injure
*vermögen to be capable of,
be able to do
(vermag), vermochte,
vermocht
verpassen to miss (a train)
verschieden different
*verstehen to understand
(versteht), verstand, verstanden
der Verteidigungsminister, —
secretary (minister) of
defense
das Verwaltungsgebäude, —
administration building
der Verwandte, –n (adj. noun)
relative
viel, mehr, meist– much

viele many
vieles many things
viertel (das Viertel) quarter
das Violinkonzert, –e violin
concerto
voll full
völlig complete(ly)
von (+ dat.) from; off of;
of; by
vor (two-way prep.) in front
of
*vorbei·fahren to drive by
(fährt . . . vorbei), fuhr . . .
vorbei, ist vorbeigefahren
*vorbei·gehen to pass, pass by
(geht . . . vorbei), ging . . .
vorbei, ist vorbeigegangen
vor·bereiten to prepare
*vor·finden to find (there)
(findet . . . vor), fand . . .
vor, vorgefunden
vorher (adv.) before, before-
hand
vorig– last
*vor·kommen to happen
(kommt . . . vor), kam . . .
vor, ist vorgekommen
der Vormittag, –e forenoon,
morning
vorne up front
der Vorschlag, ÷e suggestion
die Vorsicht (vor + dat.) care,
caution; Be careful of . . . !
vorsichtig careful
vor·stellen to introduce
sich etwas vor·stellen to imagine

*wachsen to grow
(wächst), wuchs, ist
gewachsen

der **Wagen,** — car
wahr true
während (*conj.*) while
    (*prep.*) during
wahrscheinlich probably
der **Wald,** ⸗er woods, forest
die **Wand,** ⸗e wall
wandern to wander
wann when
warm, wärmer, wärmst–
    warm
warten (auf + *acc.*) to wait
    (for)
warum why
was what
*****waschen** to wash
    (wäscht), wusch,
    gewaschen
was für ein what kind of
das **Wasser** water
der **Weg, –e** way, path, road
wegen (+ *gen.*) on account
    of, due to
*****weg·fahren** to drive off
    (fährt . . . weg), fuhr . . .
    weg, ist weggefahren
*****weg·laufen** to run away
    (läuft . . . weg), lief . . .
    weg, ist weggelaufen
*****weg·nehmen** to take away
    (nimmt . . . weg), nahm
    . . . weg, weggenommen
die **Weihnachten** (*pl.*) Christ-
    mas
weil because
der **Wein, –e** wine
weise wise
weit far
weiter·arbeiten to go on
    working
*****weiter·gehen** to walk on,
    walk by

(geht . . . weiter), ging . . .
    weiter, ist weitergegangen
welcher, welches, welche
    which
weltbekannt world-
    renowned
der **Weltkrieg, –e** world war
die **Weltmacht,** ⸗e world power
wenig little, few
wenige (*pl.*) few
wenn if; when, whenever
wer who
*****werden** to become, get
    (wird), wurde, ist
    geworden
*****werfen** to throw
    (wirft), warf, geworfen
das **Werk, –e** work
im Westen in the West
weswegen why, on what
    account
das **Wetter** weather
wichtig important
*****widersprechen** (+ *dat.*) to
    contradict
    (widerspricht), wider-
    sprach, widersprochen
wie how; as
wieder again
(das) **Wien** Vienna
Wiener Viennese
wieviel how much
wieviele how many
der **Wind, –e** wind
winken to wave
der **Winter,** — winter
der **Wintermonat, –e** winter
    month
wirklich real(ly)
wirtschaften to "run things"
*****wissen** to know (a fact)
    (weiß), wußte, gewußt

wo   where
die Woche, –n   week
wochenlang   for weeks
wohin   where to
wohl   probably
wohlwollend   benevolent,
   well-meaning
wohnen   to live, reside
die Wohnung, –en   apartment
das Wohnzimmer, —   living
   room
*wollen   to want, want to
   (will), wollte, gewollt
das Wort   word
die Worte (pl.)   words (in context)
die Wörter (pl.)   words (not in
   context)
wundern   to surprise
sich wundern   to be surprised
die Würde   dignity
der Wutanfall, ⁼e   fit of rage,
   tantrum

der Zahn, ⁼e   tooth
zart   gentle, delicate
zehn   ten
zeigen   to show; point at
die Zeit, –en   time
die Zeitung, –en   newspaper
zerstören   to destroy
*ziehen   to pull, drag; move
   to
   (zieht), zog, gezogen

die Zigarette, –n   cigarette
die Zigarre, –n   cigar
der Zigarrenrauch   cigar smoke
das Zimmer, —   room
zittern   to tremble
zu (+ dat.)   to; at; for
zuerst   first
der Zufall, ⁼e   chance;
   accident
zufrieden   satisfied
der Zug, ⁼e   train
zu·hören   to listen
zu·machen   to close
*zurück·bringen   to bring
   back, take back
   (bringt . . . zurück),
   brachte . . . zurück,
   zurückgebracht
*zurück·kommen   to come
   back
   (kommt . . . zurück),
   kam . . . zurück, ist
   zurückgekommen
zusammen   together
zuviel   too much
zu·winken (+ dat.)   to wave
   (to someone)
zwanzig   twenty
zweit–   second
*zwingen   to force
   (zwingt), zwang,
   gezwungen
zwischen (two-way prep.)
   between

index

8
9
0
1
2
3
4
5
6
7
8
9
0
1
2
3